THE

GENTLEMEN'S BOOK OF ETIQUETTE

AND

MANUAL OF POLITENESS;

BEING

*A COMPLETE GUIDE FOR A GENTLEMAN'S CON-
DUCT IN ALL HIS RELATIONS TOWARD SOCIETY.*

CONTAINING

RULES FOR THE ETIQUETTE TO BE OBSERVED IN THE STREET,
AT TABLE, IN THE BALL-ROOM, EVENING PARTY, AND
MORNING CALL; WITH FULL DIRECTIONS FOR PO-
LITE CORRESPONDENCE, DRESS, CONVERSATION,
MANLY EXERCISES AND ACCOMPLISHMENTS.

From the best French, English and American authorities.

BY CECIL B. HARTLEY.

BOSTON:
DeWOLFE, FISKE & CO.

INTRODUCTION.

MAN was not intended to live like a bear or a hermit, apart from others of his own nature, and, philosophy and reason will each agree with me, that man was born for sociability and finds his true delight in society. Society is a word capable of many meanings, and used here in each and all of them. Society, *par excellence;* the world at large; the little clique to which he is bound by early ties; the companionship of friends or relatives; even society *tete a tete* with one dear sympathizing soul, are pleasant states for a man to be in.

Taking the word in its most extended view, it is the world; but in the light we wish to impress in our book it is the smaller world of the changing, pleasant intercourse of each city or town in which our reader may chance to abide.

This society, composed, as it is, of many varying natures and elements, where each individual must submit to merge his own identity into the universal whole, which makes the word and state, is divided and subdivided into various cliques, and has a pastime for every disposition, grave or gay; and with each division rises up a new set of forms and ceremonies to be observed if you wish to glide down the current of polite life smoothly and pleasantly.

The young man who makes his first entrance into the world of society, should know how to choose his friends, and next how to conduct himself towards them. Experience is, of course, the best guide, but at first starting this must come second hand, from an older friend, or from books.

A judicious friend is the best guide; but how is the young man to know whom to choose? When at home this friend is easily selected; but in this country, where each bird leaves the parent nest as soon as his wings will bear him safely up, there are but few who stay amongst the friends at home.

Next then comes the instruction from books.

True a book will not fully supply the place either of experience or friendly advice, still it may be made useful, and, carefully written from the experience of heads grown gray in society, with only well authenticated rules, it will be a guide not to be despised by the young aspirant for favor in polite and refined circles.

You go into society from mixed motives; partly for pleasure, recreation after the fatigues of your daily duties, and partly that you may become known. In a republican country where one man's opportunities for rising are as good as those of another, ambition will lead every rising man into society.

You may set it down as a rule, that as you treat the world, so the world will treat you. Carry into the circles of society a refined, polished manner, and an amiable desire to please, and it will meet you with smiling grace, and lead you forward pleasantly along the flowery paths; go, on the contrary, with a *brusque*, rude manner, startling all the silky softness before you with cut and thrust remarks, carrying only the hard realities of life in your hand, and you will find society armed to meet you, showing only sharp corners and thorny places for your blundering footsteps to stumble against.

You will find in every circle that etiquette holds some sway; her rule is despotic in some places, in others mild, and easily set aside. Your first lesson in society will be to study where she reigns supreme, in her crown and holding her sceptre, and where she only glides in with a gentle hint or so, and timidly steps out if rebuked; and let your conduct be governed by the result of your observations. You will soon become familiar with the signs, and tell on your first entrance into a room whether kid gloves and exquisite finish of manner will be appropriate, or whether it is "hail, fellow, well met" with the inmates. Remember, however, "once a gentleman always a gentleman," and be sure that you can so carry out the rule, that in your most careless, joyous moments, when freest from the restraints of etiquette, you can still be recognizable as a *gentleman* by every act, word, or look.

Avoid too great a restraint of manner. Stiffness is not politeness, and, while you observe every rule, you may appear to heed none. To make your politeness part of yourself, inseparable from every action, is the height of gentlemanly elegance and finish of manner.

CONTENTS.

CHAPTER VI.

CHAPTER VII.

CHAPTER VIII.

CHAPTER IX.

CHAPTER X.

CHAPTER XI.

CHAPTER XII.

CHAPTER XIII.

CHAPTER XIV.

CHAPTER XV.

CHAPTER XVI.

CHAPTER XVII.

CHAPTER XVIII.

GENTLEMEN'S BOOK OF ETIQUETTE

CHAPTER I.

CONVERSATION.

ONE of the first rules for a guide in polite conversa·
tion, is to avoid political or religious discussions in
general society. Such discussions lead almost invariably
to irritating differences of opinion, often to open quarrels, and a coolness of feeling which might have been
avoided by dropping the distasteful subject as soon as
marked differences of opinion arose. It is but one out
of many that can discuss either political or religious differences, with candor and judgment, and yet so far
control his language and temper as to avoid either giving
or taking offence.

In their place, in circles which have met for such discussions, in a *tête à tête* conversation, in a small party
of gentlemen where each is ready courteously to listen
to the others, politics may be discussed with perfect propriety, but in the drawing-room, at the dinner-table, or
in the society of ladies, these topics are best avoided.

If you are drawn into such a discussion without in·
tending to be so, be careful that your individual opinion

11

does not lead you into language and actions unbecoming a gentleman. Listen courteously to those whose opinions do not agree with yours, and *keep your temper*. A man in a passion ceases to be a gentleman.

Even if convinced that your opponent is utterly wrong, yield gracefully, decline further discussion, or dextrously turn the conversation, but do not obstinately defend your own opinion until you become angry, or more ex cited than is becoming to a gentleman.

Many there are who, giving their opinion, not as an *opinion* but as a *law*, will defend their position by such phrases, as : "Well, if *I* were president, or governor, I would," &c.—and while by the warmth of their argument they prove that they are utterly unable to govern their own temper, they will endeavor to persuade you that they are perfectly competent to take charge of the government of the nation.

Retain, if you will, a fixed political opinion, yet do not parade it upon all occasions, and, above all, do not endeavor to *force* others to agree with you. Listen calmly to their ideas upon the same subjects, and if you cannot agree, differ politely, and while your opponent may set you down as a bad politician, let him be obliged to admit that you are a *gentleman*.

Wit and vivacity are two highly important ingredients in the conversation of a man in polite society, yet a straining for effect, or forced wit, is in excessively bad taste. There is no one more insupportable in society than the everlasting talkers who scatter puns, witticisms, and jokes with so profuse a hand that they become as tiresome as a comic newspaper, and whose loud laugh at

their own wit drowns other voices which might speak·
matter more interesting. The really witty man does
not shower forth his wit so indiscriminately; his charm
consists in wielding his powerful weapon delicately and
easily, and making each highly polished witticism come
in the right place and moment to be effectual. While
real wit is a most delightful gift, and its use a most
charming accomplishment, it is, like many other bright
weapons, dangerous to use too often. You may wound
where you meant only to amuse, and remarks which you
mean only in for general applications, may be construed
into personal affronts, so, if you have the gift, use it
wisely, and not too freely.

The most important requisite for a good conversational
power is education, and, by this is meant, not merely the
matter you may store in your memory from observation
or books, though this is of vast importance, but it also
includes the developing of the mental powers, and, above
all, the comprehension. An English writer says, "A
man should be able, in order to enter into conversation,
to catch rapidly the meaning of anything that is advanced; for instance, though you know nothing of science, you should not be obliged to stare and be silent,
when a man who does understand it is explaining a new
discovery or a new theory; though you have not read a
word of Blackstone, your comprehensive powers should
be sufficiently acute to enable you to take in the state-
ment that may be made of a recent cause; though you
may not have read some particular book, you should be
capable of appreciating the criticism which you hear of
it Without such power—simple enough, and easily at

tained by attention and practice, yet too seldom met
with in general society—a conversation which departs
from the most ordinary topics cannot be maintained
without the risk of lapsing into a lecture; with such
power, society becomes instructive as well as amusing,
and you have no remorse at an evening's end at having
wasted three or four hours in profitless banter, or sim-
pering platitudes. This facility of comprehension often
startles us in some women, whose education we know to
have been poor, and whose reading is limited. If they
did not rapidly receive your ideas, they could not, therefore, be fit companions for intellectual men, and it is,
perhaps, their consciousness of a deficiency which leads
them to pay the more attention to what you say. It is
this which makes married women so much more agreeable
to men of thought than young ladies, as a rule, can be,
for they are accustomed to the society of a husband, and
the effort to be a companion to his mind has engrafted
the habit of attention and ready reply."

The same author says: "No less important is the
cultivation of taste. If it is tiresome and deadening to
be with people who cannot understand, and will not even
appear to be interested in your better thoughts, it is
almost repulsive to find a man insensible to all beauty,
and immovable by any horror.

"In the present day an acquaintance with art, even
if you have no love for it, is a *sine quâ non* of good
society. Music and painting are subjects which will be
discussed in every direction around you. It is only in
bad society that people go to the opera, concerts, and
art-exhibitions merely because it is the fashion, or to say

they have been there; and if you confessed to such a weakness in really good society, you would be justly voted a puppy. For this, too, some book knowledge is indispensable. You should at least know the names of the more celebrated artists, composers, architects, sculptors, and so forth, and should be able to approximate their several schools.

"So too, you should know pretty accurately the pronunciation of celebrated names, or, if not, take care not to use them. It will never do to be ignorant of the names and approximate ages of great composers, especially in large cities, where music is so highly appreciated and so common a theme. It will be decidedly condemnatory if you talk of the *new* opera 'Don Giovanni,' or *Rossini's* 'Trovatore,' or are ignorant who composed 'Fidelio,' and in what opera occur such common pieces as ' *Ciascun lo dice*,' or ' *Il segreto*.' I do not say that these trifles are indispensable, and when a man has better knowledge to offer, especially with genius or 'cleverness' to back it, he will not only be pardoned for an ignorance of them, but can even take a high tone, and profess indifference or contempt of them. But, at the same time, such ignorance stamps an ordinary man, and hinders conversation. On the other hand the best society will not endure dilettantism, and, whatever the knowledge a man may possess of any art, he must not display it so as to make the ignorance of others painful to them. But this applies to every topic. To have only one or two subjects to converse on, and to discourse rather than talk on them, is always ill-bred, whether the theme be literature or horseflesh. The gentleman jockey will probably denounce the former as a 'bore,' and call us pedants for dwelling on it; but if, as is too often the case, he can give us nothing more general than the discussion of the 'points' of a horse that, perhaps, we have never seen, he is as great a pedant in his way.

"*Reason* plays a less conspicuous part in good society because its frequenters are too reasonable to be mere reasoners. A disputation is always dangerous to temper, and tedious to those who cannot feel as eager as the disputants; a discussion, on the other hand, in which every body has a chance of stating amicably and unobtrusively his or her opinion, must be of frequent occurrence. But to cultivate the reason, besides its high moral value, has the advantage of enabling one to reply as well as attend to the opinions of others. Nothing is more tedious or disheartening than a perpetual, 'Yes, just so,' and nothing more. Conversation must never be one-sided. Then, again, the reason enables us to support a fancy or an opinion, when we are asked *why* we think so. To reply, 'I don't know, but still I think so,' is silly and tedious.

"But there is a part of our education so important and so neglected in our schools and colleges, that it cannot be too highly impressed on the young man who proposes to enter society. I mean that which we learn first of all things, yet often have not learned fully when death eases us of the necessity—the art of speaking our own language. What can Greek and Latin, French and German be for us in our every-day life, if we have not acquired this? We are often encouraged to raise a laugh at Doctor Syntax and the tyranny of Grammar, but we may be certain that more misunderstandings, and, therefore, more difficulties arise between men in the commonest intercourse from a want of grammatical precision than from any other cause. It was once the fashion to neglect grammar, as it now is with certain people to write illegibly, and, in the days of Goethe, a man thought himself a genius if he could spell badly.

"Precision and accuracy must begin in the very outset; and if we neglect them in grammar, we shall scarcely acquire them in expressing our thoughts. But since there is no society without interchange of thought, and since the best society is that in which the best thoughts are interchanged in the best and most comprehensible manner, it follows that a proper mode of expressing ourselves is indispensable in good society.

"The art of expressing one's thoughts neatly and suitably is one which, in the neglect of rhetoric as a study, we must practice for ourselves. The commonest thought well put is more useful in a social point of view, than the most brilliant idea jumbled out. What is well expressed is easily seized, and therefore readily responded to; the most poetic fancy may be lost to the hearer, if the language which conveys it is obscure. Speech is the gift which distinguishes man from animals, and makes society possible. He has but a poor appreciation of his high privilege as a human being, who neglects to cultivate, 'God's great gift of speech.'

"As I am not writing for men of genius, but for ordinary beings, I am right to state that an indispensable part of education is a knowledge of the literature of the English language. But *how* to read, is, for

2

society more important than *what* we read. The man who takes up nothing but a newspaper, but reads it to *think*, to deduct conclusions from its premises, and form a judgment on its opinions, is more fitted for society than he, who having all the current literature and devoting his whole time to its perusal, swallows it all without digestion. In fact, the mind must be treated like the body, and however great its appetite, it will soon fall into bad health if it gorges, but does not ruminate. At the same time an acquaintance with the best current literature is necessary to modern society, and it is not sufficient to have read a book without being able to pass a judgment upon it. Conversation on literature is impossible, when your respondent can only say, ' Yes, I like the book, but I really don't know why.'

"An acquaintance with old English literature is not perhaps indispensable, but it gives a man great advantage in all kinds of society, and in some he is at a constant loss without it. The same may be said of foreign literature, which in the present day is almost as much discussed as our own; but, on the other hand, an acquaintance with home and foreign politics, with current history, and subjects of passing interest, is absolutely necessary ; and a person of sufficient intelligence to join in good society, cannot dispense with his daily newspaper, his literary journal, and the principal reviews and magazines. The cheapness of every kind of literature, the facilities of our well stored circulating libraries, our public reading rooms, and numerous excellent lectures on every possible subject, leave no excuse to poor or rich for an ignorance of any of the topics discussed in intellectual society. You may forget your Latin, Greek, French, German, and Mathematics, but if you frequent good company, you will never be allowed to forget that you are a citizen of the world."

A man of real intelligence and cultivated mind, is generally modest. He may feel when in every day society, that in intellectual acquirements he is above those around him; but he will not seek to make his companions feel their inferiority, nor try to display this advantage over them. He will discuss with frank simplicity the topics started by others, and endeavor to avoid starting such as they will not feel inclined to discuss. All that he says will be marked by politeness and deference to the feelings and opinions of others.

La Bruyere says, " The great charm of conversation consists less in the display of one's own wit and intelligence, than in the power to draw forth the resources of others; he who leaves you after a long conversation, pleased with himself and the part *he* has taken in the discourse, will be your warmest admirer. Men do not care to admire you, they wish you to be pleased with them; they do not seek for instruction or even amusement from your discourse, but they do wish you to be made acquainted with their talents and powers of conversation; and the true man of genius will delicately make all who come in contact with him, feel the exquisite satisfaction of knowing that they have appeared to advantage."

Having admitted the above to be an incontestable fact, you will also see that it is as great an accomplishment tc listen with an air of interest and attention, as it is to speak well.

To be a good listener is as indispensable as to be a good talker, and it is in the character of listener that you can most readily detect the man who is accustomed to good society. Nothing is more embarrassing to any one who is speaking, than to perceive signs of weariness or inattention in the person whom he addresses.

Never interrupt any one who is speaking; it is quite as rude to officiously supply a name or date about which another hesitates, unless you are asked to do so. Another gross breach of etiquette, is to anticipate the point of a story which another person is reciting, or to take it from his lips to finish it in your own language. Some persons plead as an excuse for this breach of etiquette, that the reciter was spoiling a good story by a bad manner, but this does not mend the matter. It is surely rude to give a man to understand that you do not consider him capable of finishing an anecdote that he has commenced.

It is ill-bred to put on an air of weariness during a long speech from another person, and quite as rude to look at a watch, read a letter, flirt the leaves of a book, or in any other action show that you are tired of the speaker or his subject.

In a general conversation, never speak when another person is speaking, and never try by raising your own voice to drown that of another. Never assume an air of haughtiness, or speak in a dictatorial manner; let your conversation be always amiable and frank, free from every affectation.

Put yourself on the same level as the person to whom you speak, and under penalty of being considered a pedantic idiot, refraining from explaining any expression or word that you may use.

Never, unless you are requested to do so, speak of your own business or profession in society; to confine your conversation entirely to the subject or pursuit which is your own speciality is low-bred and vulgar.

Make the subject for conversation suit the company in which you are placed. Joyous, light conversation will be at times as much out of place, as a sermon would be at a dancing party. Let your conversation be grave or gay as suits the time or place.

In a dispute, if you cannot reconcile the parties, withdraw from them. You will surely make one enemy perhaps two, by taking either side, in an argument when the speakers have lost their temper.

Never gesticulate in every day conversation, unless you wish to be mistaken for a fifth rate comedian.

Never ask any one who is conversing with you to repeat his words. Nothing is ruder than to say, "Pardon me, will you repeat that sentence—I did not hear you at first," and thus imply that your attention was wandering when he first spoke.

Never, during a general conversation, endeavor to concentrate the attention wholly upon yourself. It is quite as rude to enter into conversation with one of a group, and endeavor to draw him out of the circle of general conversation to talk with you alone.

Never listen to the conversation of two persons who have thus withdrawn from a group. If they are so near you that you cannot avoid hearing them, you may, **with** perfect propriety, change your seat.

Make your own share in conversation as modest and brief as is consistent with the subject under consideration, and avoid long speeches and tedious stories. If, **however**, another, particularly an old man, tells **a long story**, or one that is not new to you, listen respectfully **until** he has finished, before you speak again.

Speak of yourself but little. Your friends will find out your virtues without forcing you to tell them, and you may feel confident that it is equally unnecessary to expose your faults yourself.

If you submit to flattery, you must also submit to the imputation of folly and self-conceit.

In speaking of your friends, do not compare them, one with another. Speak of the merits of each one, but do not try to heighten the virtues of one by contrasting them with the vices of another.

No matter how absurd are the anecdotes that may be told in your presence, you must never give any sign of incredulity. They may be true ; and even if false, good breeding forces you to hear them with polite attention, and the appearance of belief. To show by word or sign any token of incredulity, is to give the lie to the narrator, and that is an unpardonable insult.

Avoid, in conversation all subjects which can injure the absent. A gentleman will never calumniate or listen to calumny.

Need I say that no gentleman will ever soil his mouth with an oath. Above all, to swear in a drawing-room or before ladies is not only indelicate and vulgar in the extreme, but evinces a shocking ignorance of the rules of polite society and good breeding.

For a long time the world has adopted a certain form of speech which is used in good society, and which changing often, is yet one of the distinctive marks of a gentleman. A word or even a phrase which has been used among the most refined circles, will, sometimes, by a sudden freak of fashion, from being caricatured in a farce or song, or from some other cause, go entirely out of use. Nothing but habitual intercourse with people of refinement and education, and mingling in general society, will teach a gentleman what words to use and what to avoid. Yet there are some words which are now entirely out of place in a parlor.

Avoid a declamatory style; some men, before speaking, will wave their hands as if commanding silence, and, having succeeded in obtaining the attention of the company, will speak in a tone, and style, perfectly suitable for the theatre or lecture room, but entirely out of place in a parlor. Such men entirely defeat the object of society, for they resent interruption, and, as their talk flows in a constant stream, no one else can speak without interrupting the pompous idiot who thus endeavors to engross the entire attention of the circle around him.

This character will be met with constantly, and generally joins to the other disagreeable traits an egotism as tiresome as it is ill-bred.

The wittiest man becomes tedious and ill-bred when he endeavors to engross entirely the attention of the company in which he should take a more modest part.

Avoid set phrases, and use quotations but rarely

They sometimes make a very piquant addition to conversation, but when they become a constant habit, they are exceedingly tedious, and in bad taste.

Avoid pedantry; it is a mark, not of intelligence, but stupidity.

Speak your own language correctly; at the same time do not be too great a stickler for formal correctness of phrases.

Never notice it if others make mistakes in language. To notice by word or look such errors in those around you, is excessively ill-bred.

Vulgar language and slang, though in common, unfortunately too common use, are unbecoming in any one who pretends to be a gentleman. Many of the words heard now in the parlor and drawing-room, derive their origin from sources which a gentleman would hesitate to mention before ladies, yet he will make daily use of the offensive word or phrase.

If you are a professional or scientific man, avoid the use of technical terms. They are in bad taste, because many will not understand them. If, however, you unconsciously use such a term or phrase, do not then commit the still greater error of explaining its meaning. No one will thank you for thus implying their ignorance.

In conversing with a foreigner who speaks imperfect English, listen with strict attention, yet do not supply a word, or phrase, if he hesitates. Above all, do not by a word or gesture show impatience if he makes pauses or blunders. If you understand his language, say so when you first speak to him; this is not making a display of your own knowledge, but is a kindness, as a foreigner

will be pleased to hear and speak his own language when
in a strange country.

Be careful in society never to play the part of buffoon,
for you will soon become known as the "funny" man of the
party, and no character is so perilous to your dignity as
a gentleman. You lay yourself open to both censure
and ridicule, and you may feel sure that, for every person
who laughs with you, two are laughing at you, and for
one who admires you, two will watch your antics with
secret contempt.

Avoid boasting. To speak of your money, connec-
tions, or the luxuries at your command is in very bad
taste. It is quite as ill-bred to boast of your intimacy
with distinguished people. If their names occur natu
ally in the course of conversation, it is very well; but to
be constantly quoting, "my friend, Gov. C——," or
"my intimate friend, the president," is pompous and in
bad taste.

While refusing the part of jester yourself, do not, by
stiff manners, or cold, contemptuous looks, endeavor to
check the innocent mirth of others. It is in excessively
bad taste to drag in a grave subject of conversation
when pleasant, bantering talk is going on around you.
Join in pleasantly and forget your graver thoughts for
the time, and you will win more popularity than if you
chill the merry circle or turn their innocent gayety to
grave discussions.

When thrown into the society of literary people, do
not question them about their works. To speak in
terms of admiration of any work to the author is in bad
taste; but you may give pleasure, if, by a quotation from

their writings, or a happy reference to them, you **prove** that you have read and appreciated them.

It is extremely rude and pedantic, when engaged **in** general conversation, to make quotations in a foreign language.

To use phrases which admit of a double meaning, **is** **un**gentlemanly, and, if addressed to a lady, they become **po**sitively insulting.

If you find you are becoming angry in a conversation, either turn to another subject or keep silence. You may utter, in the heat of passion, words which you would never use in a calmer moment, and which you would bitterly repent when they were once said.

"Never talk of ropes to a man whose father **was** hanged" is a vulgar but popular proverb. Avoid carefully subjects which may be construed into personalities, and keep a strict reserve upon family matters. Avoid, if you can, seeing the skeleton in your friend's closet, but if it is paraded for your special benefit, regard it **as** a sacred confidence, and never betray your knowledge **to** a third party.

If you have traveled, although you will endeavor **to** improve your mind in such travel, do not be constantly speaking of your journeyings. Nothing is more tiresome than a man who commences every phrase with, "When I was in Paris," or, "In Italy I saw ——."

When asking questions about persons who are not **k**nown to you, in a drawing-room, avoid using adjectives; **or** you may enquire of a mother, "Who is that awkward, ugly girl?" and be answered, "Sir, that is my daugh-ter."

Avoid gossip; in a woman it is detestable, but in a man it is utterly despicable.

Do not officiously offer assistance or advice in general society. Nobody will thark you for it.

Ridicule and practical joking are both marks of a vulgar mind and low breeding.

Avoid flattery. A delicate compliment is permissible in conversation, but flattery is broad, coarse, and to sensible people, disgusting. If you flatter your superiors, they will distrust you, thinking you have some selfish end; if you flatter ladies, they will despise you, thinking you have no other conversation.

A lady of sense will feel more complimented if you converse with her upon instructive, high subjects, than if you address to her only the language of compliment. In the latter case she will conclude that you consider her incapable of discussing higher subjects, and you cannot expect her to be pleased at being considered merely a silly, vain person, who must be flattered into good humor.

Avoid the evil of giving utterance to inflated expressions and remarks in common conversation.

It is a somewhat ungrateful task to tell those who would shrink from the imputation of a falsehood that they are in the daily habit of uttering untruths; and yet, if I proceed, no other course than this can be taken by me. It is of no use to adopt half measures; plain speaking saves a deal of trouble.

The examples about to be given by me of exaggerated expressions, are only a few of the many that are constantly in use. Whether you can acquit yourselves of the charge of occasionally using them, I cannot tell; but I dare not affirm for myself that I am altogether guiltless.

"I was caught in the wet last night, the rain came down in torrents." Most of us have been out in heavy rains; but a torrent of water pouring down from the skies would a little surprise us, after all.

"I am wet to the skin, and have not a dry thread upon me." Where these expressions are once used correctly, they are used twenty times in opposition to the truth.

"I tried to overtake him, but in vain; for he ran like lightning." The celebrated racehorse Eclipse is said to have run a mile in a minute, but poor Eclipse is left sadly behind by this expression.

"He kept me standing out in the cold so long, I thought I should have waited for ever." There is not a particle of probability that such a thought could have been for one moment entertained.

"As I came across the common, the wind was as keen as a razor." This is certainly a very keen remark, but the worst of it is that its keenness far exceeds its correctness.

"I went to the meeting, but had hard work to get in; for the place was crowded to suffocation." In this case, in justice to the veracity of the relater, it is necessary to suppose that successful means had been used for his recovery.

"It must have been a fine sight; I would have given the world to have seen it." Fond as most of us are of sight-seeing, this would be buying pleasure at a dear price indeed; but it is an easy thing to proffer to part with that which we do not possess.

"It made me quite low spirited; my heart felt as heavy as lead." We most of us know what a heavy heart is; but lead is by no means the most correct metaphor to use in speaking of a heavy heart.

"I could hardly find my way, for the night was as dark as pitch." I am afraid we have all in our turn calumniated the sky in this manner; pitch is many shades darker than the darkest night we have ever known.

"I have told him of that fault fifty times over." Five times would, in all probability, be much nearer the fact than fifty.

"I never closed my eyes all night long." If this be true, you acted unwisely; for had you closed your eyes, you might, perhaps, have fallen asleep, and enjoyed the blessing of refreshing slumber; if it be not true, you acted more unwisely still, by stating that as a fact which is altogether untrue.

"He is as tall as a church-spire." I have met with some tall fellows in my time, though the spire of a church is somewhat taller than the tallest of them.

"You may buy a fish at the market as big as a jackass, for five shillings." I certainly have my doubts about this matter; but if it be really true, the market people must be jackasses indeed to sell such large fishes for so little money.

"He was so fat he could hardly come in at the door." Most likely the difficulty here alluded to was never felt by any one but the relater; supposing it to be otherwise, the man must have been very broad or the door very narrow.

"You don't say so!—why, it was enough to kill him!" The fact that it did not kill him is a sufficient reply to this unfounded observation; but no remark can be too absurd for an unbridled tongue.

Thus might I run on for an hour, and after all leave much unsaid on the subject of exaggerated expressions. We are hearing continually the comparisons, "black as soot, white as snow, hot as fire, cold as ice, sharp as a needle, dull as a door-nail, light as a feather, heavy as lead, stiff as a poker, and crooked as a crab-tree," in cases where such expressions are quite out of order.

The practice of expressing ourselves in this inflated and thoughtless way, is more mischievous than we are aware of. It certainly leads us to sacrifice truth; to misrepresent what we mean faithfully to describe; to whiten our own characters, and sometimes to blacken the reputation of a neighbor. There is an uprightness in speech as well as in action, that we ought to strive hard to attain. The purity of truth is sullied, and the standard of integrity is lowered, by incorrect observations. Let us reflect upon this matter freely and faithfully. Let us love truth, follow truth, and practice truth in our thoughts, our words, and our deeds.

CHAPTER II.

POLITENESS.

REAL politeness is the outward expression of the most generous impulses of the heart. It enforces unselfishness, benevolence, kindness, and the golden rule, "Do unto others as you would others should do unto you." Thus its first principle is love for the neighbor, loving him as yourself.

When in society it would often be exceedingly difficult to decide how to treat those who are personally disagreeable to us, if it were not for the rules of politeness, and the little formalities and points of etiquette which these rules enforce. These evidences of polite breeding do not prove hypocrisy, as you may treat your most bitter enemy with perfect courtesy, and yet make no protestations of friendship.

If politeness is but a mask, as many philosophers tell us, it is a mask which will win love and admiration, and is better worn than cast aside. If you wear it with the sincere desire to give pleasure to others, and make all the little meetings of life pass off smoothly and agreeably, it will soon cease to be a mask, but you will find that the manner which you at first put on to give pleasure, has become natural to you, and wherever you have assumed a virtue to please others, you will find the virtue becoming habitual and finally natural, and part of yourself.

Do not look upon the rules of etiquette as deceptions. They are just as often vehicles for the expression of sincere feeling, as they are the mask to conceal a want of it.

You will in society meet with men who rail against politeness, and call it deceit and hypocrisy. Watch these men when they have an object to gain, or are desirous of making a favorable impression, and see them tacitly, but unconsciously, admit the power of courtesy, by dropping for the time, their uncouth ways, to affect the politeness, they oftentimes do not feel.

Pass over the defects of others, be prudent, discreet, at the proper time reserved, yet at other times frank, and treat others with the same gentle courtesy you would wish extended to yourself.

True politeness never embarrasses any one, because its first object is to put all at their ease, while it leaves to all perfect freedom of action. You must meet rudeness from others by perfect politeness and polish of manner on your own part, and you will thus shame those who have been uncivil to you. You will more readily make them blush by your courtesy, than if you met their rudeness by ill manners on your own part.

While a favor may be doubled in value, by a frankly courteous manner of granting it, a refusal will lose half its bitterness if your manner shows polite regret at your inability to oblige him who asks the favor at your hand.

Politeness may be extended to the lowest and meanest, an1 you will never by thus extending it detract from your own dignity. A *gentleman* may and will treat his washerwoman with respect and courtesy, and his boot-black with pleasant affability, yet preserve perfectly his own position. To really merit the name of a polite, finished gentleman, you must be polite at all times and under all circumstances.

There is a difference between politeness and etiquette. Real politeness is in-born, and may exist in the savage, while etiquette is the outward expression of politeness reduced to the rules current in good society.

A man may be polite, really so in heart, yet show in every movement an ignorance of the rules of etiquette, and offend against the laws of society. You may find him with his elbows upon the table, or tilting his chair in a parlor. You may see him commit every hour gross breaches of etiquette, yet you will never hear him intentionally utter one word to wound another, you will see that he habitually endeavors to make others comfortable, choosing for them the easiest seats, or the daintiest dishes, and putting self entirely aside to contribute to the pleasure of all around him. Such a man will learn, by contact with refined society, that his ignorance of the rules which govern it, make him, at times, disagreeable, and from the same unselfish motive which prompts him to make a sacrifice of comfort for the sake of others, he will watch and learn quickly, almost by instinct, where he offends against good breeding, drop one by one his errors in etiquette, and become truly a gentleman.

On the other hand, you will meet constantly, in the best society, men whose polish of manner is exquisite,
3

who will perform to the minutest point the niceties of good breeding, who never commit the least act that is forbidden by the strictest rules of etiquette; yet under all this mask of chivalry, gallantry, and politeness will carry a cold, selfish heart; will, with a sweet smile, graceful bow, and elegant language, wound deeply the feelings of others, and while passing in society for models of courtesy and elegance of manner, be in feeling as cruel and barbarous as the veriest savage.

So I would say to you, Cultivate your heart. Cherish there the Christian graces, love for the neighbor, unselfishness, charity, and gentleness, and you will be truly a gentleman; add to these the graceful forms of etiquette, and you then become a *perfect* gentleman.

Etiquette exists in every corner of the known world, from the savages in the wilds of Africa, who dare not, upon penalty of death, approach their barbarous rulers without certain forms and ceremonies, to the most refined circles of Europe, where gentle chivalry and a cultivated mind suggest its rules. It has existed in all ages, and the stringency of its laws in some countries has given rise to both ludicrous and tragic incidents.

In countries where royalty rules the etiquette, it often happens that pride will blind those who make the rules, and the results are often fatal. Believing that the same deference which their rank authorized them to demand, was also due to them as individuals, the result of such an idea was an etiquette as vain and useless as it was absurd.

For an example I will give an anecdote:

" The kings of Spain, the proudest and vainest of all

kings of the earth, made a rule of etiquette as stupid as it was useless. It was a fault punishable by death to touch the foot of the queen, and the individual who thus offended, no matter under what circumstances, was executed immediately.

A young queen of Spain, wife of Charles the Second, was riding on horseback in the midst of her attendants. Suddenly the horse reared and threw the queen from the saddle. Her foot remained in the stirrup, and she was dragged along the ground. An immense crowd stood looking at this spectacle, but no one dared, for his life, to attempt to rescue the poor woman. She would have died, had not two young French officers, ignorant of the stupid law which paralyzed the Spaniards, sprung forward and saved her. One stopped the horse, and whilst he held the bridle, his companion disengaged from its painful position the foot of the young queen, who was, by this time, insensible from fear and the bruises which she had already received. They were instantly arrested, and while the queen was carried on a litter to the palace, her young champions were marched off, accompanied by a strong guard, to prison. The next day, sick and feeble, the queen was obliged to leave her bed, and on her knees before the king, plead for the pardon of the two Frenchmen; and her prayer was only granted upon condition that the audacious foreigners left Spain immediately.

There is no country in the world where the absurdities of etiquette are carried to so great a length as in Spain, because there is no nation where the nobility are so proud. The following anecdote, which illustrates this, would seem incredible were it not a historical fact:

"Philip the Third, king of Spain, was sick, and being able to sit up, was carefully placed in an arm chair which stood opposite to a large fire, when the wood was piled up to an enormous height. The heat soon became intolerable, and the courtiers retired from around the king; but, as the Duke D'Ussede, the fire stirrer for the king, was not present, and as no one else had the right to touch the fire, those present dared not attempt to diminish the heat. The grand chamberlain was also absent, and he alone was authorized to touch the king's footstool. The poor king, too ill to rise, in vain implored those around him to move his chair, no one dared touch it, and when the grand chamberlain arrived, the king had fainted with the heat, and a few days later he died, literally roasted to death."

At almost all times, and in almost all places, good breeding may be shown; and we think a good service will be done by pointing out a few plain and simple instances in which it stands opposed to habits and manners, which, though improper and disagreeable, are n t very uncommon.

In the familiar intercourse of society, a well-bred *man* will be known by the delicacy and deference with which he behaves towards females. That man would deservedly be looked upon as very deficient in proper respect and feeling, who should take any physical advantage of one of the weaker sex, or offer any personal slight towards her. Woman looks, and properly looks, for protection to man. If is the province of the husband to shield the rife from injury ; of the father to protect the daughter; the brother has the same duty to perform towards the sister ; and, in general, every man should, in this sense, be the champion and the lover of every woman. Not only should he be ready to protect, but desirous to please, and willing to sacrifice much of his own personal ease and comfort, if, by doing so, he can increase those of any female in whose company he may find himself. Putting these principles into practice, a well-bred man, in his own house, will be kind and respectful in his behaviour to every female of the family. He will not use towards them harsh language, even if called upon to express dissatisfaction with their conduct. In conversation, he will abstain from every allusion which would put modesty to the blush. He will, as much as in his power, lighten their labors by cheerful and voluntary assistance. He will yield to them every little advantage which may occur in the regular routine of domestic life :—the most comfortable seat, if there be a difference ; the warmest position by the winter's fireside ; the nicest slice from the family joint, and so on.

In a public assembly of any kind, a well-bred man will pay regard to the feelings and wishes of the females by whom he is surrounded. He will not secure the best seat for himself, and leave the women folk to take care of themselves. He will not be seated at all, if the meeting be crowded, and a single female appear unaccomodated.

Good breeding will keep a person from making loud and startling noises, from pushing past another in entering or going out of a room ; from ostentatiously using a pocket-handkerchief; from hawking and spitting in company; from fidgeting any part of the body; from scratching the head, or picking the teeth with fork or with finger. In short, it will direct all who study its rules to abstain from every personal act which may give pain or offence to another's feelings. At the same time, it will enable them to bear much without taking offence. It will teach them when to speak and when to be silent, and how to behave with due respect to all. By attention to the rules of good breeding, and more especially to its leading principles, "the poorest man will be entitled to the character of a gentleman, and by inattention to them, the most wealthy person will be essentially vulgar. Vulgarity signifies coarseness or indelicacy of manner, and is not necessarily associated with poverty or lowliness of condition. Thus an operative artizan may be a gentleman, and worthy of our particular esteem; while an opulent merchant may be only a vulgar clown, with whom it is impossible to be on terms of friendly intercourse."

The following remarks upon the " Character of a Gentleman" by Brooke are so admirable that I need make no apology for quoting them entire. He says; " There is no term, in our language, more common than that of ' Gentleman;' and, whenever it is heard, all agree in the general idea of a man some way elevated above the vulgar. Yet, perhaps, no two living are precisely agreed respecting the qualities they think requisite for constituting this character. When we hear the epithets of a ' fine Gentleman,' ' a pretty Gentleman,' ' much of a Gentleman,' ' Gentlemanlike,' ' something of a Gentle-

man,' ' nothing of a Gentleman,' and so forth; all these
different appelations must intend a peculiarity annexed
to the ideas of those who express them; though no two
of them, as I said, may agree in the constituent qualities
of the character they have formed in their own mind.
There have been ladies who deemed fashionable dress a
very capital ingredient in the composition of—a Gentleman. A certain easy impudence acquired by low people, by casually being conversant in high life, has passed
a man current through many companies for—a Gentleman. In taverns and brothels, he who is the most of a
bully is the most of—a Gentleman. And the highway-
man, in his manner of taking your purse, may however
be allowed to have—much of the Gentleman. Plato,
among the philosophers, was ' the most of a man of
fashion;' and therefore allowed, at the court of Syracuse,
to be—the most of a Gentleman. But seriously, I apprehend that this character is pretty much upon the
modern. In all ancient or dead languages we have no
term, any way adequate, whereby we may express it
In the habits, manners, and characters of old Sparta
and old Rome, we find an antipathy to all the elements
of modern gentility. Among these rude and unpolished
people, you read of philosophers, of orators, of patriots,
heroes, and demigods; but you never hear of any character so elegant as that of—a pretty Gentleman.

" When those nations, however, became refined into
what their ancestors would have called corruption; when
luxury introduced, and fashion gave a sanction to cer
tain sciences, which Cynics would have branded with the
ll mannered appellations of drunkenness, gambling,

cheating, lying, &c. ; the practitioners assumed the new title of Gentlemen, till such Gentlemen became as plen-teous as stars in the milky-way, and lost distinction merely by the confluence of their lustre.   Wherefore as the said qualities were found to be of ready acquisition, and of easy descent to the populace from their betters, ambition judged it necessary to add further marks and criterions for severing the general herd from the nobler species—of Gentlemen.

" Accordingly, if the commonalty were observed to have a propensity to religion, their superiors affected a disdain of such vulgar prejudices ; and a freedom that cast off the restraints of morality, and a courage that spurned at the fear of a God, were accounted the distin-guishing characteristics—of a Gentleman.

" If the populace, as in China, were industrious and ingenious, the grandees, by the length of their nails and the cramping of their limbs, gave evidence that true dig-nity was above labor and utility, and that to be born to no end was the prerogative—of a Gentleman.

" If the common sort, by their conduct, declared a respect for the institutions of civil society and good gov-ernment ; their betters despised such pusillanimous con-formity, and the magistrates paid becoming regard to the distinction, and allowed of the superior liberties and privileges—of a Gentleman.

" If the lower set show a sense of common honesty and common order ; those who would figure in the world, think it incumbent to demonstrate that complaisance to inferiors, common manners, common equity, or any thing

common, is quite beneath the attention or sphere—of a
Gentleman.

"Now, as underlings are ever ambitious of imitating
and usurping the manners of their superiors; and as this
state of mortality is incident to perpetual change and
revolution, it may happen, that when the populace, by
encroaching on the province of gentility, have arrived to
their *ne plus ultra* of insolence, irreligion, &c.; the gentry, in order to be again distinguished, may assume the
station that their inferiors had forsaken, and, however
ridiculous the supposition may appear at present, humanity, equity, utility, complaisance, and piety, may in
time come to be the distinguishing characteristics—of a
Gentleman.

"It appears that the most general idea which people
have formed of a Gentleman, is that of a person of for
tune above the vulgar, and embellished by manners that
are fashionable in high life. In this case, fortune and
fashion are the two constituent ingredients in the composition of modern Gentlemen; for whatever the fashion
may be, whether moral or immoral, for or against reason
right or wrong, it is equally the duty of a Gentleman to
conform. And yet I apprehend, that true gentility is
altogether independent of fortune or fashion, of time,
customs, or opinions of any kind. The very same qualities that constituted a gentleman, in the first age of the
world, are permanently, invariably, and indispensably
necessary to the constitution of the same character to
the end of time.

"Hector was the finest gentleman of whom we read in
history, and Don Quixote the finest gentleman we read

of in romance ; as was instanced from the tenor of theil
principles and actions.

" Some time after the battle of Cressy, Edward the
Third of England, and Edward the Black Prince, the
more than heir of his father's renown, pressed John King
of France to indulge them with the pleasure of his company at London.   John was desirous of embracing the
.nvitation, and accordingly laid the proposal before his
parliament at Paris.   The parliament objected, that the
invitation had been made with an insidious design of
seizing his person, thereby to make the cheaper and
easier acquisition of the crown, to which Edward at that
time pretended.   But John replied, with some warmth,
that he was confident his brother Edward, and more
especially his young cousin, were too much of the GEN-
TLEMAN, to treat him in that manner.   He did not say
too much of the king, of the hero, or of the saint, bu:
too much of the GENTLEMAN to be guilty of any base-
ness.

" The sequel verified this opinion.   At the battle of
Poictiers King John was made prisoner, and soon after
conducted by the Black Prince to England.   The prince
entered London in triumph, amid the throng and accla-
mations of millions of the people.   But then this rather
appeared to be the triumph of the French king than
that of his conqueror.   John was seated on a proud
steed, royally robed, and attended by a numerous and
gorgeous train of the British nobility; while his conqueror endeavored, as much as possible, to disarrear,
and rode by his side in plain attire, and degradingly
seated on a little Irish hobby.

" As Aristotle and the Critics derived their rules for epic poetry and the sublime from a poem which Homer had written long before the rules were formed, or laws established for the purpose : thus, from the demeanor and innate principles of particular gentlemen, art has borrowed and instituted the many modes of behaviour, which the world has adopted, under the title of good manners.

" One quality of a gentleman is that of charity to the poor; and this is delicately instanced in the account which Don Quixote gives, to his fast friend Sancho Pancha, of the valorous but yet more pious knight-errant Saint Martin. On a day, said the Don, Saint Martin met a poor man half naked, and taking his cloak from his shoulders, he divided, and gave him the one half. Now, tell me at what time of the year this happened. Was I a witness? quoth, Sancho; how the vengeance should I know in what year or what time of the year it happened? Hadst thou Sancho, rejoined the knight, anything within thee of the sentiment of Saint Martin, thou must assuredly have known that this happened in winter; for, had it been summer, Saint Martin would had given the whole cloak.

" Another characteristic of the true gentleman, is a delicacy of behaviour toward that sex whom nature has entitled to the protection, and consequently entitled to the tenderness, of man.

" The same gentleman-errant, entering into a wood on a summer's evening, found himself entangled among nets of green thread that, here and there, hung from tree to tree; and conceiving it some matter of purposed conjuration, pushed valorously forward to break through the enchantment. Hereupon some beautiful shepherd esses interposed with a cry, and besought him to spare the implements of their innocent recreation. The knight, surprised and charmed by the vision, replied,— Fair creatures! my province is to protect, not to injure; to seek all means of service, but never of offence, more especially to any of your sex and apparent excellences Your pretty nets take up but a small piece of favored ground; but, did they inclose the world, I would seek out new worlds, whereby I might win a passage, rather than break them.

"Two very lovely but shamefaced girls had a cause, of some consequence, depending at Westminster, that indispensably required their personal appearance. They were relations of Sir Joseph Jeckel, and, on this tremendous occasion, requested his company and countenance at the court. Sir Joseph attended accordingly; and the cause being opened, the judge demanded whether he was to entitle those ladies by the denomination of spinsters. 'No, my Lord,' said Sir Joseph; 'they are lilies of the valley, they toil not, neither do they spin, yet you see that no monarch, in all his glory, was ever arrayed like one of these.'

"Another very peculiar characteristic of a gentleman is, the giving place and yielding to all with whom he has to do. Of this we have a shining and affecting instance in Abraham, perhaps the most accomplished character that may be found in history, whether sacred or profane. A contention had arisen between the herdsmen of Abraham and the herdsmen of his nephew, Lot, respecting the propriety of the pasture of the lands wherein they dwelled, that could now scarce contain the abundance of their cattle. And those servants, as is universally the case, had respectively endeavored to kindle and inflame their masters with their own passions. When Abraham, in consequence of this, perceived that the countenance of Lot began to change toward him, he called, and generously expostulated with him as followeth: 'Let there be no strife, I pray thee, between me and thee, or between my herdsmen and thy herdsmen; for we be brethren. If it be thy desire to separate thyself from me, is not the whole land before thee? If thou wilt take the left hand, then will I go to the right; or if thou depart to the right hand, then I will go to the left.'

"Another capital quality of the true gentleman is, that of feeling himself concerned and interested in others. Never was there so benevolent, so affecting, so pathetic a piece of oratory exhibited upon earth, as that of Abraham's pleading with God for averting the judgments that then impended over Sodom. But the matter is already so generally celebrated, that I am constrained to refer my reader to the passage at full; since the smallest abridgment must deduct from its beauties, and that nothing can be added to the excellences thereof.

" Honor, again, is said, in Scripture, peculiarly to distinguish the character of a gentleman; where it is written of Sechem, the son of Hamor, 'that he was more honorable than all the house of his father.'

" From hence it may be inferred, that human excel lence, or human amiableness, doth not so much consist in a freedom from frailty as in our recovery from lapses, our detestation of our own transgressions, and our desire of atoning, by all possible means, the injuries we have done, and the offences we have given. Herein, therefore, may consist the very singular distinction which the great apostle makes between his estimation of a just and of a good man. 'For a just or righteous man,' says he, 'one would grudge to die; but for a good man one would even dare to die.' Here the just man is supposed to adhere strictly to the rule of right or equity, and to exact from others the same measure that he is satisfied to mete; but the good man, though occasionally he may fall short of justice, has, properly speaking, no measure to his benevolence, his general propensity is to give more than the due. The just man condemns, and is desirous of punishing the transgressors of the line prescribed to himself; but the good man, in the sense of his own falls and failings, gives latitude, indulgence, and pardon. to others; he judges, he condemns no one save himself. The just man is a stream that deviates not to the right or left from its appointed channel, neither is swelled by the flood of passion above its banks; but the heart of the good man, the man of honor, the gentleman, is as a lamp lighted by the breath of GOD, and none save GOD himself can set limits to the efflux or irradiations thereof.

"Again, the gentleman never envies any superior excellence, but grows himself more excellent, by being the admirer, promoter, and lover thereof. Saul said to his son Jonathan, 'Thou son of the perverse, rebellious woman, do not I know that thou hast chosen the son of Jesse to thine own confusion? For as long as the son of Jesse liveth upon the ground, thou shalt not be established, nor thy kingdom, wherefore send and fetch him unto me, for he shall surely die.' Here every in teresting motive that can possibly be conceived to have an influence on man, united to urge Jonathan to the destruction of David; he would thereby have obeyed his king, and pacified a father who was enraged against him. He would thereby have removed the only luminary that then eclipsed the brightness of his own achievements. And he saw, as his father said, that the death of David alone could establish the kingdom in himself and his posterity. But all those considerations were of no avail to make Jonathan swerve from honor, to slacken the bands of his faith, or cool the warmth of his friendship. O Jonathan ! the sacrifice which thou then madest to virtue, was incomparably more illustrious in the sight of God and his angels than all the subsequent glories to which David attained. What a crown was thine, 'Jonathan, when thou wast slain in thy high places !'

"Saul of Tarsus had been a man of bigotry, blood, and violence; making havoc, and breathing out threatenings and slaughter, against all who were not of his own sect and persuasion. But, when the spirit of that INFANT, who laid himself in the manger of human flesh, came upon him, he acquired a new heart and a new nature; and he offered himself a willing subject to all the sufferings and persecutions which he had brought upon others.

"Saul from that time, exemplified in his own person, all those qualities of the gentleman, which he afterwards specifies in his celebrated description of that charity, which, as he says, alone endureth forever.

When Festus cried with a loud voice, 'Paul, thou art beside thyself, much learning doth make thee mad;' Paul stretched the hand, and answered, 'I am not mad, most noble Festus, but speak forth the words of truth and soberness. For the king knoweth of these things, before whom also I speak freely; for I am persuaded that none of these things are hidden from him. King Agrippa, believest thou the prophets? I know that thou believest.' Then Agrippa said unto Paul, 'Almost thou persuadest me to be a Christian.' And Paul said, 'I would to God that not only thou, but also all that hear me this day, were not only almost but altogether such as I am,—except these bonds.' Here, with what an inimitable elegance did this man, in his own person, at once sum up the orator, the saint, and the gentleman!

"From these instances, my friend, you must have seen that the character, or rather quality of a GENTLE-MAN, does not, in any degree, depend on fashion or mode, on station or opinion; neither changes with customs, climate, or ages. But, as the Spirit of God can alone inspire it into man, so it is, as God is the same, yesterday, to-day, and forever."

In concluding this chapter I would say:

"In the common actions and transactions of life, there is a wide distinction between the well-bred and the ill-bred. If a person of the latter sort be in a superior condition in life, his conduct towards those below him, or dependent upon him, is marked by haughtiness, or by unmannerly condescension. In the company of his equals in station and circumstances, an ill-bred man is

either captious and quarrelsome, or offensively familiar.
He does not consider that:

'The man who hails you Tom or Jack,
    And proves, by thumps upon your back,
        How he esteems your merit,
    Is such a friend, that one had need
    Be very much a friend indeed,
        To pardon or to bear it.'

"And if a man void of good breeding have to transact
business with a superior in wealth or situation, it is more
than likely that he will be needlessly humble, uninten-
tionally insolent, or, at any rate, miserably embarrassed.
On the contrary, a well-bred person will instinctively
avoid all these errors. 'To inferiors, he will speak
kindly and considerately, so as to relieve them from any
feeling of being beneath him in circumstances. To
equals, he will be plain, unaffected, and courteous. To
superiors, he will know how to show becoming respect,
without descending to subserviency or meanness. In
short, he will act a manly, inoffensive, and agreeable
part, in all the situations in life in which he may be
placed.'"

CHAPTER III.

TABLE ETIQUETTE.

It may seem a very simple thing to eat your meals, yet there is no occasion upon which the gentleman, and the low-bred, vulgar man are more strongly contrasted, than when at the table. The rules I shall give for table etiquette when in company will apply equally well for the home circle, with the exception of some few points, readily discernible, which may be omitted at your own table.

A well-bred man, receiving an invitation to dine with a friend should reply to it immediately, whether he accepts or declines it.

He should be punctual to the hour named in the invitation, five or ten minutes earlier if convenient, but not one instant later. He must never, unless he has previously asked permission to do so, take with him any friend not named in his invitation. His host and hostess have the privilege of inviting whom they will, and it is an imper tinence to force them to extend their hospitality, as they must do if you introduce a friend at their own house.

Speak, on entering the parlor of your friend, first to the hostess, then to the host.

When dinner is announced, the host or hostess will

give the signal for leaving the drawing-room, and you will probably be requested to escort one of the ladies to the table. Offer to her your left arm, and at the table wait until she is seated, indeed wait until every lady is seated, before taking your own place.

In leaving the parlor you will pass out first, and the lady will follow you, still holding your arm. At the door of the dining-room, the lady will drop your arm. Pass in, then wait on one side of the entrance till she passes you, to her place at the table.

If there are no ladies, you may go to the table with any gentleman who stands near you, or with whom you may be conversing when dinner is announced. If your companion is older than yourself, extend to him the same courtesy which you would use towards a lady.

There are a thousand little points to be observed in your conduct at table which, while they are not absolutely necessary, are yet distinctive marks of a well-bred man.

If, when at home, you practice habitually the courtesies of the table, they will sit upon you easily when abroad; but if you neglect them at home, you will use them awkwardly when in company, and you will find yourself recognized as a man who has " company manners," only when abroad.

I have seen men who eat soup, or chewed their food, in so noisy a manner as to be heard from one end of the table to the other; fill their mouths so full of food, as to threaten suffocation or choking; use their own knife for the butter, and salt; put their fingers in the sugar bowl, and commit other faults quite as monstrous, yet seem perfectly unconscious that they were doing anything to attract attention.

Try to sit easily and gracefully, but at the same time avoid crowding those beside you.

Far from eating with avidity of whatever delicacies which may be upon the table, and which are often served in small quantities, partake of them but sparingly, and decline them when offered the second time.

Many men at their own table have little peculiar notions, which a guest does well to respect. Some will feel hurt, even offended, if you decline a dish which they recommend; while others expect you to eat enormously, as if they feared you did not appreciate their hospitality unless you tasted of every dish upon the table. Try to pay respect to such whims at the table of others, but avoid having any such notions when presiding over your own board.

Observe a strict sobriety; never drink of more than one kind of wine, and partake of that sparingly.

The style of serving dinner is different at different houses; if there are many servants they will bring you your plate filled, and you must keep it. If you have the care of a lady, see that she has what she desires, before you give your own order to the waiter; but if there are but few domestics, and the dishes are upon the table, you may with perfect propriety help those near you, from any dish within your reach.

If your host or hostess passes you a plate, keep it, especially if you have chosen the food upon it, for others have also a choice, and by passing it, you may give your neighbor dishes distaseful to him, and take yourself those which he would much prefer.

If in the leaves of your salad, or in a plate of fruit you find a worm or insect, pass your plate to the waiter, without any comment, and he will bring you another.

Be careful to avoid the extremes of gluttony or over daintiness at table. To eat enormously is disgusting; but if you eat too sparingly, your host may think that you despise his fare.

Watch that the lady whom you escorted to the table is well helped. Lift and change her plate for her, pass her bread, salt, and butter, give her orders to the waiter, and pay her every attention in your power.

Before taking your place at table, wait until your place is pointed out to you, unless there are cards bearing the names of the guests upon the plates; in the latter case, take the place thus marked for you.

Put your napkin upon your lap, covering your knees. It is out of date, and now looked upon as a vulgar habit to put your napkin up over your breast.

Sit neither too near nor too far from the table. Never hitch up your coat-sleeves or wristbands as if you were going to wash your hands. Some men do this habitually, but it is a sign of very bad breeding.

Never tip your chair, or lounge back in it during dinner.

All gesticulations are out of place, and in bad taste at the table. Avoid making them.

Converse in a low tone to your neighbor, yet not with any air of secresy if others are engaged in *tête-à-tête* conversation: if, however, the conversation is general, avoid conversing *tête-à-tête*. Do not raise your voice too much; if you cannot make those at some distance from you hear you when speaking in a moderate tone, confine your remarks to those near you.

If you wish for a knife, plate, or anything from the side table, never address those in attendance as "Waiter!" as you would at a hotel or *restaurant*, but call one of them by name; if you cannot do this, make him a sign without speaking.

Unless you are requested to do so, never select any particular part of a dish; but, if your host asks you what part you prefer, name some part, as in this case the incivility would consist in making your host choose as well as carve for you.

Never blow your soup if it is too hot, but wait until it cools. Never raise your plate to your lips, but eat with your spoon.

Never touch either your knife or your fork until after you have finished eating your soup. Leave your spoon in your soup plate, that the servant may remove them both. Never take soup twice.

In changing your plate, or passing it during dinner, remove your knife and fork, that the plate *alone* may be taken, but after you have finished your dinner, cross the knife and fork on the plate, that the servant may take all away, before bringing you clean ones for dessert.

Do not bite your bread from the roll or slice, nor cut it with your knife; break off small pieces and pat these in your mouth with your fingers.

At dinner do not put butter on your bread. Never dip a piece of bread into the gravy or preserves upon yo·ır plate and then bite it, but if you wish to eat them together, break the bread into small pieces, and carry these to your mouth with your fork.

Use always the salt-spoon, sugar-tongs, and butter knife; to use your own knife, spoon, or fingers, evinces a shocking want of good-breeding.

Never criticize any dish before you.

If a dish is distasteful to you, decline it, but make no remarks about it. It is sickening and disgusting to explain at a table how one article makes you sick, or why some other dish has become distasteful to you. I have seen a well-dressed tempting dish go from a table untouched, because one of the company told a most disgusting anecdote about finding vermin served in a similar dish. No wit in the narration can excuse so palpably an error of politeness.

Never put bones, or the seeds of fruit upon the tablecloth. Put them upon the edge of your plate.

Never use your knife for any purpose but to *cut* your food. It is not meant to be put in your mouth. Your fork is intended to carry the food from your plate to your mouth, and no gentleman ever eats with his knife.

If the meat or fish upon your plate is too rare or too well-done, do not eat it; give for an excuse that you prefer some other dish before you; but never tell your host that his cook has made the dish uneatable.

Never speak when you have anything in your mouth. Never pile the food on your plate as if you were starving, but take a little at a time; the dishes will not run away.

Never use your own knife and fork to help either

yourself or others. There is always one before the dish at every well-served table, and you should use that.

It is a good plan to accustom yourself to using your fork with the left hand, when eating, as you thus avoid the awkwardness of constantly passing the fork from your left hand to your right, and back again, when cutting your food and eating it.

Never put fruit or bon-bons in your pocket to carry them from the table.

Do not cut fruit with a steel knife. Use a silver one.

Never eat so fast as to hurry the others at the table, nor so slowly as to keep them waiting.

If you do not take wine, never keep the bottle standing before you, but pass it on. If you do take it, pass it on as soon as you have filled your glass.

If you wish to remove a fish bone or fruit seed from your mouth, cover your lips with your hand or napkin, that others may not see you remove it.

If you wish to use your handkerchief, and have not time to leave the table, turn your head away, and as quickly as possible put the handkerchief in your pocket again.

Always wipe your mouth before drinking, as nothing is more ill-bred than to grease your glass with your lips.

If you are invited to drink with a friend, and do not drink wine, bow, raise your glass of water and drink with him.

Do not propose to take wine with your host; it is his privilege to invite you

Do not put your glass upside down on the table to signify that you do not wish to drink any more; it is sufficient to refuse firmly. Do not be persuaded to touch another drop of wine after your own prudence warns you that you have taken enough.

Avoid any air of mystery when speaking to those next you; it is ill-bred and in excessively bad taste.

If you wish to speak of any one, or to any one at the table, call them by name, but never point or make a signal when at table.

When taking coffee, never pour it into your saucer, but let it cool in the cup, and drink from that.

If at a gentleman's party, never ask any one to sing or tell a story; your host alone has the right thus to call upon his guests.

If invited yourself to sing, and you feel sufficiently sure that you will give pleasure, comply immediately with the request.

If, however, you refuse, remain firm in your refusal, as to yield after once refusing is a breach of etiquette.

When the finger-glasses are passed, dip your fingers into them and then wipe them upon your napkin.

Never leave the table till the mistress of the house gives the signal.

On leaving the table put your napkin on the table, but do not fold it.

Offer your arm to the lady whom you escorted to the table.

It is excessively rude to leave the house as soon as dinner is over. Respect to your hostess obliges you to stay in the drawing-room at least an hour.

If the ladies withdraw, leaving the gentlemen, after dinner, rise when they leave the table, and remain standing until they have left the room.

I give, from a recent English work, some humorously written directions for table etiquette, and, although they are some of them repetitions of what I have already given, they will be found to contain many useful hints:

" We now come to habits at table, which are very important. However agreeable a man may be in society, if he offends or disgusts by his table traits, he will soon be scouted from it, and justly so. There are some broad rules for behavior at table. Whenever there is a servant to help you, never help yourself. Never put a knife into your mouth, not even with cheese, which should be eaten with a fork. Never use a spoon for anything but liquids. Never touch anything edible with your fingers.

" Forks were, undoubtedly, a later invention than fingers, but, as we are not cannibals, I am inclined to think they were a good one. There are some few things which you may take up with your fingers. Thus an epicure will eat even macaroni with his fingers; and as sucking asparagus is more pleasant than chewing it, you may, as an epicure, take it up *au naturel*. But both these things are generally eaten with a fork. Bread is, of course, eaten with the fingers, and it would be absurd to carve it with your knife and fork. It must, on the contrary, always be broken when not buttered, and you should never put a slice of dry bread to your mouth to bite a piece off. Most fresh fruit, too, is eaten with the natural prongs, but when you have peeled an orange or apple, you should cut it with the aid of the fork, unless you can succeed in breaking it. Apropos of which, I may hint that no epicure ever yet put a knife to an apple, and that an orange should be peeled with a spoon. But the art of peeling an orange so as to hold its own juice, and its own sugar too, is one that can scarcely be taught in a book.

"However, let us go to dinner, and I will soon tell you whether you are a well-bred man or not; and here let me premise that what is good manners for a small dinner is good manners for a large one, and *vice versâ*. Now, the first thing you do is to sit down. Stop, sir! pray do not cram yourself into the table in that way; no, nor sit a yard from it, like that. How graceless, inconvenient, and in the way of conversation! Why, dear me! you are positively putting your elbows on the table, and now you have got your hands fumbling about with the spoons and forks, and now you are nearly knocking my new hock glasses over. Can't you take your hands down, sir? Didn't you learn that in the nursery? Didn't your mamma say to you, 'Never put your hands above the table except to carve or eat?' Oh! but come, no nonsense, sit up, if you please. I can't have your fine head of hair forming a side dish on my table; you must not bury your face in the plate, you came to show it, and it ought to be alive. Well, but there is no occasion to throw your head back like that, you look like an alderman, sir, *after* dinner. Pray, don't lounge in that sleepy way. You are here to eat, drink, and be merry. You can sleep when you get home.

"Well, then, I suppose you can see your napkin

Got none, indeed! Very likely, in *my* house. You may be sure. that I never sit down to a meal without napkins. I don't want to make my tablecloths unfit for use, and I don't want to make my trousers unwearable. Well, now, we are all seated, you can unfold it on your knees; no, no; don't tuck it into your waistcoat like an alderman; and what! what on earth do you mean by wiping your forehead with it? Do you take it for a towel? Well, never mind, I am consoled that you did not go farther, and use it as a pocket-handkerchief. So talk away to the lady on your right, and wait till soup is handed to you. By the way, that waiting is the most important part of table manners, and, as much as possible, you should avoid asking for anything or helping yourself from the table. Your soup you eat with a spoon—I don't know what else you *could* eat it with— but then it must be one of good size   Yes, that will do, but I beg you will not make that odious noise in drinking your soup. It is louder than a dog lapping water, and a cat would be quite genteel to it. Then you need not scrape up the plate in that way, nor even tilt it to get the last drop. I shall be happy to send you some more; but I must just remark, that it is not the custom to take two helpings of soup, and it is liable to keep other people waiting, which, once for all, is a selfish and intolerable habit. But don't you hear the servant offering you sherry? I wish you would attend, for my servants have quite enough to do, and can't wait all the evening while you finish that very mild story to Miss Goggles. Come, leave that decanter alone. I had the wine put on the table to fill up; the servants will hand it directly, or, as we are a small party, I will tell you to help yourself: but, pray, do not be so officious. (There, I have sent him some turbot to keep him quiet. I declare he cannot make up his mind.) You are keeping my servant again, sir. Will you, or will you not, do turbot? Don't ex amine it in that way; it is quite fresh, I assure you, take or decline it. Ah, you take it, but that is no reason why you should take up a knife too. Fish, I re- peat, must never be touched with a knife. Take a fork in the right and a small piece of bread in the left hand. Good, but—? Oh! that is atrocious; of course you must not swallow the bones, but you should rather do so than spit them out in that way. Put up your napkin like this, and land the said bone on your plate. Don't rub your head in the sauce, my good man, nor go prog- ging about after the shrimps or oysters therein. Oh! how horrid! I declare your mouth was wide open and full of fish. Small pieces, I beseech you; and once for all, whatever you eat, keep your mouth *shut*, and never attempt to talk with it full.

"So now you have got a pâté. Surely you are not taking two on your plate. There is plenty of dinner to come, and one is quite enough. Oh! dear me, you are incorrigible. What! a knife to cut that light, brittle pastry? No, nor fingers, never. Nor a spoon—almost as bad. Take your fork, sir, your fork; and, now you have eaten, oblige me by wiping your mouth and mous- tache with your napkin, for there is a bit of the pastry hanging to the latter, and looking very disagreeable. Well, you can refuse a dish if you like. There is no positive necessity for you to take venison if you don't

want it. But, at any rate, do not be in that terrific
hurry. You are not going off by the next train. Wait
for the sauce and wait for vegetables; but whether you
eat them or not do not begin before everybody else.
Surely you must take my table for that of a railway re-
freshment-room, for you have finished before the person
I helped first. Fast eating is bad for the digestion, my
good sir, and not very good manners either. What! are
you trying to eat meat with a fork alone? Oh! it is
sweetbread, I beg your pardon, you are quite right.
Let me give you a rule,—Everything that can be cut
without a knife, should be cut with a fork alone. Eat
your vegetables, therefore, with a fork. No, there is no
necessity to take a spoon for peas; a fork in the right
hand will do. What! did I really see you put your
knife into your mouth? Then I must give you up.
Once for all, and ever, the knife is to cut, not to help
with. Pray, do not munch in that noisy manner; chew
your food well, but softly. *Eat slowly.* Have you not
heard that Napoleon lost the battle of Leipsic by eating
too fast? It is a fact though. His haste caused indigestion, which made him incapable of attending to the
details of the battle. You see you are the last person
eating at table. Sir, I will not allow you to speak to
my servants in that way. If they are so remiss as to
oblige you to ask for anything, do it gently, and in a
row tone, and thank a servant just as much as you would
his master. Ten to one he is as good a man; and because he is your inferior in position, is the very reason
you should treat him courteously. Oh! it is of no use
to ask me to take wine; far from pacifying me, it will

only make me more angry, for I tell you the custom is quite gone out, except in a few country villages, and at a mess-table. Nor need you ask the lady to do so. However, there is this consolation, if you should ask any one to take wine with you, he or she *cannot* refuse, so you have your own way. Perhaps next you will be asking me to hob and nob, or *trinquer* in the French fashion with arms encircled. Ah! you don't know, perhaps, that when a lady *trinques* in that way with you, you have a right to finish off with a kiss. Very likely, indeed! But it *is* the custom in familiar circles in France, but then we are not Frenchmen. *Will* you attend to your lady, sir? You did not come merely to eat, but to make yourself agreeable. Don't sit as glum as the Memnon at Thebes; talk and be pleasant. Now, you have some pudding. No knife—no, *no*. A spoon if you like, but better still, a fork. Yes, ice requires a spoon; there is a small one handed you, take that.

"Say 'no.' This is the fourth time wine has been handed to you, and I am sure you have had enough. Decline this time if you please. Decline that dish too. Are you going to eat of everything that is handed? I pity you if you do. No, you must not ask for more cheese, and you must eat it with your fork. Break the rusk with your fingers. Good. You are drinking a glass of old port. Do not quaff it down at a gulp in that way. Never drink a whole glassful of anything at once.

"Well, here is the wine and dessert. Take whichever wine you like, but remember you must keep to that, and not change about. Before you go up stairs I will allow you a glass of sherry after your claret, but otherwise drink of one wine only. You don't mean to say you are helping yourself to wine before the ladies. At least, offer it to the one next to you, and then pass it on, gently, not with a push like that. Do not drink so fast; you will hurry me in passing the decanters, if I see that your glass is empty. You need not eat dessert till the ladies are gone, but offer them whatever is nearest to you. And now they are gone, draw your chair near mine, and I will try and talk more pleasantly to you. You will come out admirably at your next dinner with all my teaching. What! you are excited, you are talking loud to the colonel. Nonsense. Come and talk easily to me or to your nearest neighbor. There, don't drink any more wine, for I see you are getting romantic. You oblige me to make a move. You have had enough of those walnuts; you are keeping me, my dear sir. So now to coffee [one cup] and tea, which I beg you will not pour into your saucer to cool. Well, the dinner has done you good, and me too. Let us be amiable to the ladies, but not too much so."

" *Champ, champ; Smack, smack; Smack, smack; Champ, champ;*—It is one thing to know how to make a pudding, and another to know now to eat it when made. Unmerciful and monstrous are the noises with which some persons accompany the eating—no, the devouring of the food for which, we trust, they are thankful. To sit down with a company of such masticators is like joining 'a herd of swine feeding.' Soberly, at no time, probably, are the rules of good breeding less regarded than at 'feeding time,' and at no place is a departure from these rules more noticeable than at table. Some persons gnaw at a crust as dogs gnaw a bone, rattle knives and spoons against their teeth as though anxious to prove which is the harder, and scrape their plates with an energy and perseverance which would be very commendable if bestowed upon any object worth the trouble. Others, in defiance of the old nursery rhyme—

'I must not dip, howe'er I wish,
My spoon or finger in the dish;'

are perpetually helping themselves in this very straightforward and unsophisticated manner. Another, with a mouth full of food contrives to make his teeth and tongue perform the double duty of chewing and talking at the same time. Another, quite in military style, in the intervals of cramming, makes his knife and fork keep guard over the jealously watched plate, being held upright on either side in the clenched fist, like the musket of a raw recruit. And another, as often as leisure serves, fidgets his plate from left to right, and from right to left, or round and round, until the painful operation of feeding is over.

"There is, we know, such a thing as being 'too nice' —'more nice than wise.' It is quite possible to be fastidious. But there are also such inconsiderable matters as decency and good order; and it surely is better to err on the right than on the wrong side of good breeding."

5

CHAPTER IV.

ETIQUETTE IN THE STREET.

A GENTLEMAN will be always polite, in the parlor, dining-room, and in the street. This last clause will especially include courtesy towards ladies, no matter what may be their age or position. A man who will annoy or insult a woman in the street, lowers himself to a brute, no matter whether he offends by look, word, or gesture. There are several little forms of etiquette, given below, the observance of which will mark the gentleman in the street.

When walking with a lady, or with a gentleman who is older than yourself, give them the upper side of the pavement, that is, the side nearest the house.

When walking alone, and you see any one coming towards you on the same side of the street, give the upper part of the pavement, as you turn aside, to a man who may carry a heavy bundle, to a priest or clergyman, to a woman, or to any elderly person.

In a crowd never rudely push aside those who impede your progress, but wait patiently until the way is clear If you are hurried by business of importance or an engagement, you will find that a few courteous words will

open the way before you more quickly than the mos
violent pushing and loud talking.

If obliged to cross a plank, or narrow path, let any
lady or old person who may also be passing, precede
you. In case the way is slippery or in any way unsafe,
you may, with perfect propriety, offer to assist either a
a lady or elderly person in crossing it.

Do not smoke in the street until after dark, and then
remove your cigar from your mouth, if you meet a lady.

Be careful about your dress. You can never know
whom you may meet, so it is best to never leave the
house otherwise than well-dressed. Bright colors, and
much jewelry are both unbecoming to a gentleman in
the street.

Avoid touching any one with your elbows in passing,
and do not swing your arms as you walk.

Be careful when walking with or near a lady, not to
put your foot upon her dress.

In carrying an umbrella, hold it so that you can see
the way clear before you; avoid striking your umbrella
against those which pass you; if you are walking with a
lady, let the umbrella cover her perfectly, but hold it so
that you will not touch her bonnet. If you have the
care of two ladies, let them carry the umbrella between
them, and walk outside yourself. Nothing can be more
absurd than for a gentleman to walk between two ladies,
holding the umbrella himself; while, in this way, he is
perfectly protected, the ladies receive upon their dresses
and cloaks the little streams of water which run from
the points of the umbrella.

In case of a sudden fall of rain, you may, with per-

fect propriety, offer your umbrella to a lady who is un‹
provided with one. If she accepts it, and asks your
address to return it, leave it with her ; if she hesitates,
and does not wish to deprive you of the use of it, you
may offer to accompany her to her destination, and then,
do not open a conversation ; let your manner be respectful, and when you leave her, let her thank you, assure
her of the pleasure it has given you to be of service,
bow, and leave her.

In meeting a lady friend, wait for her to bow to you,
and in returning her salutation, remove your hat. To
a gentleman you may bow, merely touching your hat,
if he is alone or with another gentleman ; but if he has
a lady with him, raise your hat in bowing to him. If
you stop to speak to a lady, hold your hat in your hand,
until she leaves you, unless she requests you to replace it.
With a gentleman you may replace it immediately.

Never join a lady whom you may meet, without first
asking her permission to do so.

If you stop to converse with any one in the street,
stand near the houses, that you may not interfere with
others who are passing.

You may bow to a lady who is seated at a windcw, if
you are in the street ; but you must not bow from a
window to a lady in the street.

Do not stop to join a crowd who are collected round
a street show, or street merchant, unless you wish to
pass for a countryman taking a holiday in the city.

If you stop any one to enquire your own way, or if
you are called upon to direct another, remove your hat
while asking or answering the question.

If you see a lady leaving a carriage unattended, or hesitating at a bad crossing, you may, with propriety, offer your hand or arm to assist her, and having seen her safely upon the pavement, bow, and pass on.

In a car or omnibus, when a lady wishes to get out, stop the car for her, pass up her fare, and in an omnibus alight and assist her in getting out, bowing as you leave her.

Be gentle, courteous, and kind to children. There is no surer token of a low, vulgar mind, than unkindness to little ones whom you may meet in the streets.

A true gentleman never stops to consider what may be the position of any woman whom it is in his power to aid in the street. He will assist an Irish washerwoman with her large basket or bundle over a crossing, or carry over the little charges of a distressed negro nurse, with the same gentle courtesy which he would extend toward the lady who was stepping from her private carriage. The true spirit of chivalry makes the courtesy due to the *sex*, not to the position of the individual.

When you are escorting a lady in the street, politeness does not absolutely require you to carry her bundle or parasol, but if you are gallant you will do so. You must regulate your walk by hers, and not force her to keep up with your ordinary pace.

Watch that you do not lead her into any bad places, and assist her carefully over each crossing, or wet place on the pavement.

If you are walking in the country, and pass any

streamlet, offer your hand to assist your companion in crossing.

If you pass over a fence, and she refuses your assistance in crossing it, walk forward, and do not look back, until she joins you again. The best way to assist a lady over a fence, is to stand yourself upon the upper rail, and while using one hand to keep a steady position, stoop, offer her the other, and with a firm, steady grasp, hold her hand until she stands beside you; then let her go down on the other side first, and follow her when she is safe upon the ground.

In starting for a walk with a lady, unless she is a stranger in the place towards whom you act as guide, let her select your destination.

Where there are several ladies, and you are required to escort one of them, select the elderly, or those whose personal appearance will probably make them least likely to be sought by others. You will probably be repaid by finding them very intelligent, and with a fund of conversation. If there are more ladies than gentlemen, you may offer an arm to two, with some jest about the difficulty of choosing, or the double honor you enjoy.

Offer your seat in any public conveyance, to a lady who is standing. It is often quite as great a kindness and mark of courtesy to take a child in your lap.

When with a lady you must pay her expenses as well as your own; if she offers to share the expense, decline unless she insists upon it, in the latter case yield gracefully. Many ladies, who have no brother or father, and are dependent upon their gentlemen friends for escort, make it a rule to be under no pecuniary obligations to them, and you will, in such a case, offend more by in-insisting upon your right to take that expense, than by quietly pocketing your dignity and their cash together.

I know many gentlemen will cry out at my assertion; but I have observed this matter, and know many *ladies* who will sincerely agree with me in my opinion.

In a carriage always give the back seat to the lady or ladies accompanying you. If you have but one lady with you, take the seat opposite to her, unless she invites you to sit beside her, in which case accept her offer.

Never put your arm across the seat, or around her, as many do in riding. It is an impertinence, and if she is a lady of refinement, she will resent it as such.

If you offer a seat in your carriage to a lady, or another gentleman whom you may meet at a party or picnic, take them home, before you drive to your own destination, no matter how much you may have to drive out of your own way.

Be the last to enter the carriage, the first to leave it. If you have ladies with you, offer them your hand to assist them in entering and alighting, and you should take the arm of an old gentleman to assist him.

If offered a seat in the carriage of a gentleman friend, stand aside for him to get in first, but if he waits for you, bow and take your seat before he does.

When driving a lady in a two-seated vehicle, you should assist her to enter the carriage, see that her dress is not in danger of touching the wheels, and that her shawl, parasol, and fan, are where she can reach them, before you take your own seat. If she wishes to stop, and you remain with the horses, you should alight before she does, assist her in alighting, and again alight to help her to her seat when she returns, even if you keep your place on the seat whilst she is gone.

When attending a lady in a horse-back ride, never mount your horse until she is ready to start. Give her your hand to assist her in mounting, arrange the folds of her habit, hand her her reins and her whip, and then take your own seat on your saddle.

Let her pace be yours. Start when she does, and le. her decide how fast or slowly she will ride. Never let the head of your horse pass the shoulders of hers, and be watchful and ready to render her any assistance she may require.

Never, by rapid riding, force her to ride faster than she may desire.

Never touch her bridle, reins, or whip, except she particularly requests your assistance, or an accident, or threatened danger, makes it necessary.

If there is dust or wind, ride so as to protect her from it as far as possible.

If the road is muddy be careful that you do not ride so as to bespatter her habit. It is best to ride on the side away from that upon which her habit falls. Some ladies change their side in riding, from time to time, and you must watch and see upon which side the skirt falls, that, on a muddy day, you may avoid favoring the habit with the mud your horse's hoofs throw up.

If you ride with a gentleman older than yourself, or one who claims your respect, let him mount before you do. Extend the same courtesy towards any gentleman whom you have invited to accompany you, as he is, for the ride, your guest.

The honorable place is on the right. Give this to a lady, an elderly man, or your guest.

A modern writer says:—"If walking with a female relative or friend, a well-bred man will take the outer side of the pavement, not only because the wall-side is the most honorable side of a public walk, but also because it is generally the farthest point from danger in the street. If walking alone, he will be ready to offer assistance to any female whom he may see exposed to real peril from any source. Courtesy and manly courage will both incite him to this line of conduct. In general, this is a point of honor which almost all men are proud to achieve. It has frequently happened that even where the savage passions of men have been excited, and when mobs have been in actual conflict, women have been gallantly escorted through the sanguinary crowd unharmed, and their presence has even been a protection to their protectors. This is as it should be; and such incidents have shown in a striking manner, not only the excellency of good breeding, but have also brought it out when and where it was least to be expected.

"In streets and all public walks, a well-bred person will be easily distinguished from another who sets at defiance the rules of good breeding. He will not, whatever be his station, hinder and annoy his fellow pedestrians, by loitering or standing still in the middle of the footway. He will, if walking in company, abstain from making impertinent remarks on those he meets; he will even be careful not to appear indelicately to notice them.

He will not take ' the crown of the causeway' to himself, but readily fall in with the convenient custom which ne- cessity has provided, and walk on the right side of the path, leaving the left side free for those who are walkir g in the opposite direction. Any departure from these plain rules of good breeding is downright rudeness and insult; or, at all events, it betrays great ignorance or disregard for propriety. And yet, how often are they departed from! It is, by no means, uncommon, espe- cially in country places, for groups of working men to obstruct the pathway upon which they take a fancy to lounge, without any definite object, as far as appears, but that of making rude remarks upon passers-by. But it is not only the laboring classes of society who offend against good breeding in this way; too many others of- fend in the same, and by stopping to talk in the middle of the pavement put all who pass to great inconvenience."

In meeting a lady do not offer to shake hands with her, but accept her hand when *she* offers it for you to take.

" In France, where politeness is found in every class, the people do not run against each other in the streets nor brush rudely by each other, as they sometimes do in our cities. It adds much to the pleasure of walking, to be free from such annoyance; and this can only be brought about by the well-taught few setting a good ex- ample to the many. By having your wits about you, you can win your way through a thronged street without touching even the extreme circumference of a balloon sleeve; and, if each one strove to avoid all contact, it would be easily accomplished."

CHAPTER V.

ETIQUETTE FOR CALLING.

A GENTLEMAN in society must calculate to give a certain portion of his time to making calls upon his friends,
both ladies and gentlemen. He may extend his visiting
list to as large a number as his inclination and time will
permit him to attend to, but he cannot contract it after
passing certain limits. His position as a man in society
obliges him to call,

Upon any stranger visiting his city, who brings a letter of introduction to him;

Upon any friend from another city, to whose hospitality he has been at any time indebted;

Upon any gentleman after receiving from his hands a
favor or courtesy;

Upon his host at any dinner or supper party, (such
calls should be made very soon after the entertainment
given);

Upon any friend whose joy or grief calls for an
expression of sympathy, whether it be congratulation or
condolence;

Upon any friend who has lately returned from a voyage or long journey;

Upon any lady who has accepted his services as an

escort, either for a journey or the return from a ball or evening party; this call must be made the day after he has thus escorted the lady;

Upon his hostess after any party to which he has been invited, whether he has accepted or declined such invitation;

Upon any lady who has accepted his escort for an evening, a walk or a drive;

Upon any friend whom long or severe illness keeps confined to the house;

Upon his lady friends on New Year's day, (if it is the custom of the city in which he resides;)

Upon any of his friends when they receive bridal calls;

Upon lady friends in any city you are visiting; if gentlemen friends reside in the same city, you may either call upon them or send your card with your address and the length of time you intend staying, written upon it; if a stranger or friend visiting your city sends such a card, you must call at the earliest opportunity;

Upon any one of whom you wish to ask a favor; to make him, under such circumstances call upon you, is extremely rude;

Upon any one who has asked a favor of you; you will add very much to the pleasure you confer, in granting a favor, by calling to express the gratification it affords you to be able to oblige your friend; you will soften the pain of a refusal, if, by calling, and expressing your regret, you show that you feel interested in the request, and consider it of importance.

Upon intimate friends, relatives, and ladies, you may

call without waiting for any of the occasions given above.

Do not fall into the vulgar error of declaiming against the practice of making calls, declaring it a "bore," tiresome, or stupid. The custom is a good one.

An English writer says:—

"The visit or call is a much better institution than is generally supposed. It has its drawbacks. It wastes much time; it necessitates much small talk. It obliges one to dress on the chance of finding a friend at home; but for all this it is almost the only means of making an acquaintance ripen into friendship. In the visit, all the strain, which general society somehow necessitates, is thrown off. A man receives you in his rooms cordially, and makes you welcome, not to a stiff dinner, but an easy chair and conversation. A lady, who in the ball room or party has been compelled to limit her conversation, can here speak more freely. The talk can descend from generalities to personal inquiries, and need I say, that if you wish to know a young lady truly, you must see her at home, and by day light.

"The main points to be observed about visits, are the proper occasions and the proper hours. Now, between actual friends there is little need of etiquette in these respects. A friendly visit may be made at any time, on any occasion. True, you are more welcome when the business of the day is over, in the afternoon rather than 'n the morning, and you must, even as a friend, avoid calling at meal times. But, on the other hand, many people receive visits in the evening, and certainly this is the best time to make them."

Any first call which you receive must be returned promptly. If you do not wish to continue the acquaintance any farther, you need not return a second call, but politeness imperatively demands a return of the first one.

A call may be made upon ladies in the morning or afternoon; but in this country, where almost every man has some business to occupy his day, the evening is the best time for paying calls. You will gain ground in easy intercourse and friendly acquaintance more rapidly in one evening, than in several morning calls.

Never make a call upon a lady before eleven o'clock in the morning, or after nine in the evening.

Avoid meal times. If you inadvertently call at dinner or tea time, and your host is thus forced to invite you to the table, it is best to decline the civility. If, however, you see that you will give pleasure by staying, accept the invitation, but be careful to avoid calling again at the same hour.

No man in the United States, excepting His Excellency, the President, can expect to receive calls unless he returns them.

"Visiting," says a French writer, "forms the cord which binds society together, and it is so firmly tied, that were the knot severed, society would perish."

A ceremonious call should never extend over more than fifteen minutes, and it should not be less than ten minutes.

If you see the master of the house take letters or a paper from his pocket, look at the clock, have an absent air, beat time with his fingers or hands, or in any other way show weariness or *ennui*, you may safely conclude that it is time for you to leave, though you may not nave been five minutes in the house. If you are host to the most wearisome visitor in existence, if he stays hours, and converses only on subjects which do not interest you, in the least; unless he is keeping you from an important engagement, you must not show the least sign of weariness. Listen to him politely, endeavor to entertain him, and preserve a smiling composure, though you may long to show him the door. In case he is keeping you from business of importance, or an imperative engagement, you may, without any infringement upon the laws of politeness, inform him of the fact, and beg him to excuse you; you must, however, express polite regret at your enforced want of hospitality, and invite him to call again.

It is quite an art to make a graceful exit after a call. To know how to choose the moment when you will be regretted, and to retire leaving your friends anxious for a repetition of the call, is an accomplishment worth acquiring.

When you begin to tire of your visit, you may generally feel sure that your entertainers are tired of you, and if you do not want to remain printed upon their memory as " the man who makes such long, tiresome calls," you will retire.

If other callers come in before you leave a friend's parlor, do not rise immediately as if you wished to avoid them, but remain seated a few moments, and then leave, that your hostess may not have too many visitors to entertain at one time.

If you have been enjoying a *tête-à-tête* interview with a lady, and other callers come in, do not hurry away, as if detected in a crime, but after a few courteous, graceful words, and the interchange of some pleasant remarks, leave her to entertain her other friends.

To endeavor when making a call to "sit out" others in the room, is very rude.

When your host or hostess urges you to stay longer, after you have risen to go, be sure that that is the best time for departure. You will do better to go then, when you will be regretted, than to wait until you have worn your welcome out.

When making a visit of condolence, take your tone from your host or hostess. If they speak of their misfortune, or, in case of death, of the departed relative, join them. Speak of the talents or virtues of the deceased, and your sympathy with their loss. If, on the other hand, they avoid the subject, then it is best for you to avoid it too. They may feel their inability to sustain a conversation upon the subject of their recent affliction, and it would then be cruel to force it upon them. If you see that they are making an effort, perhaps a painful one, to appear cheerful, try to make them forget for the time their sorrows, and chat on cheerful subjects. At the same time, avoid jesting, merriment, or undue levity, as it will be out of place, and appear heartless.

A visit of congratulation, should, on the contrary, be cheerful, gay, and joyous. Here, painful subjects would be out of place. Do not mar the happiness of your friend by the description of the misery of your own position or that of a third person, but endeavor to show by joyous sympathy that the pleasure of your friend is also your happiness. To laugh with those who laugh, weep with those who are afflicted, is not hypocrisy, but kindly friendly sympathy.

Always, when making a friendly call, send up your card, by the servant who opens the door.

There are many times when a card may be left, even if the family upon which you call is at home. Visits of condolence, unless amongst relatives or very intimate friends, are best made by leaving a card with enquiries for the health of the family, and offers of service.

If you see upon entering a friend's parlor, that your call is keeping him from going out, or, if you find a lady friend dressed for a party or promenade, make your visit very brief. In the latter case, if the lady seems unattended, and urges your stay, you may offer your services as an escort.

Never visit a literary man, an artist, any man whose profession allows him to remain at home, at the hours when he is engaged in the pursuit of his profession. The fact that you know he is at home is nothing; he will not care to receive visits during the time allotted to his daily work.

Never take another gentleman to call upon one of your lady friends without first obtaining her permission to do so.

The calls made after receiving an invitation to dinner, a party, ball, or other entertainment should be made within a fortnight after the civility has been accepted.

When you have saluted the host and hostess, do not
6

take a seat until they invite you to do so, or by a motion, and themselves sitting down, show that they expect **you** to do the same.

Keep your hat in your hand when making a call. This will show your host that you do not intend to remain to dine or sup with him. You may leave an umbrella or cane in the hall if you wish, but your hat and gloves you must carry into the parlor. In making an evening call for the first time keep your hat and gloves in your hand, until the host or hostess requests you to lay them aside and spend the evening.

When going to spend the evening with a friend whom you visit often, leave your hat, gloves, and great coat in the hall.

If, on entering a parlor of a lady friend, in the evening, you see by her dress, or any other token, that she was expecting to go to the opera, concert, or an evening party, make a call of a few minutes only, and then retire. I have known men who accepted instantly the invitation given them to remain under these circumstances, and deprive their friends of an anticipated pleasure, when their call could have been made at any other time. To thus impose upon the courtesy of your friends is excessively rude. Nothing will pardon such an acceptance but the impossibility of repeating your call, owing to a short stay in town, or any other cause. Even in this case it is better to accompany your friends upon their expedition in search of pleasure. You can, of course, easily obtain admittance if they are going to a public entertainment, and if they invite you to join their party to a friend's house, you may without impropriety do so, as a lady is privileged to introduce you to her friends under such circumstances. It requires tact and discretion to know when to accept and when to decline such an invitation. Be careful that you do not intrude upon a party already complete in themselves, or that you do not interfere with the plans of the gentlemen who have already been accepted as escorts.

Never make a *third* upon such occasions. Neither one of a couple who propose spending the evening abroad together, will thank the intruder who spoils their tête-à-tête.

When you find, on entering a room, that your visit is for any reason inopportune, do not instantly retire unless you have entered unperceived and can so leave, in which case leave immediately; if, however, you have been seen, your instant retreat is cut off. Then endeavor by your own graceful ease to cover any embarrassment your entrance may have caused, make but a short call, and, if you can, leave your friends under the impression that you saw nothing out of the way when you entered.

Always leave a card when you find the person upon whom you have called absent from home.

A card should have nothing written upon it, but your name and address. To leave a card with your business address, or the nature of your profession written upon it, shows a shocking ignorance of polite society. Business cards are never to be used excepting when you make a business call.

Never use a card that is ornamented in any way, whether by a fancy border, painted corners, or embossing. Let it be perfectly plain, tinted, if you like, in color, but without ornament, and have your name written or printed in the middle, your address, in smaller characters, in the lower left hand corner.   Many gentlemen omit the Mr. upon their cards, writing merely their Christian and surname; this is a matter of taste, you may follow your own inclination.   Let your card be written thus:—

HENRY C. PRATT.

No. 217 L. street.

A physician will put Dr. before or M.D. after the name, and an officer in the army or navy may add his title; but for militia officers to do so is absurd.

If you call upon a lady, who invites you to be seated, place a chair for her, and wait until she takes it before you sit down yourself.

Never sit beside a lady upon a sofa, or on a chair very near her own, unless she invites you to do so.

If a lady enters the room where you are making a call, rise, and remain standing until she is seated.   Even if she is a perfect stranger, offer her a chair, if there is none near her.

You must rise if a lady leaves the room, and remain standing until she has passed out.

If you are engaged in any profession which you follow at home, and receive a caller, you may, during the daytime, invite him into your library, study, or the room in which you work, and, unless you use your pen, you may work while he is with you.

When you receive a visitor, meet him at the door, offer a chair, take his hat and cane, and, while speaking of the pleasure the call affords you, show, by your manner, that you are sincere, and desire a long call.

Do not let your host come with you any farther than the room door if he has other visitors; but if you are showing out a friend, and leave no others in the parlor, you should come to the street door.

A few hints from an English author, will not be amiss in this place. He says:—

"Visits of condolence and congratulation must be made about a week after the event. If you are intimate with the person on whom you call, you may ask, in the first case, for admission; if not, it is better only to leave a card, and make your 'kind inquiries' of the servant, who is generally primed in what manner to answer them. In visits of congratulation you should always go in, and be hearty in your congratulations. Visits of condolence are terrible inflictions to both receiver and giver, but they may be made less so by avoiding, as much as consistent with sympathy, any allusion to the past. The receiver does well to abstain from tears. A lady of my acquaintance, who had lost her husband, was receiving such a visit in her best crape. She wept profusely for some time upon the best of broad-hemmed cambric handkerchiefs, and then turning to her visitor, said: 'I am sure you will be glad to hear that Mr. B has left me most comfortably provided for.' *Hinc illæ lacrymæ.* Perhaps they would have been more sincere if he had left her without a penny. At the same time, if you have not sympathy and heart enough to pump up a little condolence, you will do better to avoid it, but take care that your conversation is not too gay. Whatever you may feel, you must respect the sorrows of others.

" On marriage, cards are sent round to such people as you wish to keep among your acquaintance, and it is then their part to call first on the young couple, when within distance.

" Having entered the house, you take up with you to the drawing-room both hat and cane, but leave an umbrella in the hall. In France it is usual to leave a great-coat down stairs also, but as calls are made in this country in morning dress, it is not necessary to do so.

" It is not usual to introduce people at morning calls in large towns; in the country it is sometimes done, not always. The law of introductions is, in fact, to force no one into an acquaintance. You should, therefore, ascertain beforehand whether it is agreeable to both to be introduced; but if a lady or a superior expresses a wish to know a gentleman or an inferior, the latter two have no right to decline the honor. The introduction is of an inferior [which position a gentleman always holds to a lady] to the superior. You introduce Mr. Smith to Mrs. Jones, or Mr. A. to Lord B., not *vice versa.* In introducing two persons, it is not necessary to lead one of them up by the hand, but it is sufficient simply to precede them. Having thus brought the person to be introduced up to the one to whom he is to be presented, it is the custom, even when the consent has been previously obtained, to say, with a slight bow, to the superior personage: 'Will you allow me to introduce Mr. ——?' The person addressed replies by bowing to the one introduced, who also bows at the same time, while the intro ducer repeats their names, and then retires, leaving them to converse. Thus, for instance, in presenting Mr. Jones to Mrs. Smith, you will say, ' Mrs. Smith, allow me to introduce Mr. Jones,' and while they are engaged in bowing you will murmur, ' Mrs. Smith—Mr. Jones,' and escape. If you have to present three or four people to said Mrs. Smith, it will suffice to utter their respective names without repeating that of the lady.

" A well-bred person always receives visitors at whatever time they may call, or whoever they may be; but if you are occupied and cannot afford to be interrupted by a mere ceremony, you should instruct the servant *beforehand* to say that you are 'not at home.' This form has often been denounced as a falsehood, but a lie is no lie unless intended to deceive; and since the words are universally understood to mean that you are engaged, it can be no harm to give such an order to a servant. But, on the other hand, if the servant once admits a visitor within the hall, you should receive him at any inconvenience to yourself."

He also gives some admirable hints upon visits made to friends in another city or the country.

He says:—

" A few words on visits to country houses before I quit this subject. Since a man's house is his castle, no one, not even a near relation, has a right to invite himself to stay in it. It is not only taking a liberty to do so, but may prove to be very inconvenient. A general invitation, too, should never be acted on. It is often given without any intention of following it up; but, if given, should be turned into a special one sooner or later   An invitation should specify the persons whom it includes, and the person invited should never presume to take with him any one not specified. If a gentleman cannot dispense with his valet, he should write to ask leave to bring a servant; but the means of your inviter, and the size of the house, should be taken into consideration, and it is better taste to dispense with a servant altogether. Children and horses are still more troublesome, and should never be taken without special mention made of them. It is equally bad taste to arrive with a wagonful of luggage, as that is naturally taken as a hint that you intend to stay a long time. The length of a country visit is indeed a difficult matter to decide, but in the present day people who receive much generally specify the length in their invitation—a plan which saves a great deal of trouble and doubt. But a custom not so commendable has lately come in of limiting the visits of acquaintance to two or three days. This may be pardonable where the guest lives at no great distance, but it is preposterous to expect a person to travel a long distance for a stay of three nights. If, however, the length be not specified, and cannot easily be discovered, a week is the limit for a country visit, except at the house of a near relation or very old friend. It will, however, save trouble to yourself, if, soon after your arrival, you state that you are come "for a few days," and, if your host wishes you to make a longer visit, he will at once press you to do so.

"The main point in a country visit is to give as little trouble as possible, to conform to the habits of your entertainers, and never to be in the way. On this principle you will retire to your own occupations soon after breakfast, unless some arrangement has been made for passing the morning otherwise. If you have nothing to do, you may be sure that your host has something to attend to in the morning. Another point of good-breeding is to be punctual at meals, for a host and hostess never sit down without their guest, and dinner may be getting cold. If, however, a guest should fail in this particular, a well-bred entertainer will not only take no notice of it, but attempt to set the late comer as much at his ease as possible. A host should provide amusements for his guests, and give up his time as much as possible to them; but if he should be a professional man or student — an author, for instance — the guest should, at the commencement of the visit, insist that he will not allow him to interrupt his occupations, and the latter will set his visitor more at his ease by accepting this arrangement. In fact, the rule on which a host should act is to make his visitors as much at home as possible; that on which a visitor should act, is to interfere as little as possible with the domestic routine of the house.

"The worst part of a country visit is the necessity of giving gratuities to the servants, for a poor man may often find his visit cost him far more than if he had stayed at home. It is a custom which ought to be put down, because a host who receives much should pay his own servants for the extra trouble given. Some people have made by-laws against it in their houses, but, like those about gratuities to railway porters, they are seldom regarded. In a great house a man-servant expects gold but a poor man should not be ashamed of offering him silver. It must depend on the length of the visit. The ladies give to the female, the gentlemen to the male servants. Would that I might see my friends without paying them for their hospitality in this indirect manner!"

CHAPTER VI.

ETIQUETTE FOR THE BALL ROOM.

OF all the amusements open for young people, none is more delightful and more popular than dancing. Lord Chesterfield, in his letters to his son, says: "Dancing is, in itself, a very trifling and silly thing; but it is one of those established follies to which people of sense are sometimes obliged to conform; and then they should be able to do it well. And, though I would not have you a dancer, yet, when you do dance, I would have you dance well, as I would have·you do everything you do well." In another letter, he writes: "Do you mind your dancing while your dancing master is with you? As you will be often under the necessity of dancing a minuet, I would have you dance it very well. Remember that the graceful motion of the arms, the giving of your hand, and the putting off and putting on of your hat genteelly, are the material parts of a gentleman's danc-ing. But the greatest advantage of dancing well is, that it necessarily teaches you to present yourself, to sit, stand, and walk genteelly; all of which are of real im-portance to a man of fashion."

Although the days are over when gentlemen carried their hats into ball rooms and danced minuets, there are

useful hints in the quotations given above. Nothing
will give ease of manner and a graceful carriage to a
gentleman more surely than the knowledge of dancing.
He will, in its practice, acquire easy motion, a light step,
and learn to use both hands and feet well. What can
be more awkward than a man who continually finds his
hands and feet in his way, and, by his fussy movements, betrays his trouble? A good dancer never feels
this embarrassment, consequently he never appears aware
of the existence of his feet, and carries his hands and
arms gracefully. Some people being bashful and afraid
of attracting attention in a ball room or evening party,
do not take lessons in dancing, overlooking the fact that
it is those who do *not* partake of the amusement on such
occasions, not those who do, that attract attention. To
all such gentlemen I would say; Learn to dance. You
will find it one of the very best plans for correcting
bashfulness. Unless you possess the accomplishments
that are common in polite society, you can neither give
nor receive all the benefits that can be derived from social intercourse.

When you receive an invitation to a ball, answer it immediately.

If you go alone, go from the dressing-room to the
ball room, find your host and hostess, and speak first to
them; if there are several ladies in the house, take the
earliest opportunity of paying your respects to each of
them, and invite one of them to dance with you the first
dance. If she is already engaged, you should endeavor
to engage her for a dance later in the evening, and are
then at liberty to seek a partner amongst the guests.

When you have engaged a partner for a dance, you should go to her a few moments before the set for which you have engaged her will be formed, that you may not be hurried in taking your places upon the floor. Enquire whether she prefers the head or side place in the set, and take the position she names.

In inviting a lady to dance with you, the words, " Will you *honor* me with your hand for a quadrille?" or, "Shall I have the *honor* of dancing this set with you?" are more used now than " Shall I have the *pleasure ?*" or, " Will you give me the *pleasure* of dancing with you ?"

Offer a lady your arm to lead her to the quadrille, and in the pauses between the figures endeavor to make the duty of standing still less tiresome by pleasant conversation. Let the subjects be light, as you will be constantly interrupted by the figures in the dance. There is no occasion upon which a pleasant flow of small talk is more *àpropos*, and agreeable than in a ball room.

When the dance is over, offer your arm to your partner, and enquire whether she prefers to go immediately to her seat, or wishes to promenade. If she chooses the former, conduct her to her seat, stand near her a few moments, chatting, then bow, and give other gentlemen an opportunity of addressing her. If she prefers to promenade, walk with her until she expresses a wish to sit down. Enquire, before you leave her, whether you can be of any service, and, if the supper-room is open, invite her to go in there with you.

You will pay a delicate compliment and one that will certainly be appreciated, if, when a lady declines your invitation to dance on the plea of fatigue or fear of fatigue, you do not seek another partner, but remain **with** the lady you have just invited, and thus imply that **the** pleasure of talking with, and being near, her, is greater than that of dancing with another.

Let your hostess understand that you are at her service for the evening, that she may have a prospect of giving her wall flowers a partner, and, however unattractive these may prove, endeavor to make yourself as agreeable to them as possible.

Your conduct will differ if you escort a lady to a ball. Then your principal attentions must be paid to her. You must call for her punctually at the hour she has appointed, and it is your duty to provide the carriage. You may carry her a bouquet if you will, this is optional. A more elegant way of presenting it is to send it in the afternoon with your card, as, if you wait until evening, she may think you do not mean to present one, and provide one for herself.

When you arrive at your destination, leave the carriage, and assist her in alighting; then escort her to the lady's dressing-room, leave her at the door, and go to the gentlemen's dressing-room. As soon as you have arranged your own dress, go again to the door of the lady's room, and wait until your companion comes out. Give her your left arm and escort her to the ball room; find the hostess and lead your companion to her. When they have exchanged greetings, lead your lady to a seat, and then engage her for the first dance. Tell her that while you will not deprive others of the pleasure of dancing with her, you are desirous of dancing with her whenever she is not more pleasantly engaged, and before seeking a partner for any other set, see whether your lady is engaged or is ready to dance again with you. You must watch during the evening, and, while you do not force your attentions upon her, or prevent others from paying her attention, you must never allow her to be alone, but join her whenever others are not speaking to her. You must take her in to supper, and be ready to leave the party, whenever she wishes to do so.

If the ball is given in your own house, or at that of a near relative, it becomes your duty to see that every lady, young or old, handsome or ugly, is provided with a partner, though the oldest and ugliest may fall to your own share.

Never stand up to dance unless you are perfect master of the step, figure, and time of that dance. If you make a mistake you not only render yourself ridiculous, but you annoy your partner and the others in the set.

If you have come alone to a ball, do not devote yourself entirely to any one lady. Divide your attentions amongst several, and never dance twice in succession with the same partner.

To affect an air of secrecy or mystery when conversing in a ball-room is a piece of impertinence for which no lady of delicacy will thank you.

When you conduct your partner to her seat, thank her for the pleasure she has conferred upon you, and do not remain too long conversing with her.

Give your partner your whole attention when dancing with her. To let your eyes wander round the room, or to make remarks betraying your interest in others, is not flattering, as she will not be unobservant of your want of taste.

Be very careful not to forget an engagement. It is an unpardonable breach of politeness to ask a lady to dance with you, and neglect to remind her of her promise when the time to redeem it comes.

A dress coat, dress boots, full suit of black, and white or very light kid gloves must be worn in a ball room. A white waistcoat and cravat are sometimes worn, but this is a matter of taste.

Never wait until the music commences before inviting a lady to dance with you.

If one lady refuses you, do not ask another who is seated near her to dance the same set. Do not go immediately to another lady, but chat a few moments with the one whom you first invited, and then join a group or gentlemen friends for a few moments, before seeking another partner.

Never dance without gloves. This is an imperative rule. It is best to carry two pair, as in the contact with dark dresses, or in handing refreshments, you may soil the pair you wear on entering the room, and will thus be under the necessity of offering your hand covered by a soiled glove, to some fair partner. You can slip unperceived from the room, change the soiled for a fresh pair, and then avoid that mortification.

If your partner has a bouquet, handkerchief, or fan in her hand, do not offer to carry them for her. If she finds they embarrass her, she will request you to hold them for her, but etiquette requires you not to notice them, unless she speaks of them first.

Do not be the last to leave the ball room. It is more elegant tc leave early, as staying too late gives others the impression that you do not often have an invitation to a ball, and must "make the most of it."

S)me gentlemen linger at a private ball until all the la lies have left, and then congregate in the supper-room, where they remain for hours, totally regardless of the fact that they are keeping the wearied host and his servants from their rest. Never, as you value your reputation as a gentleman of refinement, be among the number of these "hangers on."

The author of a recent work cn etiquette, published in England, gives the following hints for those who gc to balls. He says :—

"When inviting a lady to dance, if she replies very politely, asking to be excused, as she does not wish to dance ('with you,' being probably her mental reservation), a man ought to be satisfied. At all events, he should never press her to dance after one refusal. The set forms which Turveydrop would give for the invitation are too much of the deportment school to be used in practice. If you know a young lady slightly, it is sufficient tc say to her, 'May I have the pleasure of dancing this waltz, &c., with you?' or if intimately, 'Will you dance, Miss A—?' The young lady who has refused one gentleman, has no right to accept another for that dance; and young ladies who do not wish to be annoyed, must take care not to accept two gentlemen for the same dance. In Germany such innocent blunders often cause fatal results. Two partners arrive at the same moment to claim the fair one's hand; she vows

7

she has not made a mistake; 'was sure she was engaged
to Herr A—, and not to Herr B—;' Herr B— is equally
certain that she was engaged to him. The awkwardness
is, that if he at once gives her up, he appears to be indifferent about it; while, if he presses his suit, he must
quarrel with Herr A—, unless the damsel is clever
enough to satisfy both of them; and particularly if there
is an especial interest in Herr B—, he yields at last,
but when the dance is over, sends a friend to Herr A—.
Absurd as all this is, it is common, and I have often
seen one Herr or the other walking about with a huge
gash on his cheek, or his arm in a sling, a few days after
a ball.

"Friendship, it appears, can be let out on hire. The
lady who was so very amiable to you last night, has a
right to ignore your existence to-day. In fact, a ball
room acquaintance rarely goes any farther, until you
have met at more balls than one. In the same way a
man cannot, after being introduced to a young lady to
dance with, ask her to do so more than twice in the
same evening. A man may dance four or even five
times with the same partner. On the other hand, a
real well-bred man will wish to be useful, and there are
certain people whom it is imperative on him to ask to
dance—the daughters of the house, for instance, and
any young ladies whom he may know intimately; but
most of all the well-bred and amiable man will sacrifice
himself to those plain, ill-dressed, dull looking beings
who cling to the wall, unsought and despairing. After
all, he will not regret his good nature. The spirits re-
viving at the unexpected invitation, the wall-flower will

pour out her best conversation, will dance her best, and will show him her gratitude in some way or other.

"The formal bow at the end of a quadrille has gradually dwindled away. At the end of every dance you offer your right arm to your partner, (if by mistake you offer the left, you may turn the blunder into a pretty compliment, by reminding her that is *le bras du cœur*, nearest the heart, which if not anatomically true, is, at least, no worse than talking of a sunset and sunrise), and walk half round the room with her. You then ask her if she will take any refreshment, and, if she accepts, you convey your precious allotment of tarlatane to the refreshment room to be invigorated by an ice or negus, or what you will. It is judicious not to linger too long in this room, if you are engaged to some one else for the next dance. You will have the pleasure of hearing the music begin in the distant ball room, and of reflecting that an expectant fair is sighing for you like Marianna—

> "He cometh not," she said.
> She said, "I am a-weary a-weary,
> I would I were in bed;"

which is not an unfrequent wish in some ball rooms. A well-bred girl, too, will remember this, and always offer to return to the ball room, however interesting the conversation.

"If you are prudent you will not dance every dance, nor in fact, much more than half the number on the list; you will then escape that hateful redness of face at the time, and that wearing fatigue the next day which are among the worst features of a ball. Again, a gentleman

must remember that a ball is essentially a lady's party
and in their presence he should be gentle and delicate
almost to a fault, never pushing his way, apologizing if
he tread on a dress, still more so if he tears it, begging
pardon for any accidental annoyance he may occasion,
and addressing every body with a smile. But quite un
pardonable are those men whom one sometimes meets,
who, standing in a door-way, talk and laugh as they
would in a barrack or college-rooms, always coarsely,
often indelicately. What must the state of their minds
be, if the sight of beauty, modesty, and virtue, does not
awe them into silence! A man, too, who strolls down
the room with his head in the air, looking as if there
were not a creature there worth dancing with, is an ill-
bred man, so is he who looks bored; and worse than all
is he who takes too much champagne.

"If you are dancing with a young lady when the supper-room is opened, you must ask her if she would like
to go to supper, and if she says 'yes,' which, in 999
cases out of 1000, she certainly will do, you must take
her thither. If you are not dancing, the lady of the
house will probably recruit you to take in some chaperon.
However little you may relish this, you must not show
your disgust. In fact, no man ought to be disgusted at
being able to do anything for a lady; it should be his
highest privilege, but it is not—in these modern unchi-
valrous days—perhaps never was so. Having placed
your partner then at the supper-table, if there is room
there, but if not at a side-table, or even at none, you
must be as active as Puck in attending to her wants,
and as women take as long to settle their fancies in

edibles as in love-matters, you had better at once get her something substantial, chicken, *pâté de foie gras, mayonnaise,* or what you will. Afterwards come jelly and trifle in due course.

"A young lady often goes down half-a-dozen times to the supper-room—it is to be hoped not for the purpose of eating—but she should not do so with the same part-ner more than once. While the lady is supping you must stand by and talk to her, attending to every want, and the most you may take yourself is a glass of cham-pagne when you help her. You then lead her up stairs again, and if you are not wanted there any more, you may steal down and do a little quiet refreshment on your own account. As long, however, as there are many ladies still at the table, you have no right to begin. Nothing marks a man here so much as gorging at sup-per. Balls are meant for dancing, not eating, and un-fortunately too many young men forget this in the pre-sent day. Lastly, be careful what you say and how you dance after supper, even more so than before it, for if you in the slightest way displease a young lady, she may fancy that you have been too partial to strong fluids, and ladies never forgive that. It would be hard on the lady of the house if every body leaving a large ball thought it necessary to wish her good night. In quitting a small dance, however, a parting bow is expected. It is then that the pretty daughter of the house gives you that sweet smile of which you dream afterwards in a goose-berry nightmare of 'tum-tum-tiddy-tum,' and waltzes *à deux temps,* and masses of tarlatane and bright eyes, flushed checks and dewy glances.   See them to-morrow, my dear fellow, it will cure you.

"I think flirtation comes under the head of morals more than of manners; still I may be allowed to say that ball room flirtation being more open is less danger ous than any other.   A prudent man will never presume on a girl's liveliness or banter.   No man of taste ever made an offer after supper, and certainly nine-tenths of those who have done so have regretted it at breakfast the next morning.

"At public balls there are generally either three or four stewards on duty, or a professional master of cere-monies.   These gentlemen having made all the arrange-ments, order the dances, and have power to change them if desirable.   They also undertake to present young men to ladies, but it must be understood that such an introduction is only available for *one* dance.   It is better taste to ask the steward to introduce you simply to a partner, than to point out any lady in particular.   He will probably then ask you if you have a choice, and if not, you may be certain he will take you to an estab-lished wall-flower.   Public balls are scarcely enjoyable unless you have your own party.

"As the great charm of a ball is its perfect accord and harmony, all altercations, loud talking, &c., are doubly ill-mannered in a ball room.   Very little suffices to dis-turb the peace of the whole company."

The same author gives some hints upon dancing which are so excellent that I need make no apology for quoting them.   He says :—

" 'Thank you—aw—I do not dance,' is now a very

common reply from a well-dressed, handsome man, who is leaning against the side of the door, to the anxious, heated hostess, who feels it incumbent on her to find a partner for poor Miss Wallflower. I say the reply is not only common, but even regarded as rather a fine one to make. In short, men of the present day don't, won't, or can't dance; and you can't make them do it, except by threatening to give them no supper. I really cannot discover the reason for this aversion to an innocent amusement, for the apparent purpose of enjoying which they have spent an hour and a half on their toilet. There is something, indeed, in the heat of a ball room, there is a great deal in the ridiculous smallness of the closets into which the ball-giver crowds two hundred people, with a cruel indifference only equalled by that of the black-hole of Calcutta, expecting them to enjoy themselves, when the ladies' dresses are crushed and torn, and the gentlemen, under the despotism of theirs, are melting away almost as rapidly as the ices with which an occasional waiter has the heartlessness to insult them. Then, again, it is a great nuisance to be intro-duced to a succession of plain, uninteresting young women, of whose tastes, modes of life, &c., you have not the slightest conception: who may look gay, yet have never a thought beyond the curate and the parish, or appear to be serious, while they understand nothing but the opera and So-and-so's ball—in fact, to be in perpetual risk of either shocking their prejudices, or plaguing them with subjects in which they can have no possible interest; to take your chance whether they can dance at all, and to know that when you have lighted on a real charmer, perhaps the beauty of the room, she is only lent to you for that dance, and, when that is over, and you have salaamed away again, you and she must re-main to one another as if you had never met; to feel, in short, that you must destroy either your present com-fort or future happiness, is certainly sufficiently trying to keep a man close to the side-posts of the doorway. But these are reasons which might keep him altogether from a ball room, and, if he has these and other objec-tions to dancing, he certainly cannot be justified in com-ing to a place set apart for that sole purpose.

" But I suspect that there are other reasons, and that, in most cases, the individual can dance and does dance at times, but has now a vulgar desire to be distinguished from the rest of his sex present, and to appear indiffer-ent to the pleasures of the evening. If this be his laudable desire, however he might, at least, be consistent, and continue to cling to his door-post, like St. Sebastian to his tree, and reply throughout the evening, 'Thank you, I don't take refreshments;' 'Thank you, I can't eat supper;' 'Thank you, I don't talk;' 'Thank you, I don't drink champagne,'—for if a ball room be purga-tory, what a demoniacal conflict does a supper-room pre-sent; if young ladies be bad for the heart, champagne is worse for the head.

" No, it is the will, not the power to dance which is wanting, and to refuse to do so, unless for a really good reason, is not the part of a well-bred man. To mar the pleasure of others is obviously bad manners, and, though at the door-post, you may not be in the way, you may be certain that there are some young ladies longing to dance, and expecting to be asked, and that the hostess is vexed and annoyed by seeing them fixed, like pictures, to the wall. It is therefore the duty of every man who has no scruples about dancing, and purposes to appear at balls, to learn how to dance.

"In the present day the art is much simplified, and if you can walk through a quadrille, and perform a polka, waltz, or galop, you may often dance a whole evening through. Of course, if you can add to these the Lancers, Schottische, and Polka-Mazurka, you will have more variety, and can be more generally agreeable. But if your master or mistress [a man learns better from the former] has stuffed into your head some of the three hundred dances which he tells you exist, the best thing you can do is to forget them again. Whether right or wrong, the number of usual dances is limited, and unusual ones should be very sparingly introduced into a ball, for as few people know them, their dancing, on the one hand, becomes a mere display, and, on the other, interrupts the enjoyment of the majority.

"The quadrille is pronounced to be essentially a conversational dance, but, inasmuch as the figures are perpetually calling you away from your partner, the first necessity for dancing a quadrille is to be supplied with a fund of small talk, in which you can go from subject to subject like a bee from flower to flower. The next point is to carry yourself uprightly. Time was when—as in the days of the *minuet de la cour*—the carriage constituted the dance. This is still the case with the quadrille, in which, even if ignorant of the figures, you may acquit yourself well by a calm, graceful carriage. After all, the most important figure is the *smile*, and the feet may be left to their fate, if we know what to do with our hands; of which I may observe that they should never be pocketed.

"The smile is essential. A dance is supposed to amuse, and nothing is more out of place in it than a gloomy scowl, unless it be an ill-tempered frown. The gaiety of a dance is more essential than the accuracy of its figures, and if you feel none yourself, you may, at least, look pleased by that of those around you. A defiant manner is equally obnoxious. An acquaintance of mine always gives me the impression, when he advances in *l'été*, that he is about to box the lady who comes to meet him. But the most objectionable of all is the supercilious manner. Dear me, if you really think you do your partner an honor in dancing with her, you should, at least, remember that your condescension is annulled by the manner in which you treat her.

"A lady—beautiful word!—is a delicate creature, one who should be reverenced and delicately treated. It is, therefore, unpardonable to rush about in a quadrille, to catch hold of a lady's hand as if it were a door-handle, or to drag her furiously across the room, as if you were Bluebeard and she Fatima, with the mysterious closet opposite to you. This *brusque* violent style of dancing is, unfortunately, common, but immediately stamps a man. Though I would not have you wear a perpetual simper, you should certainly smile when you take a lady's hand, and the old custom of bowing in doing so, is one that we may regret; for, does she not confer an honor on us by the action? To squeeze it, on the other hand, is a gross familiarity, for which you would deserve to be kicked out of the room.

" 'Steps,' as the *chasser* of the quadrille is called, belong to a past age, and even ladies are now content to walk through a quadrille. It is, however, necessary to keep time with the music, the great object being the general harmony. To preserve this, it is also advisable, where the quadrille, as is now generally the case, is danced by two long lines of couples down the room, that in *l'été*, and other figures, in which a gentleman and lady advance alone to meet one another, none but gentlemen should advance from the one side, and, therefore, none but ladies from the other.

" Dancing masters find it convenient to introduce new figures, and the fashion of *La Trénise* and the *Grande Ronde* is repeatedly changing. It is wise to know the last mode, but not to insist on dancing it. A quadrille cannot go on evenly if any confusion arises from the ignorance, obstinacy, or inattention of any one of the dancers. It is therefore useful to know every way in which a figure may be danced, and to take your cue from the others. It is amusing, however, to find how even such a trifle as a choice of figures in a quadrille can help to mark caste, and give a handle for supercilious sneers. Jones, the other day, was protesting that the Browns were 'vulgar.' Why so? they are well-bred.' 'Yes, so they are.' 'They are well-informed.' 'Certainly.' 'They are polite, speak good English, dress quietly and well, are graceful and even elegant." 'I grant you all that.' 'Then what fault can you find with them?' My dear fellow, they are people who gal-

lop round in the last figure of a quadrille,' he replied,
triumphantly.   But to a certain extent Jones is right.
Where a choice is given, the man of taste will always
select for a quadrille (as it is a conversational dance)
the quieter mode of performing a figure, and so the
Browns, if perfect in other respects, at least were wanting in taste.   There is one alteration lately introduced
from France, which I sincerely trust, will be universally
accepted.   The farce of that degrading little performance
called 'setting'—where you dance before your partner
somewhat like Man Friday before Robinson Crusoe, and
then as if your feelings were overcome, seize her hands
and whirl her round—has been finally abolished by a
decree of Fashion, and thus more opportunity is given
for conversation, and in a crowded room you have no
occasion to crush yourself and partner between the couples on each side of you.

"I do not attempt to deny that the quadrille, as now
walked, is ridiculous ; the figures, which might be graceful, if performed in a lively manner, have entirely lost
their spirit, and are become a burlesque of dancing ;
but, at the same time, it is a most valuable dance.   Old
and young, stout and thin, good dancers and bad, lazy
and active, stupid and clever, married and single, can all
join in it, and have not only an excuse and opportunity
for *tête-à-tête* conversation, which is decidedly the easiest, but find encouragement in the music, and in some
cases convenient breaks in the necessity of dancing.   A
person of few ideas has time to collect them while the
partner is performing, and one of many can bring them
out with double effect.   Lastly, if you wish to be polite

or friendly to an acquaintance who dances atrociously, you can select a quadrille for him or her, as the case may be.

"Very different in object and principle are the so-called round dances, and there are great limitations as to those who should join in them. Here the intention is to enjoy a peculiar physical movement under peculiar conditions, and the conversation during the intervals of rest is only a secondary object. These dances demand activity and lightness, and should therefore be, as a rule, confined to the young. An old man sacrifices all his dignity in a polka, and an old woman is ridiculous in a waltz. Corpulency, too, is generally a great impediment, though some stout people prove to be the lightest dancers.

"The morality of round dances scarcely comes within my province. They certainly can be made very indelicate; so can any dance, and the French *cancan* proves that the quadrille is no safer in this respect than the waltz. But it is a gross insult to our daughters and sisters to suppose them capable of any but the most innocent and purest enjoyment in the dance, while of our young men I will say, that to the pure all things are pure. Those who see harm in it, are those in whose mind evil thoughts must have arisen. *Honi soit qui mal y pense.* Those who rail against dancing are perhaps not aware that they do but follow in the steps of the Romish Church. In many parts of the Continent, bishops who have never danced in their lives, and perhaps never seen a dance, have laid a ban of excommunication on waltzing. A story was told to me in Normandy of the worthy Bishop of Bayeux, one of this number. A priest of his diocese petitioned him to put down round dances 'I know nothing about them,' replied the prelate, 'I have never seen a waltz.' Upon this the younger ecclesiastic attempted to explain what it was and wherein the danger lay, but the bishop could not see it. 'Will Monseigneur permit me to show him?' asked the priest. 'Certainly. My chaplain here appears to understand the subject; let me see you two waltz.' How the reverend gentlemen came to know so much about it does not appear, but they certainly danced a polka, a gallop, and a *trois-temps* waltz. 'All these seem harmless enough.' 'Oh! but Monseigneur has not seen the worst;' and thereupon the two gentlemen proceeded to flounder through a *valse à deux-temps*. They must have murdered it terribly, for they were not half round the room when his Lordship cried out, 'Enough, enough, that is atrocious, and deserves excommunication.' Accordingly this waltz was forbid, while the other dances were allowed. I was at a public ball at Caen soon after this occurrence, and was amused to find the *trois-temps* danced with a peculiar shuffle, by way of compromise between conscience and pleasure.

"There are people in this country whose logic is as good as that of the Bishop of Bayeux, but I confess my inability to understand it. If there is impropriety in round dances, there is the same in all. But to the waltz, which poets have praised and preachers denounced. The French, with all their love of danger, waltz atrociously, the English but little better; the Germans and Russians alone understand it. I could rave through three pages about the innocent enjoyment of a good waltz, its grace

and beauty, but I will be practical instead, and give you
a few hints on the subject.

"The position is the most important point. The lady
and gentleman before starting should stand exactly opposite to one another, quite upright, and not, as is so
common, painfully close to one another. If the man's
hand be placed where it should be, at the centre of the
lady's waist, and not all round it, he will have as firm a
hold and not be obliged to stoop, or bend to his right.
The lady's head should then be turned a little towards
her left shoulder, and her partner's somewhat less towards his right, in order to preserve the proper balance.
Nothing can be more atrocious than to see a lady lay
her head on her partner's shoulder; but, on the other
hand, she will not dance well, if she turns it in the opposite direction. The lady again should throw her head
and shoulders a little back, and the man lean a very
little forward.

"The position having been gained, the step is the
next question. In Germany the rapidity of the waltz is
very great, but it is rendered elegant by slackening the
pace every now and then, and thus giving a *crescendo*
and *decrescendo* time to the movement. The Russian
men undertake to perform in waltzing the same feat as
the Austrians in riding, and will dance round the room
with a glass of champagne in the left hand without spill-
ing a drop. This evenness in waltzing is certainly very
graceful, but can only be attained by a long sliding step,
which is little practised where the rooms are small, and
people, not understanding the real pleasure of dancing
well, insist on dancing all at the same time. In Ger-

many they are so alive to the necessity of ample space, that in large balls a rope is drawn across tne room ; its two ends are held by the masters of the ceremonies *pro-tem.*, and as one couple stops and retires, another is allowed to pass under the rope and take its place. But then in Germany they dance for the dancing's sake. However this may be, an even motion is very desirable, and all the abominations which militate against it, sucn as hop-waltzes, the Schottische, and ridiculous *Varsovienne*, are justly put down in good society. The pace, again, should not be sufficiently rapid to endanger other couples. It is the gentleman's duty to *steer*, and is crowded rooms nothing is more trying. He must keep his eyes open and turn them in every direction, if he would not risk a collision, and the chance of a fall, or what is as bad, the infliction of a wound on his partner's arm. I have seen a lady's arm cut open in such a collision by the bracelet of that of another lady ; and the sight is by no means a pleasant one in a ball room, to say nothing of a new dress covered in a moment with blood.

" The consequences of violent dancing may be really serious. Not only do delicate girls bring on, thereby, a violent palpitation of the heart, and their partners appear in a most disagreeable condition of solution, but dangerous falls ensue from it. I have known instances of a lady's head being laid open, and a gentleman's foot being broken in such a fall, resulting, poor fellow ! in lameness for life.

" It is, perhaps, useless to recommend flat-foot waltzing in this country, where ladies allow themselves to be almost hugged by their partners, and where men think it necessary to lift a lady almost off the ground, but I am persuaded that if it were introduced, the outcry against the impropriety of waltzing would soon cease. Nothing can be more delicate than the way in which a German holds his partner. It is impossible to dance on the flat foot unless the lady and gentleman are quite free of one another. His hand, therefore, goes no further round her waist than to the hooks and eyes of her dress, hers, no higher than to his elbow. Thus danced, the waltz is smooth, graceful, and delicate, and we could never in Germany complain of our daughter's languishing on a young man's shoulder. On the other hand, nothing is more graceless and absurd than to see a man waltzing on the tips of his toes, lifting his partner off the ground, or twirling round and round with her like the figures on a street organ. The test of waltzing in time is to be able to stamp the time with the left foot. A good flat-foot waltzer can dance on one foot as well as on two, but I would not advise him to try it in public, lest, like Mr. Rarey's horse on three legs, he should come to the ground in a luckless moment. The legs should be very little bent in dancing, the body still less so. I do not know whether it be worse to see a man *sit down* in a waltz, or to find him with his head poked forward over your young wife's shoulder, hot, red, wild, and in far too close proximity to the partner of your bosom, whom he makes literally the partner of his own.

"The 'Lancers' are a revival, after many long years, and, perhaps, we may soon have a drawing-room adaptation of the Morris-dance.

8

"The only advice, therefore, which it is necessary to give to these who wish to dance the polka may be summed up in one word, 'don't.' Not so with the galop. The remarks as to the position in waltzing apply to all round dances, and there is, therefore, little to add with regard to the galop, except that it is a great mistake to suppose it to be a rapid dance. It should be danced as slowly as possible. It will then be more graceful and less fatiguing. It is danced quite slowly in Germany and on the flat foot. The polka-mazurka is still much danced, and is certainly very graceful. The remarks on the quadrille apply equally to the lancers, which are great favorites, and threaten to take the place of the former. The schottische, hop-waltz, redowa, varsovienne, cellarius, and so forth, have had their day, and are no longer danced in good society.

"The calm ease which marks the man of good taste, makes even the swiftest dances graceful and agreeable. Vehemence may be excused at an election, but not in a ball room. I once asked a beautiful and very clever young lady how she, who seemed to pass her life with books, managed to dance so well. 'I enjoy it,' she replied; 'and when I dance I give my *whole mind* to it.' And she was quite right. Whatever is worth doing at all, is worth doing well; and if it is not beneath your dignity to dance, it is not unworthy of your mind to give itself, for the time, wholly up to it. You will never enjoy dancing till you do it well; and, if you do not enjoy it, it is folly to dance. But, in reality, dancing, if it be a mere trifle, is one to which great minds have not been ashamed to stoop. Locke, for instance, has written on its utility, and speaks of it as manly, which was certainly not Michal's opinion, when she looked out of the window and saw her lord and master dancing and playing.   Plato recommended it, and Socrates learned the Athenian polka of the day when quite an old gentleman, and liked it very much.   Some one has even gone the length of calling it 'the logic of the body;' and Addison defends himself for making it the subject of a disquisition."

CHAPTER VIl.

DRESS.

BETWEEN the sloven and the coxconb there is generally a competition which shall be the more contemptible:
the one in the total neglect of every thing which might
make his appearance in public supportable, and the
other in the cultivation of every superfluous ornament.
The former offends by his negligence and dirt, and the
latter by his finery and perfumery. Each entertains a
supreme contempt for the other, and while both are
right in their opinion, both are wrong in their practice.
It is not in either extreme that the man of real elegance
and refinement will be shown, but in the happy medium
which allows taste and judgment to preside over the
wardrobe and toilet-table, while it prevents too great an
attention to either, and never allows personal appearance
to become the leading object of life.

The French have a proverb, " It is not the cowl which
makes the monk," and it might be said with equal truth,
" It is not the dress which makes the gentleman," yet,
as the monk is known abroad by his cowl, so the true
gentleman will let the refinement of his mind and education be seen in his dress.

The first rule for the guidance of a man, in matters

of dress, should be, " Let the dress suit the occasion."
It is as absurd for a man to go into the street in
the morning with his dress-coat, white kid gloves, and
dancing-boots, as it would be for a lady to promenade
the fashionable streets, in full evening dress, or for the
same man to present himself in the ball-room with heavy
walking-boots, a great coat, and riding-cap.

It is true that there is little opportunity for a gentleman to exercise his taste for coloring, in the black and
white dress which fashion so imperatively declares to be
the proper dress for a *dress* occasion. He may indulge
in light clothes in the street during the warm months of
the year, but for the ball or evening party, black and
white are the only colors (or no colors) admissible, and
in the midst of the gay dresses of the ladies, the unfortunate man in his sombre dress appears like a demon who
has found his way into Paradise among the angels.
N'importe ! Men should be useful to the women, and
how can they be better employed than acting as a foil
for their loveliness of face and dress !

Notwithstanding the dress, however, a man may make
himself agreeable, even in the earthly Paradise, a ball-
room. He can rise above the mourning of his coat, to
the joyousness of the occasion, and make himself valued
for himself, not his dress. He can make himself admired
for his wit, not his toilette ; his elegance and refinement,
not the price of his clothes.

There is another good rule for the dressing-room :
While you are engaged in dressing give your whole
attention to it. See that every detail is perfect, and
that each article is neatly arranged. From the curl of

your hair to the tip of your boot, let all be perfect in its
make and arrangement, but, as soon as you have left
your mirror, forget your dress. Nothing betokens the
coxcomb more decidedly than to see a man always fuss-
ing about his dress, pulling down his wristbands, playing
with his moustache, pulling up his shirt collar, or arranging the bow of his cravat. Once dressed, do not attempt
to alter any part of your costume until you are again in
the dressing-room.

In a gentleman's dress any attempt to be conspicuous
is in excessively bad taste. If you are wealthy, let the
luxury of your dress consist in the fine quality of each
article, and in the spotless purity of gloves and linen,
but never wear much jewelry or any article conspicuous
on account of its money value. Simplicity should always
preside over the gentleman's wardrobe.

Follow fashion as far as is necessary to avoid eccentricity or oddity in your costume, but avoid the extreme
of the prevailing *mode*. If coats are worn long, yours
need not sweep the ground, if they are loose, yours may
still have some fitness for your figure; if pantaloons are
cut large over the boot, yours need not cover the whole
foot, if they are tight, you may still take room to walk.
Above all, let your figure and style of face have some
weight in deciding how far you are to follow fashion.
For a very tall man to wear a high, narrow-brimmed
hat, long-tailed coat, and tight pantaloons, with a pointed
beard and hair brushed up from the forehead, is not
more absurd than for a short, fat man, to promenade the
street in a low, broad-brimmed hat, loose coat and pants,

and the latter made of large plaid material, and yet bur
lesques quite as broad may be met with every day.

An English writer, ridiculing the whims of Fashion,
says :—

" To be in the fashion, an Englishman must wear six
pairs of gloves in a day :

" In the morning, he must drive his hunting wagon in
reindeer gloves.

" In hunting, he must wear gloves of chamois skin.

" To enter London in his tilbury, beaver skin gloves.

" Later in the day, to promenade in Hyde Park. colored kid gloves, dark.

" When he dines out, colored kid gloves, light.

" For the ball-room, white kid gloves."

Thus his yearly bill for gloves alone will amount to a
most extravagant sum.

In order to merit the appellation of a well-dressed
man, you must pay attention, not only to the more pro-
minent articles of your wardrobe, coat, pants, and vest,
but to the more minute details. A shirtfront which fits
badly, a pair of wristbands too wide or too narrow, a
badly brushed hat, a shabby pair of gloves, or an ill-fit-
ting boot, will spoil the most elaborate costume. Purity
of skin, teeth, nails ; well brushed hair ; linen fresh and
snowy white, will make clothes of the coarsest material,
if well made, look more elegant, than the finest material
of cloth, if these details are neglected.

Frequent bathing, careful attention to the teeth,
nails, ears, and hair, are indispensable to a finished
toilette.

Use but very little perfume, much of it is in **bad** taste.

Let your hair, beard, and moustache, be always **per**fectly smooth, well arranged, and scrupulously clean.

It is better to clean the teeth with a piece of sponge, or very soft brush, than with a stiff brush, and there is no dentifrice so good as White Castile Soap.

Wear always gloves and boots, which fit well and are fresh and whole. Soiled or torn gloves and boots ruin a costume otherwise faultless.

Extreme propriety should be observed in dress. Be careful to dress according to your means. Too great saving is meanness, too great expense is extravagance.

A young man may follow the fashion farther than a middle-aged or elderly man, but let him avoid going to the extreme of the mode, if he would not be taken for an empty headed fop.

It is best to employ a good tailor, as a suit of coarse broadcloth which fits you perfectly, and is stylish in cut, will make a more elegant dress than the finest material badly made.

Avoid eccentricity; it marks, not the man of genius, but the fool.

A well brushed hat, and glossy boots must be always worn in the street.

White gloves are the only ones to be worn with full dress.

A snuff box, watch, studs, sleeve-buttons, watch-chain, and one ring are all the jewelry a well-dressed man can wear.

An English author, in a recent work, gives the following rules for a gentleman's dress:

"The best bath for general purposes, and one which
can do little harm, and almost always some good, is a
sponge bath. It should consist of a large, flat metal
basin, some four feet in diameter, filled with cold water.
Such a vessel may be bought for about fifteen shillings.
A large, coarse sponge—the coarser the better—will cost
another five or seven shillings, and a few Turkish towels
complete the ' properties.' The water should be plenti-
ful and fresh, that is, brought up a little while before the
bath is to be used; not placed over night in the bed-
room. Let us wash and be merry, for we know not how
soon the supply of that precious article which here costs
nothing may be cut off. In many continental towns
they buy their water, and on a protracted sea voyage
the ration is often reduced to half a pint a day *for all
purposes*, so that a pint per diem is considered luxurious.
Sea-water, we may here observe, does not cleanse, and
a sensible man who bathes in the sea will take a bath of
pure water immediately after it. This practice is shamefully neglected, and I am inclined to think that in many
cases a sea-bath will do more harm than good without
it, but, if followed by a fresh bath, cannot but be ad-
vantageous.

"Taking the sponge bath as the best for ordinary purposes, we must point out some rules in its use. The
sponge being nearly a foot in length, and six inches
broad, must be allowed to fill completely with water, and
the part of the body which should be first attacked is
the stomach. It is there that the most heat has col-

lected during the night, and the application of cold water quickens the circulation at once, and sends the blood which has been employed in digestion round the whole body. The head should next be soused, unless the person be of full habit, when the head should be attacked before the feet touch the cold water at all. Some persons use a small hand shower bath, which is less powerful than the common shower bath, and does almost as much good. The use of soap in the morning bath is an open question. I confess a preference for a rough towel, or a hair glove. Brummell patronized the latter, and applied it for nearly a quarter of an hour every morning.

"The ancients followed up the bath by anointing the body, and athletic exercises. The former is a mistake: the latter, an excellent practice, shamefully neglected in the present day. It would conduce much to health and strength if every morning toilet comprised the vigorous use of the dumb-bells, or, still better, the exercise of the arms without them. The best plan of all is, to choose some object in your bed-room on which to vent your hatred, and box at it violently for some ten minutes, till the perspiration covers you. The sponge must then be again applied to the whole body. It is very desirable to remain without clothing as long as possible, and I should therefore recommend that every part of the toilet which can conveniently be performed without dressing, should be so

"The next duty, then, must be to clean the TEETH. Dentists are modern inquisitors, but their torture-rooms are meant only for the foolish. Everybody is born with good teeth, and everybody might keep them good by a

proper diet, and the avoidance of sweets and smoking.
Of the two the former are, perhaps, the more dangerous.
Nothing ruins the teeth so soon as sugar in one's tea,
and highly sweetened tarts and puddings, and as it is *la
premier pas qui coûte*, these should be particularly
avoided in childhood. When the teeth attain their full
growth and strength it takes much more to destroy either
their enamel or their substance.

"It is upon the teeth that the effects of excess are first
seen, and it is upon the teeth that the odor of the breath
depends. If I may not say that it is a Christian duty
to keep your teeth clean, I may, at least, remind you
that you cannot be thoroughly agreeable without doing
so. Let words be what they may, if they come with an
impure odor, they cannot please. The butterfly loves
the scent of the rose more than its honey.

"The teeth should be well rubbed inside as well as
outside, and the back teeth even more than the front.
The mouth should then be rinsed, if not seven times, according to the Hindu legislator, at least several times,
with fresh, cold water. This same process should be repeated several times a day, since eating, smoking, and
so forth, naturally render the teeth and mouth dirty
more or less, and nothing can be so offensive, particularly
to ladies, whose sense of smell seems to be keener than
that of the other sex, and who can detect at your first
approach whether you have been drinking or smoking.
But, if only for your own comfort, you should brush
your teeth both morning and evening, which is quite
requisite for the preservation of their soundness and
color; while, if you are to mingle with others, they

should be brushed, or, at least, the mouth well rinsed after every meal, still more after smoking, or drinking wine, beer, or spirits. No amount of general attractiveness can compensate for an offensive odor in the breath; and none of the senses is so fine a gentleman, none so unforgiving, if offended, as that of smell.

"Strict attention must be paid to the condition of the nails, and that both as regards cleaning and cutting The former is best done with a liberal supply of soap on a small nail-brush, which should be used before every meal, if you would not injure your neighbor's appetite. While the hand is still moist, the point of a small penknife or pair of stumpy nail-scissors should be passed under the nails so as to remove every vestige of dirt; the skin should be pushed down with a towel, that the white half-moon may be seen, and the finer skin removed with the knife or scissors. Occasionally the edges of the nails should be filed, and the hard skin which forms round the corners of them cut away. The important point in cutting the nails is to preserve the beauty of their shape. That beauty, even in details, is worth preserving, I have already remarked, and we may study it as much in paring our nails, as in the grace of our attitudes, or any other point. The shape, then, of the nail should approach, as nearly as possible, to the oblong. The length of the nail is an open question. Let it be often cut, but always long, in my opinion. Above all, let it be well cut, and *never* bitten.

"Perhaps you tell me these are childish details. Details, yes, but not childish. The attention to details is the true sign of a great mind, and he who can in necessity consider the smallest, is the same man who can com pass the largest subjects. Is not life made up of details! Must not the artist who has conceived a picture, descend from the dream of his mind to mix colors on a palette? Must not the great commander who is bowling down nations and setting up monarchies care for the health and comfort, the bread and beef of each individual soldier? I have often seen a great poet, whom I knew personally, counting on his fingers the feet of his verses, and fretting with anything but poetic language, because he could not get his sense into as many syllables. What if his nails were dirty? Let genius talk of abstract beauty, and philosophers dogmatize on order. If they do not keep their nails clean, I shall call them both charlatans. The man who really loves beauty will cultivate it in everything around him. The man who upholds order is not conscientious if he cannot observe it in his nails. The great mind can afford to descend to details; it is only the weak mind that fears to be narrowed by them. When Napoleon was at Munich he declined the grand four-poster of the Witelsbach family, and slept, as usual, in his little camp-bed. The power to be little is a proof of greatness.

"For the hands, ears, and neck we want something more than the bath, and, as these parts are exposed and really lodge fugitive pollutions, we cannot use too much soap, or give too much trouble to their complete purification.. Nothing is lovelier than a woman's small, white, shell-like ear; few things reconcile us better to earth than the cold hand and warm heart of a friend; but, to complete the charm, the hand should be both clean and soft. Warm water, a liberal use of the nail-brush, and no stint of soap, produce this amenity far more effectually than honey, cold cream, and almond paste. Of wearing gloves I shall speak elsewhere, but for weak people who are troubled with chilblains, they are indispensable all the year round. I will add a good prescription for the cure of chilblains, which are both a disfigurement, and one of the *petites misères* of human life.

" 'Roll the fingers in linen bandages, sew them up well, and dip them twice or thrice a day in a mixture, consisting of half a fluid ounce of tincture of capsicum, and a fluid ounce of tincture of opium.'

" The person who invented razors libelled Nature, and added a fresh misery to the days of man.

" Whatever *Punch* may say, the moustache and beard movement is one in the right direction, proving that men are beginning to appreciate beauty and to acknowledge that Nature is the best valet. But it is very amusing to hear men excusing their vanity on the plea of health, and find them indulging in the hideous 'Newgate frill' as a kind of compromise between the beard and the razor. There was a time when it was thought a presumption and vanity to wear one's own hair instead of the frightful elaborations of the wig-makers, and the false curls which Sir Godfrey Kneller did his best to make graceful on canvas. Who knows that at some future age some *Punch* of the twenty-first century may not ridicule the wearing of one's own teeth instead of the dentist's? At any rate Nature knows best, and no man need be ashamed of showing his manhood in the hair of his face. Of razors and shaving, therefore, I shall only speak from necessity, because, until everybody is sensible on this point, they will still be used.

"Napoleon shaved himself. 'A born king,' said he, 'has another to shave him. A made king can use his own razor.' But the war he made on his chin was very different to that he made on foreign potentates. He took a very long time to effect it, talking between whiles to his hangers-on. The great man, however, was right, and every sensible man will shave himself, if only as an exercise of character, for a man should learn to live, in every detail without assistance. Moreover, in most cases, we shave ourselves better than barbers can do. If we shave at all, we should do it thoroughly, and every morning. Nothing, except a frown and a hay-fever, makes the face look so unlovely as a chin covered with short stubble. The chief requirements are hot water, a large, soft brush of badger hair, a good razor, soft soap that will not dry rapidly, and a steady hand. Cheap razors are a fallacy. They soon lose their edge, and no amount of stropping will restore it. A good razor needs no strop. If you can afford it, you should have a case of seven razors, one for each day of the week, so that no one shall be too much used. There are now much used packets of papers of a certain kind on which to wipe the razor, and which keep its edge keen, and are a substitute for the strop.

"Beards, moustaches, and whiskers, have always been most important additions to the face. In the present day literary men are much given to their growth, and in that respect show at once their taste and their vanity

Let no man be ashamed of his beard, if it be well kep⁴ and not fantastically cut. The moustache should be kept within limits. The Hungarians wear it so long that they can tie the ends round their heads. The style of the beard should be adopted to suit the face. A broad face should wear a large, full one ; a long face is improved by a sharp-pointed one. Taylor, the water poet, wrote verses on the various styles, and they are almost numberless. The chief point is to keep the beard well-combed and in neat trim.

"As to whiskers, it is not every man who can achieve a pair of full length. There is certainly a great vanity about them, but it may be generally said that foppishness should be avoided in this as in most other points. Above all, the whiskers should never be curled, nor pulled out to an absurd length. Still worse is it to cut them close with the scissors. The moustache should be neat and not too large, and such fopperies as cutting the points thereof, or twisting them up to the fineness of needles—though patronized by the Emperor of the French—are decidedly a proof of vanity. If a man wear the hair on his face which nature has given him, in the manner that nature distributes it, keeps it clean, and prevents its overgrowth, he cannot do wrong. All extravagances are vulgar, because they are evidence of a pretence to being better than you are; but a single extravagance unsupported is perhaps worse than a number together, which have at least the merit of consistency. If you copy puppies in the half-yard of whisker, you should have their dress and their manner too, if you would not appear doubly absurd.

"The same remarks apply to the arrangement of the hair in men, which should be as simple and as natural as possible, but at the same time a little may be granted to beauty and the requirements of the face. For my part I can see nothing unmanly in wearing long hair, though undoubtedly it is inconvenient and a temptation to vanity, while its arrangement would demand an amount of time and attention which is unworthy of a man. But every nation and every age has had a different custom in this respect, and to this day even in Europe the hair is sometimes worn long. The German student is particularly partial to hyacinthine locks curling over a black velvet coat; and the peasant of Brittany looks very handsome, if not always clean, with his love-locks hanging straight down under a broad cavalier hat. Religion has generally taken up the matter severely. The old fathers preached and railed against wigs, the Calvinists raised an insurrection in Bordeaux on the same account, and English Roundheads consigned to an unmentionable place every man who allowed his hair to grow according to nature. The Romans condemned tresses as unmanly, and in France in the middle ages the privilege to wear them was confined to royalty. Our modern custom was a revival of the French revolution, so that in this respect we are now republican as well as puritanical.

If we conform to fashion we should at least make the best of it, and since the main advantage of short hair is its neatness, we should take care to keep ours neat. This should be done first by frequent visits to the barber, for if the hair is to be short at all it should be very short, and nothing looks more untidy than long, stiff, uncurled

9

masses sticking out over the ears. If it curls naturally so much the better, but if not it will be easier to keep in order. The next point is to wash the head every morning, which, when once habitual, is a great preservative against cold. A pair of large brushes, hard or soft, as your case requires, should be used, not to hammer the head with, but to pass up under the hair so as to reach the roots. As to pomatum, Macassar, and other inventions of the hair-dresser, I have only to say that, if used at all, it should be in moderation, and never sufficiently to make their scent perceptible in company. Of course the arrangement will be a matter of individual taste, but as the middle of the hair is the natural place for a parting, it is rather a silly prejudice to think a man vain who parts his hair in the centre. He is less blamable than one who is too lazy to part it all, and has always the appearance of having just got up.

"Of wigs and false hair, the subject of satires and sermons since the days of the Roman Emperors, I shall say nothing here except that they are a practical falsehood which may sometimes be necessary, but is rarely successful. For my part I prefer the snows of life's winter to the best made peruke, and even a bald head to an inferior wig.

"When gentlemen wore armor, and disdained the use of their legs, an esquire was a necessity; and we can understand that, in the days of the Beaux, the word "gentleman" meant a man and his valet. I am glad to say that in the present day it only takes one man to make a gentleman, or, at most, a man and a ninth— that is, including the tailor. It is an excellent thing for the character to be neat and orderly, and, if a man neglects to be so in his room, he is open to the same temptation sooner or later in his person. A dressing-case is, therefore, a desideratum. A closet to hang up cloth clothes, which should never be folded, and a small dressing-room next to the bed-room, are not so easily attainable. But the man who throws his clothes about the room, a boot in one corner, a cravat in another, and his brushes anywhere, is not a man of good habits. The spirit of order should extend to everything about him.

"This brings me to speak of certain necessities of dress; the first of which I shall take is appropriateness. The age of the individual is an important consideration in this respect; and a man of sixty is as absurd in the style of nineteen as a young man in the high cravat of Brummell's day. I know a gallant colonel who is master of the ceremonies in a gay watering-place, and who, afraid of the prim old-fashioned *tournure* of his *confrères* in similar localities, is to be seen, though his hair is gray and his age not under five-and-sixty, in a light cut-away, the 'peg-top' continuations, and a turned-down collar. It may be what younger blades will wear when they reach his age, but in the present day the effect is ridiculous. We may, therefore, give as a general rule, that after the turning-point of life a man should eschew the changes of fashion in his own attire, while he avoids complaining of it in the young. In the latter, on the other hand, the observance of these changes must depend partly on his taste and partly on his position. If wise, he will adopt with alacrity any new fashions which improve the grace, the ease, the healthfulness, and the con-

venience of his garments. He will be glad of greater freedom in the cut of his cloth clothes, of boots with elastic sides
instead of troublesome buttons or laces, of the privilege
to turn down his collar, and so forth, while he will avoid
as extravagant, elaborate shirt-fronts, gold bindings on
the waistcoat, and expensive buttons.   On the other
hand, whatever his age, he will have some respect to his
profession and position in society.   He will remember
how much the appearance of the man aids a judgment
of his character, and this test, which has often been cried
down, is in reality no bad one; for a man who does not
dress appropriately evinces a want of what is most necessary to professional men—tact and discretion.

"Position in society demands appropriateness.   Well
knowing the worldly value of a good coat, I would yet
never recommend a man of limited means to aspire to
a fashionable appearance.   In the first place, he becomes
thereby a walking falsehood; in the second, he cannot,
without running into debt, which is another term for dis-
honesty, maintain the style he has adopted.   As he cannot afford to change his suits as rapidly as fashion alters,
he must avoid following it in varying details.   He will
rush into wide sleeves one month, in the hope of being
fashionable, and before his coat is worn out, the next
month will bring in a narrow sleeve.   We cannot, unfortunately, like Samuel Pepys, take a long cloak now-a-
days to the tailor's, to be cut into a short one, 'long
cloaks being now quite out,' as he tells us.   Even when
there is no poverty in the case, our position must not
be forgotten.   The tradesman will win neither customers
nor friends by adorning himself in the mode of the club-

lounger, and the clerk, or commercial traveler, who dresses fashionably, lays himself open to inquiries as to his antecedents, which he may not care to have investigated. In general, it may be said that there is vulgarity in dressing like those of a class above us, since it must be taken as a proof of pretension.

"As it is bad taste to flaunt the airs of the town among the provincials, who know nothing of them, it is worse taste to display the dress of a city in the quiet haunts of the rustics. The law, that all attempts at distinction by means of dress is vulgar and pretentious, would be sufficient argument against wearing city fashions in the country.

"While in most cases a rougher and easier mode of dress is both admissible and desirable in the country, there are many occasions of country visiting where a town man finds it difficult to decide. It is almost peculiar to the country to unite the amusements of the daytime with those of the evening; of the open air with those of the drawing-room. Thus, in the summer, when the days are long, you will be asked to a pic-nic or an archery party, which will wind up with dancing in-doors, and may even assume the character of a ball. If you are aware of this beforehand, it will always be safe to send your evening dress to your host's house, and you will learn from the servants whether others have done the same, and whether, therefore, you will not be singular in asking leave to change your costume. But if you are ignorant how the day is to end, you must be guided partly by the hour of invitation, and partly by the extent of your intimacy with the family. I have actually known gentlemen arrive at a large pic-nic at mid-day in complete evening dress, and pitied them with all my heart, compelled as they were to suffer, in tight black clothes, under a hot sun for eight hours, and dance after all in the same dress. On the other hand, if you are asked to come an hour or two before sunset, after six in summer, in the autumn after five, you cannot err by appearing in evening dress. It is always taken as a compliment to do so, and if your acquaintance with your hostess is slight, it would be almost a familiarity to do otherwise. In any case you desire to avoid singularity, so that if you can discover what others who are invited intend to wear, you can always decide on your own attire. In Europe there is a convenient rule for these matters; never appear after four in the afternoon in morning dress; but then gray trousers are there allowed instead of black, and white waistcoats are still worn in the evening. At any rate, it is possible to effect a compromise between the two styles of costume, and if you are likely to be called upon to dance in the evening, it will be well to wear thin boots, a black frock-coat, and a small black neck-tie, and to put a pair of clean white gloves in your pocket. You will thus be at least less conspicuous in the dancing-room than in a light tweed suit.

"Not so the distinction to be made according to size. As a rule, tall men require long clothes—some few perhaps even in the nurse's sense of those words—and short men short clothes. On the other hand, Falstaff should beware of Jenny Wren coats and affect ample wrappers, while Peter Schlemihl, and the whole race of thin men, must eschew looseness as much in their garments as their morals.

"Lastly we come to what is appropriate to different occasions, and as this is an important subject, I shall treat of it separately. For the present it is sufficient to point out that, while every man should avoid not only extravagance, but even brilliance of dress on ordinary occasions, there are some on which he may and ought to pay more attention to his toilet, and attempt to look gay. Of course, the evenings are not here meant. For evening dress there is a fixed rule, from which we can depart only to be foppish or vulgar; but in morning dress there is greater liberty, and when we undertake to mingle with those who are assembled avowedly for gayety, we should not make ourselves remarkable by the dinginess of our dress. Such occasions are open air entertainments, *fêtes*, flower-shows, archery-meetings, *matinées*, and *id genus omne*, where much of the pleasure to be derived depends on the general effect on the enjoyers, and where, if we cannot pump up a look of mirth, we should, at least, if we go at all, wear the semblance of it in our dress. I have a worthy little friend, who. I believe, is as well disposed to his kind as Lord Shaftesbury himself, but who, for some reason, perhaps a twinge of philosophy about him, frequents the gay meetings to which he is asked in an old coat and a wide-awake. Some people take him for a wit, but he soon shows that he does not aspire to that character; others for a philosopher, but he is too good-mannered for that; others, poor man! pronounce him a cynic, and all are agreed that whatever he may be, he looks out of place, and spoils the general effect. I believe, in my heart, that he is the mildest of men, but will not take the trouble to dress more than once a day. At any rate, he has a character for eccentricity, which, I am sure, is precisely what he would wish to avoid. That character is a most delightful one for a bachelor, and it is generally Cœlebs who holds it, for it has been proved by statistics that there are four single to one married man among the inhabitants of our mad houses; but eccentricity yields a reputation which requires something to uphold it, and even in Diogenes of the Tub it was extremely bad taste to force himself into Plato's evening party without sandals. and nothing but a dirty tunic on him.

"Another requisite in dress is its simplicity, with which I may couple harmony of color. This simplicity is the only distinction which a man of taste should aspire to in the matter of dress, but a simplicity in appearance must proceed from a nicety in reality. One should not be simply ill-dressed, but simply well-dressed. Lord Castlereah would never have been pronounced the most distinguished man in the gay court of Vienna, because he wore no orders or ribbons among hundreds decorated with a profusion of those vanities, but because besides this he was dressed with taste. The charm of Brummell's dress was its simplicity; yet it cost him as much thought, time, and care as the portfolio of a minister. The rules of simplicity, therefore, are the rules of taste. All extravagance, all splendor, and all profusion must be avoided. The colors, in the first place, must harmonize both with our complexion and with one another; perhaps most of all with the color of our hair

All bright colors should be avoided, such as red, yellow, sky-blue, and bright green. Perhaps only a successful Australian gold digger would think of choosing such colors for his coat, waistcoat, or trousers; but there are hundreds of young men who might select them for their gloves and neck-ties. The deeper colors are, some how or other, more manly, and are certainly less striking. The same simplicity should be studied in the avoidance of ornamentation. A few years ago it was the fashion to trim the evening waistcoat with a border of gold lace. This is an example of fashions always to be rebelled against. Then, too, extravagance in the form of our dress is a sin against taste. I remember that long ribbons took the place of neck-ties some years ago. At a commemoration, two friends of mine determined to cut a figure in this matter, having little else to distinguish them. The one wore two yards of bright pink; the other the same quantity of bright blue ribbon, round their necks. I have reason to believe they think now that they both looked superbly ridiculous. In the same way, if the trousers are worn wide, we should not wear them as loose as a Turk's; or, if the sleeves are to be open, we should not rival the ladies in this matter. And so on through a hundred details, generally remembering that to exaggerate a fashion is to assume a character, and therefore vulgar. The wearing of jewelry comes under this head. Jewels are an ornament to women, but a blemish to men. They bespeak either effeminacy or a love of display. The hand of a man is honored in working, for labor is his mission; and the hand that wears its riches on its fingers, has rarely worked honestly to win them. The best jewel a man can wear is his h<nor. Let that be bright and shining, well set in pru dence, and all others must darken before it. But as we are savages, and must have some silly trickery to hang about us, a little, but very little concession may be made to our taste in this respect. I am quite serious when I disadvise you from the use of nose-rings, gold anklets, and hat-bands studded with jewels; for when I see an incred-ulous young man of the nineteenth century, dangling from his watch-chain a dozen silly 'charms' (often the only ones he possesses), which have no other use than to give a fair coquette a legitimate subject on which to ap-proach to closer intimacy, and which are revived from the lowest superstitions of dark ages, and sometimes darker races, I am quite justified in believing that some South African chieftain, sufficiently rich to cut a dash, might introduce with success the most peculiar fashions of his own country. However this may be, there are al-ready sufficient extravagances prevalent among our young men to attack.

"The man of good taste will wear as little jewelry as possible. One handsome signet-ring on the little finger of the left hand, a scarf-pin which is neither large, nor showy, nor too intricate in its design, and a light, rather thin watch-guard with a cross-bar, are all that he ought to wear. But, if he aspires to more than this, he should observe the following rules:- –

"1. Let everything be real and good. False jewelry is not only a practical lie, but an absolute vulgarity, since its use arises from an attempt to appear richer cr grandei than its wearer is.

"2 Let it be simple. Elaborate studs waistcoat-buttons, and wrist-links, are all abominable. The last, particularly, should be as plain as possible, consisting of plain gold ovals, with, at most, the crest engraved upon them. Diamonds and brilliants are quite unsuitable to men, whose jewelry should never be conspicuous. If you happen to possess a single diamond of great value you may wear it on great occasions as a ring, but no more than one ring should ever be worn by a gentleman.

" 3. Let it be distinguished rather by its curiosity than its brilliance. An antique or bit of old jewelry possesses more interest, particularly if you are able to tell its history, than the most splendid production of the goldsmith's shop.

" 4. Let it harmonize with the colors of your dress.

" 5. Let it have some use. Men should never, like women, wear jewels for mere ornament, whatever may be the fashion of Hungarian noblemen, and deposed Indian rajahs with jackets covered with rubies.

"The precious stones are reserved for ladies, and even our scarf-pins are more suitable without them.

"The dress that is both appropriate and simple can never offend, nor render its wearer conspicuous, though it may distinguish him for his good taste. But it will not be pleasing unless clean and fresh. We cannot quarrel with a poor gentleman's thread-bare coat, if his linen be pure, and we see that he has never attempted to dress beyond his means or unsuitably to his station. But the sight of decayed gentility and dilapidated fashion may call forth our pity, and, at the same time prompt a moral: 'You have evidently sunken;' we say to our selves, 'But whose fault was it? Am I not led to suppose that the extravagance which you evidently once revelled in has brought you to what I now see you?' While freshness is essential to being well-dressed, it will be a consolation to those who cannot afford a heavy tailor's bill, to reflect that a visible newness in one's clothes is as bad as patches and darns, and to remember that there have been celebrated dressers who would never put on a new coat till it had been worn two or three times by their valets. On the other hand, there is no excuse for untidiness, holes in the boots, a broken hat, torn gloves, and so on. Indeed, it is better to wear no gloves at all than a pair full of holes. There is nothing to be ashamed of in bare hands, if they are clean, and the poor can still afford to have their shirts and shoes mended, and their hats ironed. It is certainly better to show signs of neatness than the reverse, and you need sooner be ashamed of a hole than a darn.

"Of personal cleanliness I have spoken at such length that little need be said on that of the clothes. If you are economical with your tailor, you can be extravagant with your laundress. The beaux of forty years back put on three shirts a day, but except in hot weather one is sufficient. Of course, if you change your dress in the evening you must change your shirt too. There has been a great outcry against colored flannel shirts in the place of linen, and the man who can wear one for three days is looked on as little better than St. Simeon Stylites. I should like to know how often the advocates of linen change their own under-flannel, and whether the same rule does not apply to what is seen as to what is concealed. But while the flannel is perl aps healthier as absɔrbing the moisture more rapidly, the linen has the advantage of *looking* cleaner, ar.d may therefore be preferred. As to economy, if the flannel costs less to wash, it also wears out sooner ; but, be this as it may, a man's wardrobe is not complete without half a dozen or so of these shirts, which he will find most useful, and ten times more comfortable than linen in long excursions, or when exertion will be required. Flannel, too, has the advantage of being warm in winter and cool in summer, for, being a non-conductor, but a retainer of heat, it protects the body from the sun, and, on the other hand, shields it from the cold. But the best shirt of all, particularly in winter, is that which wily monks and hermits pretended to wear for a penance, well knowing that they could have no garment cooler, more comfortable, or more healthy. I mean, of course, the rough hair-shirt. Like flannel, it is a non-conductor of heat ; but then, too, it acts the part of a shampooer, and with its perpetual friction soothes the surface of the skin, and prevents the circulation from being arrested at any one point of the body. Though I doubt if any of my readers will take a hint from the wisdom of the merry anchorites, they will perhaps allow me to suggest that the next best thing to wear next the skin is flannel, and that too of the coarsest description.

" Quantity is better than quality in linen. Nevertheless it should be fine and well spun. The loose cuff, which we borrowed from the French some four years ago, is a great improvement on the old tight wrist-band, and, indeed, it must be borne in mind that anything which binds any part of the body tightly impedes the circulation, and is therefore unhealthy as well as un-graceful.

"The necessity for a large stock of linen depends on a rule far bettter than Brummell's, of three shirts a day, viz :—

"Change your linen whenever it is at all dirty.

"This is the best guide with regard to collars, socks, pocket-handkerchiefs, and our under garments. No rule can be laid down for the number we should wear per week, for everything depends on circumstances. Thus in the country all our linen remains longer clean than in town; in dirty, wet, or dusty weather, our socks get soon dirty and must be changed; or, if we have a cold, to say nothing of the possible but not probable case of tear-shedding on the departure of friends, we shall want more than one pocket-handkerchief per diem. In fact, the last article of modern civilization is put to so many uses, is so much displayed, and liable to be called into action on so many various engagements, that we should always have a clean one in our pockets. Who knows when it may not serve us is in good stead? Who can tell how often the corner of the delicate cam-bric will have to represent a tear which, like difficult passages in novels is 'left to the imagination.' Can a man of any feeling call on a disconsolate widow, for in-stance, and listen to her woes, without at least pulling out that expressive appendage? Can any one believe in our sympathy if the article in question is a dirty one? There are some people who, like the clouds, only exist to weep; and King Solomon, though not one of them, has given them great encouragement in speaking of the house of mourning. We are bound to weep with tlem, and we are bound to weep elegantly.

" A man whose dress is neat, clean, simple, and appropriate, will pass muster anywhere.

" A well-dressed man does not require so much an extensive as a varied wardrobe. He wants a different costume for every season and every occasion; but if what he selects is simple rather than striking, he may appear in the same clothes as often as he likes, as long as they are fresh and appropriate to the season and the object. There are four kinds of coats which he must have : a morning-coat, a frock-coat, a dress-coat, and an over-coat. An economical man may do well with four of the first, and one of each of the others per annum. The dress of a gentleman in the present day should not cost him more than the tenth part of his income on an average. But as fortunes vary more than position, if his income is large it will take a much smaller proportion, if small a larger one. If a man, however, mixes in society, and I write for those who do so, there are some things which are indispensable to even the proper dressing, and every occasion will have its proper attire.

" In his own house then, and in the morning, there is no reason why he should not wear out his old clothes. Some men take to the delightful ease of a dressing-gown and slippers; and if bachelors, they do well. If family men, it will probably depend on whether the lady or the gentleman wears the pantaloons. The best walking-dress for a non-professional man is a suit of tweed of the same color, ordinary boots, gloves not too dark for the coat, a scarf with a pin in winter, or a small tie of one color in summer, a respectable black hat and a cane. The last item is perhaps the most important, and though its use varies with fashion, I confess I am sorry when I see it go out. The best substitute for a walking-stick is an umbrella, *not* a parasol unless it be given you by a lady to carry. The main point of the walking-dress is the harmony of colors, but this should not be carried to the extent of M. de Maltzan, who some years ago made a bet to wear nothing but pink at Baden-Baden for a whole year, and had boots and gloves of the same lively hue. He won his wager, but also the soubriquet of 'Le Diable enflammé.' The walking-dress should vary according to the place and hour. In the country or at the sea-side a straw hat or wide-awake may take the place of the beaver, and the nuisance of gloves be even dispensed with in the former. But in the city where a man is supposed to make visits as well as lounge in the street, the frock coat of very dark blue or black, or a black cloth cut-away, the white waistcoat, and lavender gloves, are almost indispensable. Very thin boots should be avoided at all times, and whatever clothes one wears they should be well brushed. The shirt, whether seen or not, should be quite plain. The shirt collar should never have a color on it, but it may be stiff or turned down according as the wearer is Byronically or Brummellically disposed. The scarf, if simple and of modest colors, is perhaps the best thing we can wear round the neck; but if a neck-tie is preferred it should not be too long, nor tied in too stiff and studied a manner. The cane should be extremely simple, a mere stick in fact, with no gold head, and yet for the town not rough, thick, or clumsy. The frock-coat should be ample and loose, and a tall well-built man may throw it back. At any rate, it should never be buttoned up. Great-coats should be buttoned up, of a dark color, not quite black, longer than the frock-coat, but never long enough to reach the ankles. If you have visits to make you should do away with the great-coat, if the weather allows you to do so. The frock-coat, or black cut-away, with a white waistcoat in summer, is the best dress for making calls in.

"It is simple nonsense to talk of modern civilization, and rejoice that the cruelties of the dark ages can never be perpetrated in these days and this country. I maintain that they are perpetrated freely, generally, daily, with the consent of the wretched victim himself, in the compulsion to wear evening clothes. Is there anything at once more comfortless or more hideous? Let us begin with what the delicate call limb-covers, which we are told were the invention of the Gauls, but I am inclined to think, of a much worse race, for it is clearly an anachronism to ascribe the discovery to a Venetian called Piantaleone, and it can only have been Inquisitors or demons who inflicted this scourge on the race of man, and his ninth-parts, the tailors, for I take it that both are equally bothered by the tight pantaloon. Let us pause awhile over this unsightly garment, and console ourselves with the reflection that as every country, and almost every year, has a different fashion in its make of it, we may at last be emancipated from it altogether, or at least be able to wear it *à la Turque.*

"But it is not all trousers that I rebel against. If
10

I might wear linen appendices in summer, and fur con-tinuations in winter, I would not groan, but it is the evening-dress that inflicts on the man who likes society the necessity of wearing the same trying cloth all the year round, so that under Boreas he catches colds, and under the dog-star he melts. This unmentionable, but most necessary disguise of the 'human form divine,' is one that never varies in this country, and therefore I must lay down the rule :—

" For all evening wear—black cloth trousers.

" But the tortures of evening dress do not end with our lower limbs. Of all the iniquities perpetrated under the Reign of Terror, none has lasted so long as that of the strait-jacket, which was palmed off on the people as a 'habit de compagnie.' If it were necessary to sing a hymn of praise to Robespierre, Marat, and Co., I would rather take the guillotine as my subject to extol than the swallow tail. And yet we endure the stiffness, unsight-liness, uncomfortableness, and want of grace of the lat-ter, with more resignation than that with which Char-lotte Corday put her beautiful neck into the 'trou d'en-fer' of the former. Fortunately modern republicanism has triumphed over ancient etiquette, and the tail-coat of to-day is looser and more easy than it was twenty years ago. I can only say, let us never strive to make it bearable, till we have abolished it. Let us abjure such vulgarities as silk collars, white silk linings, and so forth, which attempt to beautify this monstrosity, as a hangman might wreathe his gallows with roses. The plainer the manner in which you wear your misery, the better.

"Then, again, the black waistcoat, stiff, tight, and comfortless. Fancy Falstaff in a ball-dress, such as we now wear. No amount of embroidery, gold-trimmings, or jewel-buttons will render such an infliction grateful to the mass. The best plan is to wear thorough mourning for your wretchedness. In France and America, the cooler white waistcoat is admitted. However, as we have it, let us make the best of it, and not parade our misery by hideous ornamentation. The only evening waistcoat for all purposes for a man of taste is one of simple black, with the simplest possible buttons.

"These three items never vary for dinner-party, muffin-worry, or ball. The only distinction allowed is in the neck-tie. For dinner, the opera, and balls, this must be white, and the smaller the better. It should be too, of a washable texture, not silk, nor netted, nor hanging down, nor of any foppish production, but a simple, white tie, without embroidery. The black tie is admitted for evening parties, and should be equally simple. The shirt-front, which figures under the tie should be plain, with unpretending small plaits. The glove must be white, not yellow. Recently, indeed, a fashion has sprung up of wearing lavender gloves in the evening. They are economical, and as all economy is an abomination, must be avoided. Gloves should always be worn at a ball. At a dinner-party in town they should be worn on entering the room, and drawn off for dinner. While, on the one hand, we must avoid the awkwardness of a gallant sea-captain who, wearing no gloves at a dance, excused himself to his partner by saying, 'Never mind, miss, I can wash my hands when I've done danc-

ing,' we have no need, in the present day, to copy the
Roman gentleman mentioned by Athenæus, who wore
gloves at dinner that he might pick his meat from the
hot dishes more rapidly than the bare-handed guests.
As to gloves at tea-parties and so forth, we are generally
safer with than without them. If it is quite a small
party, we may leave them in our pocket, and in the
country they are scarcely expected to be worn; but
'touch not a cat but with a glove;' you are always safer
with them.

"I must not quit this subject without assuring myself
that my reader knows more about it now than he did before. In fact I have taken one thing for granted, viz.,
that he knows what it is to be dressed, and what undressed. Of course I do not suppose him to be in the
blissful state of ignorance on the subject once enjoyed
by our first parents. I use the words 'dressed' and 'undressed' rather in the sense meant by a military tailor,
or a cook with reference to a salad. You need not be
shocked. I am one of those people who wear spectacles
for fear of seeing anything with the naked eye. I am
the soul of scrupulosity. But I am wondering whether
everybody arranges his wardrobe as our ungrammatical
nurses used to do ours, under the heads of 'best, second-
best, third-best,' and so on, and knows what things ought
to be placed under each. To be 'undressed' is to be
dressed for work and ordinary occupations, to wear a
coat which you do not fear to spoil, and a neck-tie which
your ink-stand will not object to, but your acquaintance
might. To be 'dressed,' on the other hand, since by
dress we show our respect for society at large, or the

persons with whom we are to mingle, is to be clothed in the garments which the said society pronounces as suitable to particular occasions; so that evening dress in the morning, morning dress in the evening, and top boots and a red coat for walking, may all be called 'undress,' if not positively 'bad dress.' But there are shades of being 'dressed;' and a man is called 'little dressed,' 'well dressed,' and 'much dressed,' not according to the quantity but the quality of his coverings.

"To be 'little dressed,' is to wear old things, of a make that is no longer the fashion, having no pretension to elegance, artistic beauty, or ornament. It is also to wear lounging clothes on occasions which demand some amount of precision. To be 'much dressed' is to be in the extreme of the fashion, with bran new clothes, jewelry, and ornaments, with a touch of extravagance and gaiety in your colors. Thus to wear patent leather boots and yellow gloves in a quiet morning stroll is to be much dressed, and certainly does not differ immensely from being badly dressed. To be 'well dressed' is the happy medium between these two, which is not given to every one to hold, inasmuch as good taste is rare, and is a *sine quâ non* thereof. Thus while you avoid ornament and all fastness, you must cultivate fashion, that is *good* fashion, in the make of your clothes. A man must not be made by his tailor, but should make him, educate him, give him his own good taste. To be well dressed is to be dressed precisely as the occasion, place, weather, your height, figure, position, age, and, remember it, your *means* require. It is to be clothed without peculiarity, pretension, or eccentricity; without violent colors, elab orate ornament, or senseless fashions, introduced, often, by tailors for their own profit. Good dressing is to wear as little jewelry as possible, to be scrupulously neat, clean, and fresh, and to carry your clothes as if you did not give them a thought.

"Then, too, there is a scale of honor among clothes, which must not be forgotten. Thus, a new coat is more honorable than an old one, a cut-away or shooting-coat than a dressing-gown, a frock-coat than a cut-away, a dark blue frock-coat than a black frock-coat, a tail-coat than a frock-coat. There is no honor at all in a blue tail-coat, however, except on a gentleman of eighty, accompanied with brass buttons and a buff waistcoat. There is more honor in an old hunting-coat than in a new one, in a uniform with a bullet hole in it than one without, in a fustian jacket and smock-frock than in a frock-coat, because they are types of labor, which is far more honorable than lounging. Again, light clothes are generally placed above dark ones, because they cannot be so long worn, and are, therefore, proofs of expenditure, *alias* money, which in this world is a commodity more honored than every other; but, on the other hand, tasteful dress is always more honorable than that which has only cost much. Light gloves are more esteemed than dark ones, and the prince of glove-colors is, undeniably, lavender.

"'I should say Jones was a fast man,' said a friend to me one day, 'for he wears a white hat.' If this idea of my companion's be right, fastness may be said to consist mainly in peculiarity. There is certainly only one step from the sublimity of fastness to the ridiculousness of snobberry, and it is not always easy to say where the one ends and the other begins. A dandy, on the other hand, is the clothes on a man, not a man in clothes, a living lay figure who displays much dress, and is quite satisfied if you praise it without taking heed of him. A bear is in the opposite extreme; never dressed enough, and always very roughly; but he is almost as bad as the other, for he sacrifices everything to his ease and comfort. The off-hand style of dress only suits an off-hand character. It was, at one time, the fashion to affect a certain negligence, which was called poetic, and supposed to be the result of genius. An ill-tied, if not positively untied cravat was a sure sign of an unbridled imagination; and a waistcoat was held together by one button only, as if the swelling soul in the wearer's bosom had burst all the rest. If, in addition to this, the hair was unbrushed and curly, you were certain of passing for a 'man of soul.' I should not recommend any young gentleman to adopt this style, unless, indeed, he can mouth a great deal, and has a good stock of quotations from the poets. It is of no use to show me the clouds, unless I can positively see you in them, and no amount of negligence in your dress and person will convince me you are a genius, unless you produce an octavo volume of poems published by yourself. I confess I am glad that the *négligé* style, so common in novels of ten years back, has been succeeded by neatness. What we want is real ease in the clothes, and, for my part, I should rejoice to see the Knickerbocker style generally adopted.

"Besides the ordinary occasions treated of before, there are several special occasions requiring a change of dress. Most of our sports, together with marriage (which some people include in sports), come under this head. Now, the less change we make the better in the present day, particularly in the sports, where, if we are dressed with scrupulous accuracy, we are liable to be subjected to a comparison between our clothes and our skill. A man who wears a red coat to hunt in, should be able to hunt, and not sneak through gates or dodge over gaps. A few remarks on dresses worn in different sports may be useful. Having laid down the rule that a strict accuracy of sporting costume is no longer in good taste, we can dismiss shooting and fishing at once, with the warning that we must not dress *well* for either. An old coat with large pockets, gaiters in one case, and, if necessary, large boots in the other, thick shoes at any rate, a wide-awake, and a well-filled bag or basket at the end of the day, make up a most respectable sportsman of the lesser kind. Then for cricket you want nothing more unusual than flannel trousers, which should be quite plain, unless your club has adopted some colored stripe thereon, a colored flannel shirt of no very violent hue, the same colored cap, shoes with spikes in them, and a great coat.

"For hunting, lastly, you have to make more change, if only to insure your own comfort and safety. Thus cord-breeches and some kind of boots are indispensable. So are spurs, so a hunting-whip or crop; so too, if you do not wear a hat, is the strong round cap that is to save your valuable skull from cracking if you are thrown on your head. Again, I should pity the man who would attempt to hunt in a frock-coat or a dress-coat; and

scarf with a pin in it is much more convenient than a
tie. But beyond these you need nothing out of the com
mon way, but a pocketful of money. The red coat, for
instance, is only worn by regular members of a hunt, and
boys who ride over the hounds and like to display their
'pinks.' In any case you are better with an ordinary
riding-coat of dark color, though undoubtedly the red is
prettier in the field. If you *will* wear the latter, see
that it is cut square, for the swallow-tail is obsolete, and
worn only by the fine old boys who 'hunted, sir, fifty
years ago, sir, when I was a boy of fifteen, sir. Those
were hunting days, sir; such runs and such leaps.'
Again, your ' cords' should be light in color and fine in
quality; your waistcoat, if with a red coat, quite light
too; your scarf of cashmere, of a buff color, and fastened
with a small simple gold pin; your hat should be old,
and your cap of dark green or black velvet, plated inside, and with a small stiff peak, should be made to look
old. Lastly, for a choice of boots. The Hessians are
more easily cleaned, and therefore less expensive to keep;
the ' tops' are more natty. Brummell, who cared more
for the hunting-dress than the hunting itself, introduced the fashion of pipe-claying the tops of the latter,
but the old original 'mahoganies,' of which the upper
leathers are simply polished, seem to be coming into
fashion again."

CHAPTER VIII.

MANLY EXERCISES.

BODILY exercise is one of the most important means provided by nature for the maintenance of health, and in order to prove the advantages of exercise, we must show what is to be exercised, why exercise is necessary, and the various modes in which it may be taken.

The human body may be regarded as a wonderful machine, the various parts of which are so wonderfully adapted to each other, that if one be disturbed all must suffer. The bones and muscles are the parts of the human frame on which motion depends. There are four hundred muscles in the body; each one has certain functions to perform, which cannot be disturbed without danger to the whole. They assist the tendons in keeping the bones in their places, and put them in motion. Whether we walk or run, sit or stoop, bend the arm or head, or chew our food, we may be said to open and shut a number of hinges, or ball and socket joints. And it is a wise provision of nature, that, to a certain extent, the more the muscles are exercised, the stronger do they become; hence it is that laborers and artisans are stronger and more muscular than those persons whose lives are passed in easy occupations or professional duties.

Besides strengthening the limbs, muscular exercise has a most beneficial influence on respiration and the circulation of the blood. The larger blood-vessels are generally placed deep among the muscles, consequently when the latter are put into motion, the blood is driven through the arteries and veins with much greater rapidity than when there is no exercise; it is more completely purified, as the action of the insensible perspiration is promoted, which relieves the blood of many irritating matters, chiefly carbonic acid and certain salts, taken up in its passage through the system, and a feeling of lightness and cheerfulness is diffused over body and mind.

We have said that a good state of health depends in a great measure on the proper exercise of *all the muscles.* But on looking at the greater portion of our industrial population,—artisans and workers in factories generally —we find them, in numerous instances, standing or sitting in forced or unnatural positions, using only a few of their muscles, while the others remain, comparatively speaking, unused or inactive. Sawyers, filers, tailors, and many others may be easily recognized as they walk the streets, by the awkward movement and bearing impressed upon them by long habit. The stooping position especially tells most fatally upon the health; weavers, shoemakers, and cotton-spinners have generally a sallow and sickly appearance, very different from that of those whose occupation does not require them to stoop, or to remain long in a hurtful posture. Their common affections are indigestion and dull headache, with giddiness especially during summer. They attribute their complaints to two causes, one of which is the posture of the body, bent for twelve or thirteen hours a day, the other the heat of the working-room.

Besides the trades above enumerated, there are many others productive of similar evils by the position into which they compel workmen, or by the close and confined places in which they are carried on; and others, again, in their very natures injurious. Plumbers and painters suffer from the noxious materials which they are constantly using, grinders and filers from dust, and bakers from extremes of temperature and irregular hours. Wherever there is physical depression, there is a disposition to resort to injurious stimulants; and "the time of relief from work is generally spent, not in invigorating the animal frame, but in aggravating complaints, and converting functional into organic disease."

But there are others who suffer from artificial poisons and defective exercise as well as artisans and operatives —the numerous class of shopkeepers; the author above quoted says, "Week after week passes without affording them one pure inspiration. Often, also, they have not exercise even in the open air of the town; a furlong's walk to church on Sunday being the extent of their rambles. When they have the opportunity they want the inclination for exercise. The father is anxious about his trade or his family, the mother is solicitous about her children. Each has little taste for recreation or amusement. The various disorders, generally known under the name of indigestion, disorders dependant on a want

of circulation of blood through the bowels, biliary de-
rangements, and headache, are well known to be the
general attendants on trade, closely pursued. Indeed,
in almost every individual, this absorbing principle produces one or other of the various maladies to which I
have alluded.

The great remedy for the evils here pointed out is
bodily exercise, of some kind, every day, and as much
as possible in the open air. An opinion prevails that an
occasional walk is sufficient to maintain the balance of
health; but if the intervals of inaction be too long, the
good effect of one walk is lost before another is taken.
Regularity and sufficiency are to be as much regarded
in exercise as in eating or sleeping. Sir James Clark
says, that "the exercise which is to benefit the system
generally, must be in the open air, and extend to the
whole muscular system. Without regular exercise out
of doors, no young person can continue long healthy;
and it is the duty of parents in fixing their children at
boarding schools to ascertain that sufficient time is occupied daily in this way. They may be assured that attention to this circumstance is quite as essential to the
moral and physical health of their children, as any
branch of education which they may be taught."

Exercise, however, must be regulated by certain rules,
the principal of which is, to avoid carrying it to excess
—to proportion it always to the state of health and habit
of the individual. Persons of short breath predisposed
to determination of blood to the head, subject to palpitation of the heart, or general weakness, are not to believe that a course of severe exercise will do them good;

on the contrary, many serious results often follow over-fatigue. For the same reason it is desirable to avoid active exertion immediately after a full meal, as the foundation of heart diseases is sometimes laid by leaping or running after eating. The great object should be so to blend exercise and repose, as to ensure the highest possible amount of bodily vigor. It must be recollected that exhausted muscles can be restored only by the most perfect rest.

In the next place, it is a mistake to consider the labor of the day as equivalent to exercise. Work, generally speaking, is a mere routine process, carried on with but little variety of circumstances, in a confined atmosphere, and in a temperature frequently more exhaustive than restorative. The workman requires something more than this to keep him in health; he must have exercise as often as possible in the open air,—in fields, parks, or pleasure grounds; but if these are not at his command, the streets of the town are always open to him, and a walk in these is better than no walk at all. The mere change of scene is beneficial, and in walking he generally sets in motion a different set of muscles from those he has used while at work.

To derive the greatest amount of good from exercise, it must be combined with amusement, and be made pleasureable and recreative. This important fact ought never to be lost sight of, since to ignorance of it alone we owe many of the evils which afflict society. And it would be well if those who have been accustomed to look on social amusements as destructive of the morals of the people, would consider how much good may be done by giving the mind a direction which, while promotive of health, would fill it with cheerfulness and wean it from debasing habits. The character of our sports at the presen; time, partake but little of the robust and boisterous spirit of our forefathers; but with the refinement of amusements, the opportunity for enjoying them has been grievously diminished. Cheering signs of a better state of things are, however, visible in many quarters, and we trust that the good work will be carried on until the whole of our population shall be in possession of the means and leisure for pleasurable recreation.

While indulging in the recreative sports which are to restore and invigorate us, we must be mindful of the many points of etiquette and kindness which will do much, if properly attended to, to promote the enjoyment of our exercise, and we propose to review the principal exercises used among us, and to point out in what places the delicate and gentlemanly attention to our companions will do the most to establish, for the person who practices them, the reputation of a polished gentleman.

RIDING.

There are no amusements, probably, which give us so wide a scope for the rendering of attention to a friend as riding and driving. Accompanied, as we may be at any time, by timid companions, the power to convince them, by the management of the horse we ride, and the watch kept at the same time on theirs, that we are competent to act the part of companion and guardian, will enable us to impart to them a great degree of reliance on

us, and will, by lessening their fear do much to enhance
the enjoyment of the excursion.

With ladies, in particular, a horseman cannot be too
careful to display a regard for the fears of their companions, and by a constant watch on all the horses in the
cavalcade, to show at once his ability and willingness to
assist his companions.

There are few persons, comparatively speaking, even
among those who ride often, who can properly assist a
lady in mounting her horse. An over-anxiety to help a
lady as gracefully as possible, generally results in a nervous trembling effort which is exceedingly disagreeable
to the lady, and, at the same time, dangerous; for were
the horse to shy or start, he could not be so easily
quieted by a nervous man as by one who was perfectly
cool. In the mount the lady must gather her skirt into
her left hand, and stand close to the horse, her face toward his head, and her right hand resting on the pommel.
The gentleman, having asked permission to assist her,
stands at the horse's shoulder, facing the lady, and stooping low, he places his right hand at a proper elevation
from the ground. The lady then places her left foot on
the gentleman's palm, and as he raises his hand she
springs slightly on her right foot, and thus reaches the
saddle. The gentleman must not jerk his hand upward,
but lift it with a gentle motion. This method of mounting is preferable to a step or horse-block. Keep a *firm*
hand, for a sinking foot-hold will diminish the confidence
of a lady in her escort, and, in many cases cause her
unnecessary alarm while mounting. To any one who is
likely to be called on to act as cavalier to ladies in horse-

back excursions, we would recommend the following
practice: Saddle a horse with a side saddle, and ask a
gentleman friend to put on the skirt of a lady's habit,
and with him, practice the mounting and dismounting
until you have thoroughly conquered any difficulties you
may have experienced at first :

After the seat is first taken by the lady, the gentle·
man should always stand at the side of the lady's horse
until she is firmly fixed in the saddle, has a good foot-
hold on the stirrup, and has the reins and whip well in
hand.   Having ascertained that his companion is firmly
and comfortably fixed in the saddle, the gentleman
should mount his horse and take his riding position on
the right or "off" side of the lady's horse, so that, in
case of the horse's shying in such a way as to bring him
against the other horse, the lady will suffer no inconvenience.   In riding with two ladies there are two rules
in regard to the gentleman's position.

If both ladies are good riders, they should ride side
by side, the ladies to the left; but, if the contrary should
be the case, the gentleman should ride *between* the ladies
in order to be ready in a moment to assist either in case
of one of the horses becoming difficult to manage.   Before allowing a lady to mount, the entire furniture of
her horse should be carefully examined by her escort.
The saddle and girths should be tested to see if they are
firm, the stirrup leather examined, in case of the tongue
of the buckle being in danger of slipping out by not be
ing well buckled at first, and most particularly the bri
dle, curb, headstall, and reins should be carefully and
thoroughly examined, for on them depends the entire

11

control of the horse. These examinations should *never* be left to the stablehelps, as the continual harnessing of horses by them often leads to a loose and careless **way** of attending to such matters, which, though seemingly trivial, may lead to serious consequences.

On the road, the constant care of the gentleman should be to render the ride agreeable to his companion, by the pointing out of objects of interest with which she may not be acquainted, the reference to any peculiar beauty of landscape which may have escaped her notice, and a general lively tone of conversation, which will, if she be timid, draw her mind from the fancied dangers of horseback riding, and render her excursion much more agreeable than if she be left to imagine horrors whenever her horse may prick up his ears or whisk his tail. And, while thus conversing, keep an eye always on the lady's horse, so that in case he should really get frightened, you may be ready by your instruction and assistance to aid the lady in quieting his fears.

In dismounting you should offer your right hand to the lady's left, and allow her to use *your* left as a step to dismount on, gently declining it as soon as the lady has left her seat on the saddle, and just before she springs. Many ladies spring from the saddle, but this generally confuses the gentleman and is dangerous to the lady, for the horse *may* move at the instant she springs, which would inevitably throw her backward and might result in a serious injury.

DRIVING.

In the indulgence of this beautiful pastime there are

many points of care and attention to be observed; they
will render to the driver himself much gratification by
the confidence they will inspire in his companion, by
having the knowledge that he or she is being driven by
a careful horseman, and thus knowing that half of what
danger may attend the pleasure, is removed.

On reaching the door of your companion's residence,
whom we will suppose to be in this case a lady,—though
the same attention may well be extended to a gentleman,—drive close to the mounting-block or curb, and
by heading your horse toward the middle of the road,
and slightly backing the wagon, separate the fore and
hind wheels on the side next the block as much as possible.   This gives room for the lady to ascend into the
wagon without soiling her dress by rubbing against
either tire, and also gives the driver room to lean over
and tuck into the wagon any part of a lady's dress that
may hang out after she is seated.

In assisting the lady to ascend into the wagon, the
best and safest way is to tie the horse firmly to a hitch-
ing-post or tree, and then to give to your companion the
aid of both your hands; but, in case of there being no
post to which you can make the rein fast, the following
rule may be adopted:

Grasp the reins firmly with one hand, and draw them
just tight enough to let the horse feel that they are
held, and with the other hand assist the lady; under *no*
circumstances, even with the most quiet horse, should
you place a lady in your vehicle without *any* hold on
the horse, for, although many horses would stand per·
fectly quiet, the whole race of them are timid, and any

sudden noise or motion may start them, in which case
the life of your companion may be endangered.   In the
light *no-top* or *York* wagon, which is now used almost
entirely for pleasure drives, the right hand cushion
should always be higher by three or four inches than the
left, for it raises the person driving, thus giving him
more control, and renders the lady's seat more comfortable and more safe.   It is a mistaken idea, in driving,
that it shows a perfect horseman, to drive fast.   On the
contrary, a *good* horseman is more careful of his horse
than a poor one, and in starting, the horse is always allowed to go slowly for time; as he gradually takes up a
quicker pace, and becomes warmed up, the driver may
push him even to the top of his speed for some distance,
always, however, allowing him to slacken his pace toward
the end of his drive, and to come to the stopping-place
at a moderate gait.

Endeavor, by your conversation on the road, to make
the ride agreeable to your companion.   Never try to
show off your driving, but remember, that there is no
one who drives with so much apparent ease and so little
display as the professional jockey, who, as he devotes
his life to the management of the reins, may well be supposed to be the most thoroughly good " whip."

In helping the lady out of the wagon, the same rule
must be observed as in the start; namely, to have your
horse well in hand or firmly tied.   Should your companion be a gentleman and a horseman, the courtesy is
always to offer him the reins, though the offer, if made
to yourself by another with whom you are riding, should
always be declined; unless, indeed, the horse should be

particularly "hard-mouthed" and your friend's arms should be tired, in which case you should relieve him.

Be especially careful in the use of the whip, that it may not spring back outside of the vehicle and strike your companion. This rule should be particularly attended to in driving "tandem" or "four-in-hand," as a cut with a heavy tandem-whip is by no means a pleasant accompaniment to your drive.

In this much-abused accomplishment, there would, from the rough nature of the sport, seem to be small room for civility ; yet, in none of the many manly sports is there so great a scope for the exercise of politeness as in this. Should your adversary be your inferior in boxing, there are many ways to teach him and encourage him in his pursuit of proficiency, without knocking him about as if your desire was to injure him as much as possible. And you will find that his gratitude for your forbearance will prompt him to exercise the same indulgence to others who are inferior to himself, and thus by the exchange of gentlemanly civility the science of boxing is divested of one of its most objectionable points, viz : the danger of the combatants becoming angry and changing the sport to a brutal fight.

Always allow your antagonist to choose his gloves from the set, though, if you recommend *any* to him, let him take the hardest ones and you the softest ; thus he will receive the easier blows. Allow him the choice of ground and position, and endeavor in every way to give him the utmost chance. In this way, even if you should

be worsted in the game, your kindness and courtesy to
him will be acknowledged by any one who may be with
you, and by no one more readily than your antagonist
himself. These same rules apply to the art of fencing,
the most graceful and beautiful of exercises. Let your
opponent have his choice of the foils and sword-gloves,
give him the best position for light, and in your thrusts
remember that to make a " hit" does not require you to
force your foil as violently as you can against your antagonist's breast; but, that every touch will show if your
foils be chalked and the one who has the most " spots"
at the end of the encounter is the beaten man.

S A I L I N G .

Within a few years there has been a most decided
movement in favor of aquatic pursuits. Scarcely a town
can be found, near the sea or on the bank of a river
but what can either furnish a yacht or a barge. In all
our principal cities the "navies" of yachts and barges
number many boats. The barge clubs particularly are
well-fitted with active, healthy men, who can appreciate
the physical benefit of a few hours' work at the end of a
sixteen-foot sweep, and who prefer health and blistered
hands to a life of fashionable and unhealthy amusement.
Under the head of sailing we will give some hints of
etiquette as to sailing and rowing together. A gentleman
will never parade his superiority in these accomplishments,
still less boast of it, but rather, that the others may not feel
their inferiority, he will keep considerably within his powers. If a guest or a stranger be of the party, the best
place must be offered to him, though he may be a bad oar;

but, at the same time, if a guest knows his inferiority in this respect, he will, for more reasons than one, prefer an inferior position. So, too, when a certain amount of exertion is required, as in boating, a well-bred man will offer to take the greater share, pull the heaviest oar, and will never shirk his work. In short, the whole rule of good manners on such occasions is not to be selfish, and the most amiable man will therefore be the best bred. It is certainly desirable that a gentleman should be able to handle an oar, or to steer and work a yacht, both that when he has an opportunity he may acquire health, and that he may be able to take part in the charming excursions which are made by water. One rule should apply to all these aquatic excursions, and that is, that the gentleman who invites the ladies, should there be any, and who is, therefore, at the trouble of getting up the party, should always be allowed to steer the boat, unless he decline the post, for he has the advantage of more intimate acquaintance with the ladies, whom he will have to entertain on the trip, and the post of honor should be given him as a compliment to his kindness in undertaking the preliminaries.

HUNTING.

Gentlemen residing in the country, and keeping a stable, are generally ready to join the hunt club. We are gradually falling into the English sports and pastimes. Cricket, boxing, and hunting, are being more and more practiced every year, and our horsemen and pugilists aspire to conquer those of Britain, when a few years back, to attempt such a thing would have been considered folly. In this country the organization of hunt-clubs is made as much to rid the country of the foxes as to enjoy the sport. We differ much from the Britons in our hunting; we have often a hilly dangerous country, with high worm and post-and-rail fences crossing it, deep streams with precipitous sides and stony ground to ride over. We hunt in cold weather when the ground is frozen hard, and we take everything as it is, hills, fences, streams, and hedges, risking our necks innumerable times in a hunt. In England the hunters have a flat country, fences which do not compare to ours in height, and they hunt *after* a frost when the ground is soft.

Our hunting field at the "meet" does not show the gaudy equipment and top-boots of England, but the plain dress of the gentleman farmer, sometimes a blue coat and jockey-cap, but oftener the every-day coat and felt hat, but the etiquette of our hunting field is more observed than in England. There any one joins the meet, if it is a large one, but here no one enters the field unless acquainted with one or more of the gentlemen on the ground. The rules in the hunt are few and simple. Never attempt to hunt unless you have a fine seat in the saddle and a good horse, and never accept the loan of a friend's horse, still less an enemy's, unless you ride very well. A man may forgive you for breaking his daugh-ter's heart but never for breaking his hunter's neck. Another point is, always to be quiet at a meet, and never join one unless acquainted with some one in the field. Pluck, skill, and a good horse are essentials in hunting Never talk of your achievments, avoid enthusiastic shout-ing when you break cover, and do not ride over the

hounds. Keep a firm hand, a quick eye, an easy, calm
frame of mind, and a good, firm seat on the saddle.
Watch the country you are going over, be always ready
to help a friend who may "come to grief," and with the
rules and the quiet demeanor you will soon be a favorite
in the field.

SKATING.

Though we may, in the cold winter, sigh for the return
of spring breezes, and look back with regret on the autumn sports, or even the heat of summer, there is yet a
balm for our frozen spirits in the glorious and exhilarat-
ing sports of winter. The sleigh filled with laughing
female beauties and "beauties," too, of the sterner sex,
and the merry jingle of the bells as we fly along the
road or through the streets, are delights of which Old
Winter alone is the giver. But, pleasant as the sleigh-
ride is, the man who looks for health and exercise at all
seasons, turns from the seductive pleasures of the sleigh
to the more simple enjoyment derived from the skates.
Flying along over the glistening ice to the accompaniment of shouts of merry laughter at some novice's mis-
hap, and feeling that we have within us the speed of the
race-horse, the icy pleasure is, indeed, a good substitute
for the pleasures of the other seasons.

So universal has skating become, that instruction in
this graceful accomplishment seems almost unnecessary;
but, for the benefit of the rising generation who may
peruse our work, we will give, from a well-known authority, a few hints as to the manner of using the skates

before we add our own instruction as to the etiquette of the skating ground.

"Before going on the ice, the young skater must learn to put on the skates, and may also learn to walk with them easily in a room, balancing, alternately, on each foot. A skater's dress should be as loose and unincumbered as possible. All fullness of dress is exposed to the wind. As the exercise of skating produces perspiration, flannel next the chest, shoulders, and loins, is necessary to avoid the evils of sudden chills in cold weather.

"Either very rough or very smooth ice should be avoided. The person who, for the first time, attempts to skate, must not trust to a stick. He may take a friend's hand for support, if he requires one; but that should be soon relinquished, in order to balance himself. He will, probably, scramble about for half an hour or so, till he begins to find out where the edge of his skate is. The beginner must be fearless, but not violent; nor even in a hurry. He should not let his feet get apart, and keep his heels still nearer together. He must keep the ankle of the foot on the ice quite firm; not attempting to gain the edge of the skate by bending it, because the right mode of getting to either edge is by the inclination of the whole body in the direction required; and this inclination should be made fearlessly and decisively. The leg which is on the ice should be kept perfectly straight: for, though the knee must be somewhat bent at the time of striking, it must be straightened as quickly as possible without any jerk. The leg which is off the ice should also be kept straight, though not stiff, having an easy but straight play, the toe pointing downwards, and the heel from six to twelve inches of the other.

"The learner must not look down at the ice, nor at his feet, to see how they perform. He may, at first, incline his body a little forward, for safety, but hold his head up, and see where he goes, his person erect and his face rather elevated than otherwise.

"When once off, he must bring both feet up together, and strike again, as soon as he finds himself steady enough, rarely allowing both feet to be on the ice to gether. The position of the arms should be easy and varied; one being always more raised than the other, this elevation being alternate, and the change corresponding to that of the legs; that is, the right arm being raised as the right leg is put down, and *vice versâ*, so that the arm and leg of the same side may not be raised together. The face must be always turned in the direction of the line intended to be described. Hence in backward skating, the head will be inclined much over the shoulder; in forward skating, but slightly. All sudden and violent action must be avoided. Stopping may be caused by slightly bending the knees, drawing the feet together, inclining the body forward, and pressing on the heels. It may be also caused by turning short to the right or left, the foot on the side to which we turn being rather more advanced, and supporting part of the weight."*

When on the ice, if you should get your skates on before your companion, always wait for him; for, nothing is more disagreeable than being left behind on an occa

* Walker's Manly Exercises.

sion of this kind. Be ready at all times when skating to render assistance to any one, either lady or gentleman, who may require it. A *gentleman* may be distinguished at all times by the willingness with which he will give up his sport to render himself agreeable and kind to any one in difficulty. Should you have one of the skating-sleds so much used for taking ladies on the ice, and should your own ladies, if you are accompanied by any, not desire to use it, the most becoming thing you can do is to place it at the disposal of any other gentleman who has ladies with him, and who is not provided with such a conveyance.

Always keep to the right in meeting a person on the ice, and always skate perfectly clear of the line in which a lady is advancing, whether she be on skates or on foot. Attention to the other sex is no where more appreciated than on the ice, where they are, unless good skaters, comparatively helpless. Be always prompt to assist in the extrication of any one who may break through the ice, but let your zeal be tempered by discretion, and always get a rope or ladder if possible, in preference to going near the hole; for there is great risk of your breaking through yourself, and endangering your own life without being able to assist the person already submerged. But should the rope or ladder not be convenient, the best method is to lay flat on your breast on the ice, and push yourself cautiously along until you can touch the person's hand, and then let him climb by it out of the hole.

SWIMMING

So few persons are unable to swim, that it would be useless for us to furnish any instruction in the actual art of swimming; but a few words on the subject of assisting others while in the water may not come amiss.

It is a desirable accomplishment to be able to swim in a suit of clothes. This may be practiced by good swimmers, cautiously at first, in comparatively shallow water, and afterwards in deeper places. Occasions may frequently occur where it may be necessary to plunge into the water to save a drowning person, where the lack of time, or the presence of ladies, would preclude all possibility of removing the clothes. There are few points of etiquette in swimming, except those of giving all the assistance in our power to beginners, and to remember the fact of our being gentlemen, though the sport may be rough when we are off *terra firma*. We shall therefore devote this section of our exercise department to giving a few general directions as to supporting drowning persons, which support is, after all, the most valued attention we can render to any one.

If possible, always go to save a life in company with one or two others. One companion is generally sufficient, but two will do no harm, for, if the service of the second be not required, he can easily swim back to shore. On reaching the object of your pursuit, if he be clinging to anything, caution him, as you approach, to hold it until you tell him to let go, and then to let his arms fall to his side. Then let one of your companions place his hand under the armpit of the person to be assisted, and you doing the like, call to him to let go his support, then tread water until you get his arms on the shoulders of your companion and yourself, and then swim gently to shore. Should you be alone, the utmost you can do is to let him hold his support while you tread water near him until further assistance can be obtained. If you are alone and he has no support, let him rest one arm across your shoulder, put one of your arms behind his back, and the hand under his armpit, and tread water until help arrives. Never let a man in these circum- stances *grasp* you in any way, particularly if he be frightened, for you may both be drowned; but, try to cool and reassure him by the intrepidity of your own movements, and he will be safely and easily preserved.

CRICKET.

When in the cricket-field, we must allow ourselves to enter into the full spirit of the game; but we must not allow the excitement of the play to make us forget what is due to others and to ourselves. A gentle, easy, and, at the same time, gentlemanly manner, may be as- sumed. Always offer to your companions the use of your private bat, if they are not similarly provided; for the bats belonging to the club often lose the spring in the handle from constant use, and a firm bat with a good spring will prove very acceptable. In this way you gratify the player, and, as a reward for your kindness, he may, from being well provided, score more for the side than he would with inferior or worn-out tools.

This game is more purely democratic than any one we know of, and the most aristocratic of gentlemen takes

second rank, for the time, to the most humble cricketer,
if the latter be the more skillful.   But a good player is
not always a gentleman, and the difference in cultivation
may always be distinguished.   A *gentleman* will never
deride any one for his bad play, nor give vent to oaths,
or strong epithets, if disappointed in the playing of one
of his side.   If he has to ask another player for anything, he does so in a way to establish his claim to gen
tility.   "May I trouble you for that ball?" or, "Will
you please to hand me that bat?" are much preferable to
"Here, you! ball there!" or, "Clumsy, don't carry off
that bat!"   Again, if a gentleman makes a mistake himself, he should always acknowledge it quietly, and never
start a stormy discussion as to the merits of his batting
or fielding.   In fine, preserve the same calm demeanor
in the field that you would in the parlor, however deeply
you enter into the excitement of the game.

CHAPTER IX.

TRAVELING.

IN this country where ladies travel so much alone, a gentleman has many opportunities of making this unprotected state a pleasant one. There are many little courtesies which you may offer to a lady when travel·ing, even if she is an entire stranger to you, and by an air of respectful deference, you may place her entirely at her ease with you, even if you are both young.

When traveling with a lady, your duties commence when you are presented to her as an escort. If she is personally a stranger, she will probably meet you at the wharf or car depot; but if an old acquaintance, you should offer to call for her at her residence. Take a hack, and call, leaving, ample time for last speeches and farewell tears. If she hands you her purse to defray her expenses, return it to her if you stop for any length cf time at a place where she may wish to make purchases. If you make no stop upon your journey, keep the purse until you arrive at your destination, and then return it If she does not give you the money for her expenses when you start, you had best pay them yourself, keeping an account, and she will repay you at the journey's end.

When you start, select for your companion the plea-
santest seat, see that her shawl and bag are within her
reach, the window lowered or raised as she may prefer,
and then leave her to attend to the baggage, or, if you
prefer, let her remain in the hack while you get checks
for the trunks. Never keep a lady standing upon the
wharf or in the depot, whilst you arrange the baggage.

When you arrive at a station, place your lady in a
hack while you get the trunks.

When arriving at a hotel, escort your companion to
the parlor, and leave her there whilst you engage rooms.
As soon as her room is ready, escort her to the door,
and leave her, as she will probably wish to change her
dress or lie down, after the fatigue of traveling. If you
remain chatting in the parlor, although she may be too
polite to give any sign of weariness, you may feel sure
she is longing to go to a room where she can bathe her
face and smooth her hair.

If you remain in the hotel to any meal, ask before
you leave her, at what hour she wishes to dine, sup, or
breakfast, and at that hour, knock at her door, and
escort her to the table.

If you remain in the city at which her journey ter-
minates, you should call the day after your arrival upon
the companion of your journey. If, previous to that
journey, you have never met her, she has the privilege
of continuing the acquaintance or not as she pleases, so
if all your gallantry is repaid by a cut the next time
you meet her, you must submit, and hope for better
luck next time. In such a case, you are at liberty

12

to decline escorting her again should the request be made.

When traveling alone, your opportunities to display your gallantry will be still more numerous. To offer to carry a bag for a lady who is unattended, to raise or lower a window for her, offer to check her baggage, procure her a hack, give her your arm from car to boat or boat to car, assist her children over the bad crossings, or in fact extend any such kindness, will mark you as a gentleman, and win you the thanks due to your courtesy. Be careful however not to be too attentive, as you then become officious, and embarrass when you mean to please.

If you are going to travel in other countries, in Europe, especially, I would advise you to study the languages, before you attempt to go abroad. French is the tongue you will find most useful in Europe, as it is spoken in the courts, and amongst diplomatists; but, in order fully to enjoy a visit to any country, you must speak the language of that country. You can then visit in the private houses, see life among the peasantry, go with confidence from village to town, from city to city, learning more of the country in one day from familiar intercourse with the natives, than you would learn in a year from guide books or the explanations of your courier. The way to really enjoy a journey through a strange land, is not to roll over the high ways in your carriage, stop at the hotels, and be led to the points of interest by your guide, but to shoulder your knapsack, or take up your valise, and make a pedestrian tour through the hamlets and villages. Take a room at a hotel in the principal cities if you will, and see all that your guide book commands you to seek, and then start on your own tour of investigation, and believe me you will enjoy your independent walks and chats with the villagers and peasants, infinitely more than your visits dictated by others. Of course, to enjoy this mode of traveling, you must have some know edge of the language, and if you start with only a very slight acquaintance with it, you will be surprised to find how rapidly you will acquire the power to converse, when you are thus forced to speak in that language, or be entirely silent.

Your pocket, too, will be the gainer by the power to arrange your own affairs. If you travel with a courier and depend upon him to arrange your hotel bills and other matters, you will be cheated by every one, from the boy who blacks your boots, to the magnificent artist, who undertakes to fill your picture gallery with the works of the "old masters." If Murillo, Raphael, and Guido could see the pictures brought annually to this country as genuine works of their pencils, we are certain that they would tear their ghostly hair, wring their shadowy hands, and return to the tomb again in disgust. Ignorant of the language of the country you are visiting, you will be swindled in the little villages and the large cities by the inn-keepers and the hack-drivers, in the country and in the town, morning, noon, and evening, daily, hourly, and weekly; so, again I say, study the languages if you propose going abroad.

In a foreign country nothing stamps the difference between the gentleman and the clown more strongly than the regard they pay to foreign customs. While the latter will exclaim against every strange dress or dish and even show signs of disgust if the latter does not please him, the former will endeavor, as far as is in his power, to "do in Rome as Romans do."

Accustom yourself, as soon as possible, to the customs of the nation which you are visiting, and, as far as you can without any violation of principle, follow them. You will add much to your own comfort by so doing, for, as you cannot expect the whole nation to conform to your habits, the sooner you fall in with theirs the sooner you will feel at home in the strange land.

Never ridicule or blame any usage which seems to you ludicrous or wrong. You may wound those around you, or you may anger them, and it cannot add to the pleasure of your visit to make yourself unpopular. If in Germany they serve your meat upon marmalade, or your beef raw, or in Italy give you peas in their pods, or in France offer you frog's legs and horsesteaks, if you cannot eat the strange viands, make no remarks and repress every look or gesture of disgust. Try to adapt your taste to the dishes, and if you find that impossible, remove those articles you cannot eat from your plate, and make your meal upon the others, but do this silently and quietly, endeavoring not to attract attention.

The best travelers are those who can eat cats in China, oil in Greenland, frogs in France, and maccaroni in Italy; who can smoke a meershaum in Germany, ride an elephant in India, shoot partridges in England, and wear a turban in Turkey; in short, in every nation adapt their habits, costume, and taste to the national manners, dress and dishes.

Do not, when abroad, speak continually in praise of your own country, or disparagingly of others. If you find others are interested in gaining information about America, speak candidly and freely of its customs, scenery, or products, but not in a way that will imply a contempt of other countries. To turn up your nose at the Thames because the Mississippi is longer and wider, or to sneer at *any* object because you have seen its su-perior at home, is rude, ill-bred, and in excessively bad taste. You will find abroad numerous objects of interest which America cannot parallel, and while abroad, you will do well to avoid mention of "our rivers," "our mountains," or, "our manufactories." You will find ruins in Rome, pictures in Florence, cemeteries in France, and factories in England, which will take the lead and chal-lenge the world to compete; and you will exhibit a far better spirit if you candidly acknowledge that superiority, than if you make absurd and untrue assertions of "our" power to excel them.

You will, of course, meet with much to disapprove, much that will excite your laughter; but control the one and keep silence about the other. If you find fault, do so gently and quietly; if you praise, do so without quali-fication, sincerely and warmly.

Study well the geography of any country which you may visit, and, as far as possible, its history also. You cannot feel much interest in localities or monuments con-nected with history, if you are unacquainted with the events which make them worthy of note.

Converse with any who seem disposed to form an ac- quaintance. You may thus pass an hour or two plea- santly, obtain useful information, and you need not carry on the acquaintance unless you choose to do so. Amongst the higher circles in Europe you will find many of the customs of each nation in other nations, but it is among the peasants and the people that you find the true na- tionality.

You may carry with you one rule into every country, which is, that, however much the inhabitants may object to your dress, language, or habits, they will cheerfully acknowledge that the American stranger is perfectly amiable and polite.

CHAPTER X.

ETIQUETTE IN CHURCH.

IT is not, in this book, a question, what you must believe, but how you must act. If your conscience per-
mits you to visit other churches than your own, your first
duty, whilst in them, is not to sneer or scoff at any of
its forms, and to follow the service as closely as you can.

To remove your hat upon entering the edifice devoted
to the worship of a Higher Power, is a sign of respect
never to be omitted. Many men will omit in foreign
churches this custom so expressive and touching, and by
the omission make others believe them irreverent and
foolish, even though they may act from mere thoughtlessness. If, however, you are in a country where the
head is kept covered, and another form of humility
adopted, you need not fear to follow the custom of those
around you. You will be more respected if you pay deference to their religious views, than if you undertock to
prove your superiority by affecting a contempt for any
form of worship. Enter with your thoughts fixed upon
high and holy subjects, and your face will show your devotion, even if you are ignorant of the forms of that
particular church.

If you are with a lady, in a catholic church, offer her

the holy water with your hand ungloved, for, as it is in the intercourse with princes, that church requires all the ceremonies to be performed with the bare hand.

Pass up the aisle with your companion until you reach the pew you are to occupy, then step before her, open the door, and hold it open while she enters the pew. Then follow her, closing the door after you.

If you are visiting a strange church, request the sexton to give you a seat. Never enter a pew uninvi.ed. If you are in your own pew in church, and see strangers looking for a place, open your pew door, invite them by a motion to enter, and hold the door open for them, re-entering yourself after they are seated.

If others around you do not pay what you think a proper attention to the services, do not, by scornful glances or whispered remarks, notice their omissions. Strive, by your own devotion, to forget those near you.

You may offer a book or fan to a stranger near you, if unprovided themselves, whether they be young or old, lady or gentleman.

Remain kneeling as long as those around you do so. Do not, if your own devotion is not satisfied by your at titude, throw scornful glances upon those who remain seated, or merely bow their heads. Above all never sign to them, or speak, reminding them of the position most suitable for the service. Keep your own position, but do not think you have the right to dictate to others. I have heard young persons addressing, with words of re-proach, old men, and lame ones, whose infirmities forbade them to kneel or stand in church, but who were, doubt-less, as good Christians as their presumptuous advisers.

I kno that it often is an effort to remain silent when those in another pew talk incessantly in a low tone or whisper, or sing in a loud tone, out of all time or tune, or read the wrong responses in a voice of thunder; but, while you carefully avoid such faults yourself, you must pass them over in others, without remark.

If, when abroad, you visit a church to see the pictures or monuments within its walls, and not for worship, choose the hours when there is no service being read. Even if you are alone, or merely with a guide, speak low, walk slowly, and keep an air of quiet respect in the edifice devoted to the service of God.

Let me here protest against an Americanism of which modest ladies justly complain; it is that of gentlemen standing in groups round the doors of churches both before and after service. A well-bred man will not indulge in this practice; and, if detained upon the step by a friend, or, whilst waiting for another person, he will stand aside and allow plenty of room for others to pass in, and will never bring the blood into a woman's face by a long, curious stare.

In church, as in every other position in life, the most unselfish man is the most perfect gentleman; so, if you wish to retain your position as a well-bred man, you will, in a crowded church, offer your seat to any lady, or old man, who may be standing.

CHAPTER XI.

ONE HUNDRED HINTS FOR GENTLEMANLY DEPORTMENT.

1. ALWAYS avoid any rude or boisterous action, especially when in the presence of ladies. It is not necessary to be stiff, indolent, or sullenly silent, neither is
perfect gravity always required, but if you jest let it be
with quiet, gentlemanly wit, never depending upon
clownish gestures for the effect of a story. Nothing
marks the gentleman so soon and so decidedly as quiet,
refined ease of manner.

2. Never allow a lady to get a chair for herself, ring
a bell, pick up a handkerchief or glove she may have
dropped, or, in short, perform any service for herself
which you can perform for her, when you are in the
room. By extending such courtesies to your mother,
sisters, or other members of your family, they become
habitual, and are thus more gracefully performed when
abroad.

3. Never perform any little service for another with a
formal bow or manner as if conferring a favor, but with
a quiet gentlemanly ease as if it were, not a ceremonious,
unaccustomed performance, but a matter of course, for
you to be courteous.

4. It is not necessary to tell all that you know; that

were mere folly; but what a man says must be what he believes himself, else he violates the first rule for a gentleman's speech—Truth.

5. Avoid gambling as you would poison. Every bet made, even in the most finished circles of society, is a species of gambling, and this ruinous crime comes on by slow degrees. Whilst a man is minding his business, he is playing the best game, and he is sure to win. You will be tempted to the vice by those whom the world calls gentlemen, but you will find that loss makes you angry, and an angry man is never a courteous one; gain excites you to continue the pursuit of the vice; and, in the end you will lose money, good name, health, good conscience, light heart, and honesty; while you gain evil associates, irregular hours and habits, a suspicious, fretful temper, and a remorseful, tormenting conscience. Some one *must* lose in the game; and, if you win it, it is at the risk of driving a fellow creature to despair.

6. Cultivate tact! In society it will be an invaluable aid. Talent is something, but tact is everything. Talent is serious, sober, grave, and respectable; tact is all that and more too. It is not a sixth sense, but it is the life of all the five. It is the *open* eye, the *quick* ear, the *judging* taste, the *keen* smell, and the *lively* touch; it is the interpreter of all riddles—the surmounter of all difficulties—the remover of all obstacles. It is useful in all places, and at all times; it is useful in solitude, for it shows a man his way *into* the world; it is useful in society, for it shows him his way *through* the world. Talent is power—tact is skill; talent is weight—tact is momentum; talent knows what to do—tact knows how to do it;

talent makes a man respectable—tact will make him respected; talent is wealth—tact is ready money.   For all
the practical purposes of society tact carries against
talent ten to one.

7. Nature has left every man a capacity of being
agreeable, though all cannot *shine* in company; but there
are many men sufficiently qualified for both, who, by a
very few faults, that a little attention would soon correct,
are not so much as tolerable.   Watch, avoid such faults.

8. Habits of self-possession and self-control acquired
early in life, are the best foundation for the formation
of gentlemanly manners.   If you unite with this the
constant intercourse with ladies and gentlemen of refinement and education, you will add to the dignity of perfect self command, the polished ease of polite society.

9. Avoid a conceited manner.   It is exceedingly ill-
bred to assume a manner as if you were superior to those
around you, and it is, too, a proof, not of superiority
but of vulgarity.   And to avoid this manner, avoid the
foundation of it, and cultivate humility.   The praises
of others should be of use to you, in teaching, not what
you are, perhaps, but in pointing out what you ought to
be.

10. Avoid pride, too; it often miscalculates, and more
often misconceives.   The proud man places himself at a
distance from other men; seen through that distance,
others, perhaps, appear little to him; but he forgets that
this very distance causes him also to appear little to
others.

11. A gentleman's title suggests to him humility and
affability; to be easy of access, to pass by neglects and

offences, especially from inferiors; neither to despise any
for their bad fortune or misery, nor to be afraid to own
those who are unjustly oppressed; not to domineer over
inferiors, nor to be either disrespectful or cringing to
superiors; not standing upon his family name, or wealth,
but making these secondary to his attainments in civility,
industry, gentleness, and discretion.

12. Chesterfield says, "All ceremonies are, in themselves, very silly things; but yet a man of the world
should know them. They are the outworks of manners,
which would be too often broken in upon if it were not
for that defence which keeps the enemy at a proper distance. It is for that reason I always treat fools and
coxcombs with great ceremony, true good breeding not
being a sufficient barrier against them."

13. When you meet a lady at the foot of a flight of
stairs, do not wait for her to ascend, but bow, and go up
before her.

14. In meeting a lady at the head of a flight of stairs,
wait for her to precede you in the descent.

15. Avoid slang. It does not beautify, but it sullies
conversation. "Just listen, for a moment, to our fast
young man, or the ape of a fast young man, who thinks
that to be a man he must speak in the dark phraseology
of slang. If he does anything on his own responsibility,
he does it on his own 'hook.' If he sees anything re-
markably good, he calls it a 'stunner,' the superlative
of which is a 'regular stunner.' If a man is requested
to pay a tavern bill, he is asked if he will 'stand Sam.'
If he meets a savage-looking dog, he calls him an 'ugly
customer.' If he meets an eccentric man, he calls him

a 'rummy old cove.' A sensible man is a 'chap that is up to snuff.' Our young friend never scolds, but 'blows up;' never pays, but 'stumps up;' never finds it too difficult to pay, but is 'hard up.' He has no hat, but shelters his head beneath a 'tile.' He wears no neckcloth, but surrounds his throat with a 'choker.' He lives nowhere, but there is some place where he 'hangs out.' He never goes away or withdraws, but he 'bolts' —he 'slopes'—he 'mizzles'—he 'makes himself scarce' —he 'walks his chalks'—he 'makes tracks'—he 'cuts stick'—or, what is the same thing, he 'cuts his lucky!' The highest compliment that you can pay him is to tell him that he is a 'regular brick.' He does not profess to be brave, but he prides himself on being 'plucky.' Money is a word which he has forgotten, but he talks a good deal about 'tin,' and the 'needful,' 'the rhino,' and 'the ready.' When a man speaks, he 'spouts;' when he holds his peace, he 'shuts up;' when he is humiliated, he is 'taken down a peg or two,' and made to 'sing small.' Now, besides the vulgarity of such expressions, there is much in slang that is objectionable in a moral point of view. For example, the word 'governor,' as applied to a father, is to be reprehended. Does it not betray, on the part of young men, great ignorance of the paternal and filial relationship, or great contempt for them? Their father is to such young men merely a governor,— merely a representative of authority. Innocently enough the expression is used by thousands of young men who venerate and love their parents; but only think of it, and I am sure that you will admit that it is a cold, heartless word when thus applied, and one that ought forthwith to be abandoned."

16. There are few traits of social life more repulsive than tyranny. I refer not to the wrongs, real or imaginary, that engage our attention in ancient and moderr history; my tyrants are not those who have waded through blood to thrones, and grievously oppress their brother men. I speak of the *petty* tyrants of the fire side and the social circle, who trample like very despots on the opinions of their fellows. You meet people of this class everywhere; they stalk by your side in the streets; they seat themselves in the pleasant circle on the hearth, casting a gloom on gayety; and they start up dark and scowling in the midst of scenes of innocent mirth, to chill and frown down every participator. They "pooh! pooh!" at every opinion advanced; they make the lives of their mothers, sisters, wives, children, unbearable. Beware then of tyranny. A gentleman is ever humble, and the tyrant is never courteous.

17. Cultivate the virtues of the soul, strong principle, incorruptible integrity, usefulness, refined intellect, and fidelity in seeking for truth. A man in proportion as he has these virtues will be honored and welcomed everywhere.

18. Gentility is neither in birth, wealth, or fashion, but in the mind. A high sense of honor, a determination never to take a mean advantage of another, adherence to truth, delicacy and politeness towards those with whom we hold intercourse, are the essential characteristics of a gentleman.

19. Little attentions to your mother, your wife, and

your sister, will beget much love. The man who is a rude husband, son, and brother, cannot be a gentleman; he may ape the manners of one, but, wanting the refinement of heart that would make him courteous at home, his politeness is but a thin cloak to cover a rude, unpolished mind.

20. At table, always eat slowly, but do not delay those around you by toying with your food, or neglecting the business before you to chat, till all the others are ready to leave the table, but must wait until you repair your negligence, by hastily swallowing your food.

21. Are you a husband? Custom entitles you to be the "lord and master" over your household. But don't assume the *master* and sink the *lord*. Remember that noble generosity, forbearance, amiability, and integrity are the *lordly* attributes of man. As a husband, therefore, exhibit the true nobility of man, and seek to govern your household by the display of high moral excellence.

A domineering spirit—a fault-finding petulance—impatience of trifling delays—and the exhibition of unworthy passion at the slightest provocation can add no laurel to your own "lordly" brow, impart no sweetness to home, and call forth no respect from those by whom you may be surrounded. It is one thing to be a *master*, another to be a *man*. The latter should be the husband's aspiration; for he who cannot govern himself, is ill-qualified to rule others. You can hardly imagine how refreshing it is to occasionally call up the recollection of your courting days. How tediously the hours rolled away prior to the appointed time of meeting; how swift they seemed to fly, when met; how fond was the first greeting; how tender the last embrace; how fervent were your vows; how vivid your dreams of future happiness, when, returning to your home, you felt yourself secure in the confessed love of the object of your warm affections! Is your dream realized?—are you so happy as you expected?—why not? Consider whether as a husband you are as fervent and constant as you were when a lover. Remember that the wife's claims to your unremitting regard—great before marriage, are now ex alted to a much higher degree. She has left the world for you—the home of her childhood, the fireside of her parents, their watchful care and sweet intercourse have all been yielded up for you. Look then most jealously upon all that may tend to attract you from home, and) weaken that union upon which your temporal happiness mainly depends; and believe that in the solemn relationship of HUSBAND is to be found one of the best guarantees for man's honor and happiness.

22. Perhaps the true definition of a gentleman is this: "Whoever is open, loyal, and true; whoever is of humane and affable demeanor; whoever is honorable in himself, and in his judgment of others, and requires no law but his word to make him fulfil an engagement; such a man is a gentleman, be he in the highest or lowest rank of life, a man of elegant refinement and intellect, or the most unpolished tiller of the ground."

23. In the street, etiquette does not require a gentleman to take off his glove to shake hands with a lady, unless her hand is uncovered. In the house, however, the rule is imperative, he must not offer a lady a gloved hand. In the street, if his hand be very warm or very

13

cold, or the glove cannot be readily removed, it is much better to offer the covered hand than to offend the lady's touch, or delay the salutation during an awkward fumble to remove the glove.

24. Sterne says, "True courtship consists in a number of quiet, gentlemanly attentions, not so pointed as to alarm, not so vague as to be misunderstood." A clown will terrify by his boldness, a proud man chill by his reserve, but a gentleman will win by the happy mixture of the two.

25. Use no profane language, utter no word that will cause the most virtuous to blush. Profanity is a mark of low breeding; and the tendency of using indecent and profane language is degrading to your minds. Its injurious effects may not be felt at the moment, but they will continue to manifest themselves to you through life. They may never be obliterated; and, if you allow the fault to become habitual, you will often find at your tongue's end some expressions which you would not use for any money. By being careful on this point you may save yourself much mortification and sorrow.

"Good men have been taken sick and become delirious. In these moments they have used the most vile and indecent language. When informed of it, after a restoration to health, they had no idea of the pain they had given to their friends, and stated that they had learned and repeated the expressions in childhood, and though years had passed since they had spoken a bad word, the early impressions had been indelibly stamped upon the mind."

Think of this, ye who are tempted to use improper

language, and never let a vile word disgrace you. An oath never falls from the tongue of the man who commands respect.

Honesty, frankness, generosity, and virtue are noble traits. Let these be yours, and do not fear. You will then claim the esteem and love of all.

26. Courteous and friendly conduct may, probably will, sometimes meet with an unworthy and ungrateful return; but the absence of gratitude and similar courtesy on the part of the receiver cannot destroy the self-approbation which recompenses the giver. We may scatter the seeds of courtesy and kindness around us at little expense. Some of them will inevitably fall on good ground, and grow up into benevolence in the minds of others, and all of them will bear the fruit of happiness in the bosom whence they spring. A kindly action always fixes itself on the heart of the truly thoughtful and polite man.

27. Learn to restrain anger. A man in a passion ceases to be a gentleman, and if you do not control your passions, rely upon it, they will one day control you. The intoxication of anger, like that of the grape, shows us to others, but hides us from ourselves, and we injure our own cause in the opinion of the world when we *too* passionately and eagerly defend it. Neither will all men be disposed to view our quarrels in the same light that we do; and a man's blindness to his own defects will ever increase in proportion as he is angry with others, or pleased with himself. An old English writer says:—

"As a preventative of anger, banish all tale-bearers and slanderers from your conversation, for it is these

blow the devil's bellows to rouse up the flames of rage
and fury, by first abusing your ears, and then your cre-
dulity, and after that steal away your patience, and all
this, perhaps, for a lie.   To prevent anger, be not too
inquisitive into the affairs of others, or what people say
of yourself, or into the mistakes of your friends, for this
is going out to gather sticks to kindle a fire to burn
your own house."

28. Keep good company or none.   You will lose your
own self-respect, and habits of courtesy sooner and
more effectually by intercourse with low company, than
in any other manner; while, in good company, these
virtues will be cultivated and become habitual.

29. Keep your engagements.   Nothing is ruder than
to make an engagement, be it of business or pleasure,
and break it.   If your memory is not sufficiently retentive to keep all the engagements you make stored within
it, carry a little memorandum book and enter them there.
Especially, keep any appointment made with a lady,
for, depend upon it, the fair sex forgive any other fault
in good breeding, sooner than a broken engagement.

30. Avoid personality; nothing is more ungentlemanly.   The tone of good company is marked by its
entire absence.   Among well-informed persons there are
plenty of topics to discuss, without giving pain to any
one present.

31. Make it a rule to be always punctual in keeping
an appointment, and, when it is convenient, be a little
beforehand.   Such a habit ensures that composure and
ease which is the very essence of gentlemanly deportment; want of it keeps you always in a fever and bustle

and no man who is hurried and feverish appears so well as he whose punctuality keeps him cool and composed.

32. It is right to cultivate a laudable ambition, but do not exaggerate your capacity. The world will not give you credit for half what you esteem yourself. Some men think it so much gained to pass for more than they are worth; but in most cases the deception will be discovered, sooner or later, and the rebound will be greater than the gain. We may, therefore, set it down as a truth, that it is a damage to a man to have credit for greater powers than he possesses.

33. Be ready to apologize when you have committed a fault which gives offence. Better, far better, to retain a friend by a frank, courteous apology for offence given, than to make an enemy by obstinately denying or persisting in the fault.

34. An apology made to yourself must be accepted. No matter how great the offence, a gentleman cannot keep his anger after an apology has been made, and thus, amongst truly well-bred men, an apology is always accepted.

35. Unless you have something of real importance to ask or communicate, do not stop a gentleman in the street during business hours. You may detain him from important engagements, and, though he may be too well-bred to show annoyance, he will not thank you for such detention.

36. If, when on your way to fulfil an engagement, a friend stops you in the street, you may, without committing any breach of etiquette, tell him of your appoint

ment, and release yourself from a long talk, but do **so is a** courteous manner, expressing regret for the necessity

37. If, when meeting two gentlemen, you are obliged to detain one of them, apologize to the other for so doing, whether he is an acquaintance or a stranger, and do not keep him waiting a moment longer than is neces. sary,

38. Have you a sister? Then love and cherish her with all that pure and holy friendship which renders a brother so worthy and noble. Learn to appreciate her sweet influence as portrayed in the following words:

"He who has never known a sister's kind administration, nor felt his heart warming beneath her endearing smile and love-beaming eye, has been unfortunate indeed. It is not to be wondered at if the fountains of pure feeling flow in his bosom but sluggishly, or if the gentle emotions of his nature be lost in the sterner attributes of mankind.

"'That man has grown up among affectionate sisters,' I once heard a lady of much observation and experience remark.

"'And why do you think so?' said I.

"'Because of the rich development of all the tender feelings of the heart.'

" A sister's influence is felt even in manhood's riper years; and the heart of him who has grown cold in chilly contact with the world will warm and thrill with pure enjoyment as some accident awakens within him the soft tones, the glad melodies of his sister's voice; and he will turn from purposes which a warped and false philosophy had reasoned into expediency, and even weep for the gentle influences which moved him in his earlier years."

The man who would treat a sister with harshness, rudeness, or disrespect, is unworthy of the name of gentleman, for he thus proves that the courtesies he extends to other ladies, are not the promptings of the heart, but the mere external signs of etiquette; the husk without the sweet fruit within.

39. When walking with a friend in the street, never leave him to speak to another friend without apologizing for so doing.

40. If walking with a lady, never leave her alone in the street, under any circumstances. It is a gross violation of etiquette to do so.

41. The most truly gentlemanly man is he who is the most unselfish, so I would say in the words of the Rev. J. A. James:

"Live for some purpose in the world. Act your part well. Fill up the measure of duty to others. Conduct yourselves so that you shall be missed with sorrow when you are gone. Multitudes of our species are living in such a selfish manner that they are not likely to be remembered after their disappearance. They leave behind them scarcely any traces of their existence, but are forgotten almost as though they had never been. They are while they live, like one pebble lying unobserved amongst a million on the shore; and when they die, they are like that same pebble thrown into the sea, which just ruffles the surface, sinks, and is forgotten, without being missed from the beach. They are neither regretted by the rich, wanted by the poor, nor celebrated by the learned

Who has been the better for their life? Who has been the worse for their death? Whose tears have they dried up? whose wants supplied? whose miseries have they healed? Who would unbar the gate of life, to re-admit them to existence? or what face would greet them back again to our world with a smile? Wretched, unproductive mode of existence! Selfishness is its own curse; it is a starving vice. The man who does no good, gets none. He is like the heath in the desert, neither yielding fruit, nor seeing when good cometh—a stunted, dwarfish, miserable shrub."

42. Separate the syllables of the word gentleman, and you will see that the first requisite must be gentleness— *gentle*-man. Mackenzie says, "Few persons are sufficiently aware of the power of gentleness. It is slow in working, but it is infallible in its results. It makes no noise; it neither invites attention, nor provokes resistance; but it is God's great law, in the moral as in the natural world, for accomplishing great results. The progressive dawn of day, the flow of the tide, the lapse of time, the changes of the seasons—these are carried on by slow and imperceptible degrees, yet their progress and issue none can mistake or resist. Equally certain and surprising are the triumphs of gentleness. It assumes nothing, yet it can disarm the stoutest opposition; it yields, but yielding is the element of its strength; it endures, but in the warfare victory is not gained by doing, but by suffering."

43. Perfect composure of manner requires perfect peace of mind, so you should, as far as lies in human power, avoid the evils which make an unquiet mind, and

first of all, avoid that cheating, swindling process called "running in debt." Owe no man anything; avoid it as you would avoid war, pestilence, and famine. Hate it with a perfect hatred. As you value comfort, quiet, and independence, keep out of debt. As you value a healthy appetite, placid temper, pleasant dreams, and happy wakings, keep out of debt. It is the hardest of all task-masters; the most cruel of all oppressors. It is a mill-stone about the neck. It is an incubus on the heart. It furrows the forehead with premature wrinkles. It drags the nobleness and kindness out of the port and bearing of a man; it takes the soul out of his laugh, and all stateliness and freedom from his walk. Come not, then, under its crushing dominion.

44. Speak gently ; a kind refusal will often wound less than a rough, ungracious assent.

45. "In private, watch your thoughts , in your family, watch your temper; in society, watch your tongue."

46. The true secret of pleasing all the world, is to have an humble opinion of yourself. True goodness is invariably accompanied by gentleness, courtesy, and humility. Those people who are always "sticking on their dignity," are continually losing friends, making enemies, and fostering a spirit of unhappiness in themselves.

47. Are you a merchant? Remember that the counting-house is no less a school of manners and temper than a school of morals. Vulgarity, imperiousness, peevish-ness, caprice on the part of the heads, will produce their corresponding effects upon the household. Some mer-chants are petty tyrants. Some are too surly to be fit for any charge, unless it be that of taming a shrew

The coarseness of others, in manner and language, must either disgust or contaminate all their subordinates. In one establishment you will encounter an unmanly levity, which precludes all discipline. In another, a mock dig-nity, which supplies the juveniles with a standing theme of ridicule. In a third, a capriciousness of mood and temper, which reminds one of the prophetic hints of the weather in the old almanacks — "windy"—"cool'—"very pleasant"—"blustering"—"look out for storms" —and the like. And, in a fourth, a selfish acerbity, which exacts the most unreasonable services, and never cheers a clerk with a word of encouragement.—These are sad infirmities. Men ought not to have clerks until they know how to treat them. Their own comfort, too, would be greatly enhanced by a different deportment.

48. If you are about to enter, or leave, a store or any door, and unexpectedly meet a lady going the other way, stand aside and raise your hat whilst she passes. If she is going the same way, and the door is closed, pass be-fore her, saying, "allow me," or, "permit me,"—open the door, and hold it open whilst she passes.

49. In entering a room where you will meet ladies, take your hat, cane, and gloves in your left hand, that your right may be free to offer to them.

50. Never offer to shake hands with a lady; she will, if she wishes you to do so, offer her hand to you, and it is an impertinence for you to do so first.

51 If you are seated in the most comfortable chair in a public room, and a lady, an invalid, or an old man enters, rise, and offer your seat, even if they are strangers to you. Many men will attend to these civili-

ties when with friends or acquaintances, and neglect them amongst strangers, but the true gentleman will not wait for an introduction before performing an act of courtesy.

52. As both flattery and slander are in the highest degree blameable and ungentlemanly, I would quote the rule of Bishop Beveridge, which effectually prevents both. He says, "Never speak of a man's virtue before his face, nor of his faults behind his back."

53. Never enter a room, in which there are ladies, after smoking, until you have purified both your mouth, teeth, hair, and clothes. If you wish to smoke just before entering a saloon, wear an old coat and carefully brush your hair and teeth before resuming your own.

54. Never endeavor to attract the attention of a friend by nudging him, touching his foot or hand secretly, or making him a gesture. If you cannot speak to him frankly, you had best let him alone; for these signals are generally made with the intention of ridiculing a third person, and that is the height of rudeness.

55. Button-holding is a common but most blameable breach of good manners. If a man requires to be forcibly detained to listen to you, you are as rude in thus detaining him, as if you had put a pistol to his head and threatened to blow his brains out if he stirred.

56. It is a great piece of rudeness to make a remark in general company, which is intelligible to one person only. To call out, "George, I met D. L. yesterday, and he says he will attend to that matter," is as bad as if you went to George and whispered in his ear.

57. In your intercourse with servants, nothing will

mark you as a well-bred man, so much as a gentle, courteous manner. A request will make your wishes attended to as quickly as a command, and thanks for a service, oil the springs of the servant's labor immensely. Rough, harsh commands may make your orders obeyed well and promptly, but they will be executed unwillingly, in fear, and, probably, dislike, while courtesy and kindness will win a willing spirit as well as prompt service.

58. Avoid eccentric conduct. It does not, as many suppose, mark a man of genius. Most men of true genius are gentlemanly and reserved in their intercourse with other men, and there are many fools whose folly is called eccentricity.

59. Avoid familiarity. Neither treat others with too great cordiality nor suffer them to take liberties with you. To check the familiarity of others, you need not become stiff, sullen, nor cold, but you will find that excessive politeness on your own part, sometimes with a little formality, will soon abash the intruder.

60. Lazy, lounging attitudes in the presence of ladies are very rude.

61. It is only the most arrant coxcomb who will boast of the favor shown him by a lady, speak of her by her first name, or allow others to jest with him upon his friendship or admiration for her. If he really admires her, and has reason to hope for a future engagement with her, her name should be as sacred to him as if she were already his wife; if, on the contrary, he is not on intimate terms with her, then he adds a lie to his excessively bad breeding, when using her name familiarly.

62. "He that can please nobody is not so much to be pitied as he that nobody can please."

63. Speak without obscurity or affectation. The first is a mark of pedantry, the second a sign of folly. A wise man will speak always clearly and intelligibly.

64 To betray a confidence is to make yourself despicable. Many things are said among friends which are not said under a seal of secrecy, but are understood to be confidential, and a truly honorable man will never violate this tacit confidence. It is really as sacred as if the most solemn promises of silence bound your tongue; more so, indeed, to the true gentleman, as his sense of honor, not his word, binds him.

65. Chesterfield says, "As learning, honor, and virtue are absolutely necessary to gain you the esteem and admiration of mankind, politeness and good breeding are equally necessary to make you welcome and agreeable in conversation and common life. Great talents, such as honor, virtue, learning, and parts are above the generality of the world, who neither possess them themselves nor judge of them rightly in others; but all people are judges of the lesser talents, such as civility, affability, and an obliging, agreeable address and manner; because they feel the good effects of them, as making society easy and pleasing."

66. "Good sense must, in many cases, determine good breeding; because the same thing that would be civil at one time and to one person, may be quite otherwise at another time and to another person."

67 Nothing can be more ill-bred than to meet a polite

remark addressed to you, either with inattention or a rude answer.

68. Spirit is now a very fashionable word, but it is terribly misapplied. In the present day to act with spirit and speak with spirit means to act rashly and speak in discretely. A gentleman shows his spirit by firm, but gentle words and resolute actions. He is spirited but neither rash nor timid.

69. " Use kind words. They do not cost much. It does not take long to utter them. They never blister the tongue or lips in their passage into the world, or occasion any other kind of bodily suffering. And we have never heard of any mental trouble arising from this quarter.

"Though they do not COST much, yet they ACCOMPLISH much. They help one's own good nature and good will. One cannot be in a habit of this kind, without thereby picking away something of the granite roughness of his own nature. Soft words will soften his own soul. Philosophers tell us that the angry words a man uses, in his passion, are fuel to the flame of his wrath, and make it blaze the more fiercely. Why, then, should not words of the opposite character produce opposite results, and that most blessed of all passions of the soul, kindness, be augmented by kind words? People that are forever speaking kindly, are forever disinclining themselves to ill temper.

" Kind words make other people good natured. Cold words freeze people, and hot words scorch them, and sarcastic words irritate them, and bitter words make them bitter, and wrathful words make them wrathful.

And kin I words also produce their own image on men's souls. And a beautiful image it is. They soothe, and quiet, and comfort the hearer. They shame him out of his sour, morose, unkind feelings, and he has to become kind himself.

"There is such a rush of all other kind of words, in our days, that it seems desirable to give kind words a chance among them. There are vain words, and idle words, and hasty words, and spiteful words, and silly words, and empty words. Now, kind words are better than the whole of them, and it is a pity that, among the improvements of the present age, birds of this feather might not have more chance than they have had to spread their wings.

"Kind words are in danger of being driven from the field, like frightened pigeons, in these days of boisterous words, and warlike words, and passionate words. They have not the brass to stand up, like so many grenadiers, and fight their own way among the throng. Besides, they have been out of use so long, that they hardly know whether they have any right to make their appearance any more in our bustling world; not knowing but that, perhaps, the world was done with them, and would not like their company any more.

"Let us welcome them back. We have not done with them. We have not yet begun to use them in such abundance as they ought to be used. We cannot spare them."

70. The first step towards pleasing every one is to endeavor to offend no one. To give pain by a light or jesting remark is as much a breach of etiquette, as to

give pain by a wound made with a steel weapon, is a breach of humanity.

71. "A gentleman will never use his tongue to rail and brawl against any one; to speak evil of others in their absence; to exaggerate any of his statements; to speak harshly to children or to the poor; to swear, lie, or use improper language; to hazard random and improbable statements; to speak rashly or violently upon any subject; to deceive people by circulating false reports, or to offer up *lip*-service in religion. But he will use it to convey to mankind useful information; to instruct his family and others who need it; to warn and reprove the wicked; to comfort and console the afflicted; to cheer the timid and fearful; to defend the innocent and oppressed; to plead for the widow and orphan; to congratulate the success of the virtuous, and to confess, tearfully and prayerfully, his faults."

72. Chesterfield says, "Civility is particularly due to all women; and, remember, that no provocation whatsoever can justify any man in not being civil to every woman; and the greatest man would justly be reckoned a brute if he were not civil to the meanest woman. It is due to their sex, and is the only protection they have against the superior strength of ours; nay, even a little is allowable with women: and a man may, without weakness, tell a women she is either handsomer or wiser than she is." (Chesterfield would not have said this in the present age of strong minded, sensible women.)

73. There is much tact and good breeding to be displayed in the correction of any little error that may occur in conversation. To say, shortly,—"You are

wrong! I know better!" is rude, and your friends will much more readily admit an error if you say courteously and gently, "Pardon me, but I must take the liberty of correcting you," or, "You will allow me, I am sure, to tell you that your informant made an error." If such an error is of no real importance, it is better to let it pass unnoticed.

74. Intimate friends and relations should be careful when they go out into the world together, or admit others to their own circle, that they do not make a bad use of the knowledge which they have gained of each other by their intimacy. Nothing is more common than this; and, did it not mostly proceed from mere carelessness, it would be superlatively ungenerous. You seldom need wait for the written life of a man to hear about his weaknesses, or what are supposed to be such, if you know his intimate friends, or meet him in company with them.

75. In making your first visit anywhere, you will be less apt to offend by being too ceremonious, than by being too familiar.

76. With your friends remember the old proverb, that, "Familiarity breeds contempt."

77. If you meet, in society, with any one, be it a gentleman or a lady, whose timidity or bashfulness, shows them unaccustomed to meeting others, endeavor, by your own gentleness and courtesy, to place them more at ease, and introduce to them those who will aid you in this endeavor.

78. If, when walking with a gentleman friend, you meet a lady to whom your friend bows, you, too, must
14

touch or raise your hat, though you are not acquainted with the lady.

79. "Although it is now very much the custom, in many wealthy families, for the butler to remove the dishes from the table and carve them on the sideboard, thus saving trouble to the master or mistress of the house, and time to the guests, the practice is not so general even amongst what are called the higher classes of society that general instructions for carving will be uninteresting to them, to say nothing of the more numerous class, who, although enabled to place good dishes before their friends, are not wealthy enough to keep a butler if they were so inclined. Good carving is, to a certain extent, indicative of good society, for it proves to company that the host does not give a dinner party for the first time, but is accustomed to receive friends, and frequently to dispense the cheer of a hospitable board. The master or mistress of a house, who does not know how to carve, is not unfrequently looked upon as an ignorant *parvenu*, as a person who cannot take a hand at whist, in good society, is regarded as one who has passed his time in the parlor of a public house, playing at cribbage or all fours. Independently, however, of the importance of knowing how to carve well, for the purpose of regaling one's friends and acquaintances, the science, and it is a science, is a valuable acquirement for any man, as it enables him, at a public or private dinner, to render valuable aid. There are many diners-out who are welcome merely because they know how to carve. Some men amuse by their conversation; others are favorites because they can sing a good song; but the man

who makes himself useful and agreeable to all, is he who carves with elegance and speed. We recommend the novice in this art, to keep a watchful eye upon every superior carver whom he may meet at dinner. In this way he will soon become well versed in the art and mystery of cutting up."

80. Years may pass over our heads without affording an opportunity for acts of high beneficence or extensive utility; whereas, not a day passes, but in common transactions of life, and, especially in the intercourse of society, courtesy finds place for promoting the happiness of others, and for strengthening in ourselves the habits of unselfish politeness. There are situations, not a few, in human life, when an encouraging reception, a condescending behaviour, and a look of sympathy, bring greater relief to the heart than the most bountiful gift.

81. Cecil says, "You may easily make a sensation— but a sensation is a vulgar triumph. To keep up the sensation of an excitement, you must be always standing on your head (morally speaking), and the attitude, like everything overstrained, would become fatiguing to yourself and tedious to others. Whereas, to obtain permanent favor, as an agreeable, well-bred man, requires simply an exercise of the understanding."

82. There is no vice more truly ungentlemanly than that of using profane language. Lamont says :

"Whatever fortune may be made by perjury, I believe there never was a man who made a fortune by common swearing. It often appears that men pay for swearing, but it seldom happens that they are paid for it. It is not easy to perceive what honor or credit is connected with it. Does any man receive promotion because he is a notable blusterer? Or is any man advanced to dignity because he is expert at profane swearing? Never. Low must be the character which such impertinence will exalt: high must be the character which such impertinence will not degrade. Inexcusable, therefore, must be the practice which has neither reason nor passion to support it. The drunkard has his cups; the satirist, his revenge; the ambitious man, his preferments; the miser, his gold; but the common swearer has nothing; he is a fool at large, sells his soul for nought, and drudges in the service of the devil gratis. Swearing is void of all plea; it is not the native offspring of the soul, nor interwoven with the texture of the body, nor, anyhow, allied to our frame. For, as Tillotson expresses it, 'Though some men pour out oaths as if they were natural, yet no man was ever born of a swearing constitution.' But it is a custom, a low and a paltry custom, picked up by low and paltry spirits who have no sense of honor, no regard to decency, but are forced to substitute some rhapsody of nonsense to supply the vacancy of good sense Hence, the silliness of the practice can only be equalled by the silliness of those who adopt it."

83. Dr. Johnson says that to converse well "there must, in the first place, be knowledge—there must be materials; in the second place, there must be a command of words; in the third place, there must be imagination to place things in such views as they are not commonly seen in; and, in the fourth place, there must be a presence of mind, and a resolution that is not to be over

come by failure—-this last is an essential requisite ; for want of it, many people do not excel in conversation."

84. "Do not constantly endeavor to draw the attention of all upon yourself when in company. Leave room for your hearers to imagine something within you beyond what you speak ; and, remember, the more you are praised the more you will be envied."

85. Be very careful to treat with attention and respect those who have lately met with misfortunes, or have suffered from loss of fortune. Such persons are apt to think themselves slighted, when no such thing is intended. Their minds, being already sore, feel the least rub very severely, and who would thus cruelly add affliction to the afflicted ? Not the *gentleman* certainly.

86. There is hardly any bodily blemish which a winning behavior will not conceal or make tolerable; and there is no external grace which ill-nature or affectation will not deform.

87. Good humor is the only shield to keep off the darts of the satirist ; but if you are the first to laugh at a jest made upon yourself, others will laugh *with* you instead of *at* you.

88. Whenever you see a person insult his inferiors, you may feel assured that he is the man who will be servile and cringing to his superiors; and he who acts the bully to the weak, will play the coward when with the strong.

89. Maintain, in every word, a strict regard for perfect truth. Do not think of one falsity as harmless, another as slight, a third as unintended. Cast them all aside. They may be light and accidental, but they are

an ugly soot from the smoke of the pit for all that, and
it is better to have your heart swept clean of them,
without stopping to consider whether they are large and
black.

90. The advantage and necessity of cheerfulness and
intelligent intercourse with the world is strongly to be
recommended. A man who keeps aloof from society and
lives only for himself, does not fulfil the wise intentions
of Providence, who designed that we should be a mutual
help and comfort to each other in life.

91. Chesterfield says, "Merit and good breeding will
make their way everywhere. Knowledge will introduce
man, and good breeding will endear him to the best
companies; for, politeness and good breeding are absolutely necessary to adorn any, or all, other good qualities
or talents. Without them, no knowledge, no perfection
whatever, is seen in its best light. The scholar, without
good breeding, is a pedant; the philosopher, a cynic;
the soldier, a brute; and every man disagreeable."

92. It is very seldom that a man may permit himself to tell stories in society; they are, generally,
tedious, and, to many present, will probably have all the
weariness of a "twice-told tale." A short, brilliant anecdote, which is especially applicable to the conversation
going on, is all that a well-bred man will ever permit
himself to inflict.

93. It is better to take the tone of the society into
which you are thrown, than to endeavor to lead others
after you. The way to become truly popular is to be
grave with the grave, jest with the gay, and converse
sensibly with those who seek to display their sense.

94. Watch each of your actions, when in society, that all the habits which you contract there may be useful and good ones.   Like flakes of snow that fall un-perceived upon the earth, the seemingly unimportant events of life succeed one another.   As the snow gathers together, so are our habits formed.   No single flake that is added to the pile produces a sensible change—no single action creates, however it may exhibit, a man's character ; but, as the tempest hurls the avalanche down the moun-tain, and overwhelms the inhabitant and his habitation, so passion, acting upon the elements of mischief, which pernicious habits have brought together by imperceptible accumulation, may overthrow the edifice of truth and virtue.

95. There is no greater fault in good breeding than too great diffidence.   Shyness cramps every motion, clogs every word.   The only way to overcome the fault is to mix constantly in society, and the habitual inter-course with others will give you the graceful ease of manner which shyness utterly destroys.

96. If you are obliged to leave a large company at an early hour, take French leave.   Slip away unper-ceived, if you can, but, at any rate, without any formal leave-taking.

97. Avoid quarrels.   If you are convinced, even, that you have the right side in an argument, yield your opinion gracefully, if this is the only way to avoid a quarrel, saying, " We cannot agree, I see, but this ina-bility must not deprive me of a friend, so we will discuss the subject no further."   Few men will be able to resist your courtesy and good nature, but many would try to

combat an obstinate adherence to your own side of the question.

98. Avoid the filthy habit of which foreigners in this country so justly complain—I mean spitting.

99. If any one bows to you in the street, return the bow. It may be an acquaintance whose face you do not immediately recognize, and if it is a stranger who mistakes you for another, your courteous bow will relieve him from the embarrassment arising from his mistake.

100. The following hints on conversation conclude the chapter :—

" Conversation may be carried on successfully by persons who have no idea that it is or may be an art, as clever things are sometimes done without study. But there can be no certainty of good conversation in ordinary circumstances, and amongst ordinary minds, unless certain rules be observed, and certain errors be avoided.

"The first and greatest rule unquestionably is, that all must be favorably disposed towards each other, and willing to be pleased. There must be no sullen or uneasy-looking person—no one who evidently thinks he has fallen into unsuitable company, and whose sole aim it is to take care lest his dignity be injured—no one whose feelings are of so morose or ascetic a kind that he cannot join without observable pain and hesitation in the playfulness of the scene—no matter-of-fact person, who takes all things literally, and means all things literally, and thinks it as great a crime to say something in jest as to do it in earnest. One of any of these classes of persons is sufficient to mar the enjoyments of a hundred. The matter-of-factish may do very well with the matter-of-factish, the morose with the morose, the stilted with the stilted; and they should accordingly keep amongst themselves respectively. But, for what is generally recognized as agreeable conversation, minds exempted from these peculiarities are required.

"The ordinary rules of politeness are, of course, necessary—no rudeness, no offence to each other's self-esteem; on the contrary, much mutual deference is required, in order to keep all the elements of a company sweet. Sometimes, however, there is a very turbid kind of conversation, where there is no want of common good breeding. This, most frequently, arises from there being too great a disposition to speak, and too small a disposition to listen. Too many are eager to get their ideas expressed, or to attract attention; and the consequence is, that nothing is heard but broken snatches and fragments of discourse, in which there is neither profit nor entertainment. No man listens to what another has to say, and then makes a relative or additionally illustrative remark. One may be heard for a minute, or half a minute, but it is with manifest impatience; and the moment he is done, or stops to draw breath, the other plunges in with what *he* had to say, being something quite of another strain, and referring to another subject. He in his turn is interrupted by a third, with the enunciation of some favorite ideas of his, equally irrelative; and thus conversation becomes no conversation, but a contention for permission to speak a few hurried words, which nobody cares to hear, or takes the trouble to answer. Meanwhile, the modest and weak sit silent and

ungratified. The want of regulation is here very mani
fest. It would be better to have a president who should
allow everybody a minute in succession to speak without
interruption, than thus to have freedom, and so mon
strously to abuse it. The only remedy, as far as meetings by invitation are concerned, is to take care that no
more eager talkers are introduced than are absolutely
necessary to prevent conversation from flagging. One
to every six or eight persons is the utmost that can be
safely allowed.

"The danger of introducing politics, or any other no-
toriously controversial subject, in mixed companies, is so
generally acknowledged, that conversation is in little
danger—at least in polite circles—from that source.
But wranglements, nevertheless, are apt to arise. Very
frequently the company falls together by the ears in
consequence of the starting of some topic in which facts
are concerned—with which facts no one chances to be
acquainted.

" Conversation is often much spoilt through slight in
attentions or misapprehensions on the part of a particular member of the company. In the midst of some interesting narrative or discussion, he suddenly puts all to
a stop, in order that some little perplexity may be ex-
plained, which he could never have fallen into, if he had
been paying a fair degree of attention to what was going
on. Or he has some precious prejudice jarred upon by
something said, or supposed to be said, and all is at a
stand, till he has been, through the united exertions of a
vexed company, re-assured and put at his ease. Often
the most frivolous interruption from such causes will dis

concert the whole strain of the conversation, and spoil
the enjoyment of a score of people.

"The eager speakers, already alluded to, are a different class from those who may be called the determinedly
loquacious. A thoroughly loquacious man has no idea
of anything but a constant outpouring of talk from his
own mouth. If he stops for a moment, he thinks he
is not doing his duty to the company; and, anxious that
there should be no cause of complaint against him on
that score, he rather repeats a sentence, or gives the
same idea in different words, or hums and haws a little,
than allow the least pause to take place. The notion
that any other body can be desirous of saying a word,
never enters his head. He would as soon suppose that
a beggar was anxious to bestow alms upon him, as that
any one could wish to speak, as long as he himself was
willing to save them the trouble. Any attempt to interrupt him is quite hopeless. The only effect of the sound
of another voice is to raise the sound of his own, so as
to drown it. Even to give a slight twist or turn to the
flow of his ideas, is scarce possible. When a decided
attempt is made to get in a few words, he only says, with
an air of offended feeling, set off with a tart courtesy,
'Allow me sir,' or, 'When you are done, sir;' as if he
were a man whom nobody would allow, on any occasion,
to say all he had to say. If, however, he has been permitted to talk on and on incessantly a whole evening,
to the complete closing of the mouths of the rest, he
goes away with all the benevolent glow of feeling which
arises from a gratified faculty, remarking to the gentleman who takes his arm, 'What a great deal of pleasant

conversation we have had!' and chatters forth all the way home such sentences as, 'Excellent fellow, our host, 'charming wife,' 'delightful family altogether, 'always make everybody so happy.'

"Another class of spoilers of conversation are the loud talkers or blusterers. They are not numerous, but one is enough to destroy the comfort of thirty people for a whole evening. The least opposition to any of his ideas makes the blusterer rise in his might, and bellow, and roar, and bellow again, till the whole company is in something like the condition of Æneas's fleet after Eolus has done his worst. The society enjoyed by this kind of man is a series of *first invitations*.

"While blusterers and determinedly loquacious persons are best left to themselves, and while endless worryings on unknown things are to be avoided, it is necessary both that one or two good conversationists should be at every party, and that the strain of the conversation should not be allowed to become too tame. In all invited parties, eight of every ten persons are disposed to hold their peace, or to confine themselves to monosyllabic answers to commonplace inquiries. It is necessary, therefore, that there should be *some* who can speak, and that fluently, if not entertainingly—only not too many. But all engrossing of conversation, and all turbulence, and over-eagerness, and egotism, are to be condemned. A very soft and quiet manner has, at last, been settled upon, in the more elevated circles, as the best for conversation. Perhaps they carry it to a pitch of affectation; but, yet, when we observe the injurious consequences of the opposite style in less polite companies, it is not easy to avoid the conclusion that the great folks are, upon the whole, right. In the courtly scene, no one has his ears offended with loud and discordant tones, no one is condemned to absolute silence. All display in conversation will not depend on the accidental and external quality of strength of voice, as it must do where a loud and contentious style of talking is allowed; the soft-toned and the weak-lunged will have as good a chance as their more robust neighbors; and it will be possible for all both to speak and to hear. There may be another advantage in its being likely to produce less mental excitement than the more turbulent kind of society. But *regulation* is, we are persuaded, the thing most of all wanted in the conversational meetings of the middle classes. People interrupt each other too much —are too apt to run away into their own favorite themes, without caring for the topic of their neighbors—too frequently wrangle about trifles. The regularity of a debating society would be intolerable; but some certain degree of method might certainly be introduced with great advantage. There should, at least, be a vigorous enforcement of the rule against more than one speaking at a time, even though none of those waiting for their turn should listen to a word he says. Without this there may be much talk, and even some merriment, but no conversation."

CHAPTER XII.

PARTIES.

Now, there are many different kinds of parties. There are the evening party, the matinée, the reading, dancing, and singing parties, the picnic, the boating, and the riding parties ; and the duties for each one are distinct, yet, in many points, similar.   Our present subject is :—

THE EVENING PARTY.

These are of two kinds, large and small. For the first, you will receive a formal card, containing the compliments of your hostess for a certain evening, and this calls for full dress, a dress coat, and white or very light gloves.   To the small party you will probably be invited verbally, or by a more familiar style of note than the compliment card. Here you may wear gloves if you will, but you need not do so unless perfectly agreeable to yourself.

If you are to act as escort to a lady, you must call at the hour she chooses to name, and the most elegant way is to take a carriage for her.   If you wish to present a bouquet, you may do so with perfect propriety, even if you have but a slight acquaintance with her.

When you reach the house of your hostess for the evening, escort your companion to the dressing-room, and leave her at the door. After you have deposited your own hat and great-coat in the gentlemen's dressing room, return to the ladies' door and wait for your companion. Offer her your right arm, and lead her to the drawing-room, and, at once, to the hostess, then take her to a seat, and remain with her until she has other companions, before you seek any of your own friends in the room.

There is much more real enjoyment and sociability in a *well-arranged* party, than in a ball, though many of the points of etiquette to be observed in the latter are equally applicable to the former. There is more time allowed for conversation, and, as there are not so many people collected, there is also more opportunity for forming acquaintances. At a *soirée, par excellence,* music, dancing, and conversation are all admissible, and if the hostess has tact and discretion this variety is very pleasing. As there are many times when there is no pianist or music engaged for dancing, you will do well, if you are a performer on the piano-forte, to learn some quadrilles, and round dances, that you may volunteer your services as *orchestra.* Do not, in this case, wait to be solicited to play, but offer your services to the hostess, or, if there is a lady at the piano, ask permission to relieve her. To turn the leaves for another, and sometimes call figures, are also good natured and well-bred actions.

There is one piece of rudeness very common at parties, against which I would caution you. Young people very often form a group, and indulge in the most boisterous merriment and loud laughter, for jests known only to themselves. Do not join such a group. A well-bred man, while he is cheerful and gay, will avoid any appearance of romping in society.

If dancing is to be the amusement for the evening, your first dance should be with the lady whom you accompanied, then, invite your hostess, and, if there are several ladies in the family you must invite each of them once, in the course of the evening. If you go alone, invite the ladies of the house before dancing with any of your other lady friends.

Never attempt any dance with which you are not perfectly familiar. Nothing is more awkward and annoying than to have one dancer, by his ignorance of the figures, confuse all the others in the set, and certainly no man wants to show off his ignorance of the steps of a round dance before a room full of company.

Do not devote yourself too much to one lady. A party is meant to promote sociability, and a man who persists in a tête-à-tête for the evening, destroys this intention. Besides you prevent others from enjoying the pleasure of intercourse with the lady you thus monopolize.

Avoid any affectation of great intimacy with any lady present; and even if you really enjoy such intimacy, or she is a relative, do not appear to have confidential conversation, or, in any other way, affect airs of secrecy or great familiarity.

Dance easily and gracefully, keeping perfect time, but not taking too great pains with your steps. If you whole attention is given to your feet or carriage, you will probably be mistaken for a dancing master.

When you conduct your partner to a seat after a dance, you may sit or stand beside her to converse, un-less you see that another gentleman is waiting to invite her to dance.

Do not take the vacant seat next a lady unless you are acquainted with her.

After dancing, do not offer your hand, but your arm, to conduct your partner to her seat.

If music is called for and you are able to play or sing, do so when first invited, or, if you refuse then, do not afterwards comply. If you refuse, and then alter your mind you will either be considered a vain coxcomb, who likes to be urged; or some will conclude that you refused at first from mere caprice, for, if you had a good reason for declining, why change your mind?

Never offer to turn the leaves of music for any one playing, unless you can read the notes, for you run the risk of confusing them, by turning too soon or too late.

If you sing a good second, never sing with a lady un-less she herself invites you. Her friends may wish to hear you sing together, when she herself may not wish to sing with one to whose voice and time she is unaccus-tomed.

Do not start a conversation whilst any one is either playing or singing, and if another person commences one, speak in a tone that will not prevent others from listen-ing to the music.

If you play yourself, do not wait for silence in the room before you begin. If you play well, those really

15

fond of music will cease to converse, and listen to you; and those who do not care for it, will not stop talking if you wait upon the piano stool until day dawn.

Relatives should avoid each other at a party, as they can enjoy one another's society at home, and it is the constantly changing intercourse, and complete sociability that make a party pleasant.

Private concerts and amateur theatricals are very often the occasions for evening parties, and make a very pleasant variety on the usual dancing and small talk. An English writer, speaking of them, says:

"Private concerts and amateur theatricals ought to be very good to be successful. Professionals alone should be engaged for the former, none but real amateurs for the latter. Both ought to be, but rarely are, followed by a supper, since they are generally very fatiguing, if not positively trying. In any case, refreshments and ices should be handed between the songs and the acts. Private concerts are often given in the 'morning,' that is, from two to six P. M.; in the evening their hours are from eight to eleven. The rooms should be arranged in the same manner as for a reception, the guests should be seated, and as music is the avowed object, a general silence preserved while it lasts. Between the songs the conversation ebbs back again, and the party takes the general form of a reception. For private theatricals, however, where there is no special theatre, and where the curtain is hung, as is most common, between the folding-doors, the audience-room must be filled with chairs and benches in rows, and, if possible, the back rows raised higher than the others. These are often removed when the performance is over, and the guests then converse, or, sometimes, even dance. During the acting it is rude to talk, except in a very low tone, and, be it good or bad, you would never think of hissing."

If you are alone, and obliged to retire early from an evening party, do not take leave of your hostess, but slip away unperceived.

If you have escorted a lady, her time must be yours, and she will tell you when she is ready to go. See whether the carriage has arrived before she goes to the dressing-room, and return to the parlor to tell her. If the weather was pleasant when you left home, and you walked, ascertain whether it is still pleasant; if not, procure a carriage for your companion. When it is at the door, join her in the drawing-room, and offer your arm to lead her to the hostess for leave-taking, making your own parting bow at the same time, then take your companion to the door of the ladies' dressing-room, get your own hat and wait in the entry until she comes out.

When you reach your companion's house, do not accept her invitation to enter, but ask permission to call in the morning, or the following evening, and make that call.

CHAPTER XIII.

COURTESY AT HOME.

THERE are many men in this world, who would be horror struck if accused of the least breach of etiquette towards their friends and acquaintances abroad, and yet, who will at home utterly disregard the simplest rules of politeness, if such rules interfere in the least with their own selfish gratification. They disregard the pure and holy ties which should make courtesy at home a pleasure as well as a duty. They forget that home has a sweet poetry of its own, created out of the simplest materials, yet, haunting, more or less, the secret recesses of every human heart; it is divided into a thousand separate poems, which should be full of individual interest, little quiet touches of feeling and golden recollections, which, .n the heart of a truly noble man, are interwoven with his very being. Common things are, to him, hallowed and made beautiful by the spell of memory and associa- tion, owing all their glory to the halo of his own pure, fond affection. The eye of a stranger rests coldly on such revelations; their simple pathos is hard to be un- derstood; and they smile oftentimes at the quaintness of those passages which make others weep. With the beautiful instinct of true affection, home love retains only the good. There were clouds then, even as now, darkening the horizon of daily life, and breaking tears or wild storms above our heads ; but he remembers nothing save the sunshine, and fancies somehow that it has never shone so bright since! How little it took to make him happy in those days, aye, and sad also, but it was a pleasant sadness, for he wept only over a flower or a book. But let us turn to our first poem; and in using this term we allude, of course, to the poetry of idea, rather than that of the measure; beauty of which is so often lost to us from a vague feeling that it cannot exist without rhythm. But pause and listen, first of all, gentle reader, to the living testimony of a poet heart, brimful, and gushing over with home love :—"There are not, in the unseen world, voices more gentle and more true, that may be more implicitly relied on, or that are so certain to give none but the tenderest counsel, as the voices in which the spirits of the fireside and the hearth address themselves to human kind!"

The man who shows his contempt for these holy ties and associations by pulling off his mask of courtesy as soon as his foot passes his own threshold, is not really a gentleman, but a selfish tyrant, whose true qualities are not courtesy and politeness, but a hypocritical affectation of them, assumed to obtain a footing in society. Avoid such men. Even though you are one of the favored ones abroad who receive their gentle courtesy, you may rest assured that the heartless egotism which makes them rude and selfish at home, will make their friendship but a name, if circumstances ever put it to the test. Above all, avoid their example.

In what does the home circle consist? First, there are the parents who have watched over your infancy and childhood, and whom you are commanded by the Highest Power to "honor." Then the brothers and sisters, the wife who has left her own home and all its tender ties for your sake, and the children who look to you for example, guidance, and instruction.

Who else on the broad earth can lay the same claim to your gentleness and courtesy that they can? If you are rude at home, then is your politeness abroad a mere cloak to conceal a bad, selfish heart.

The parents who have anxiously watched over your education, have the first right to the fruits of it, and all the *gentleman* should be exerted to repay them for the care they have taken of you since your birth. All the rules of politeness, of generosity, of good nature, patience, and respectful affection should be exerted for your parents. You owe to them a pure, filial love, void of personal interest, which should prompt you to study all their tastes, their likes, and aversions, in order to indulge the one and avoid the other; you owe to them polite attention, deference to all their wishes, and compliance with their requests. Every joy will be doubled to them, if you show a frank pleasure in its course, and no comfort can soothe the grief of a parent so much as the sympathizing love of a dutiful son. If they are old, dependent upon you for support, then can you still better prove to them that the tender care they lavished upon you, when you depended upon their love for everything, was not lost, but was good seed sown upon fruitful ground. Nay, if with the infirmities of age come the crosses of bad temper, or exacting selfishness, your duty still lies as plainly before you. It is but the promptings of natural affection that will lead you to love and cherish an indulgent parent; but it is a pure, high virtue which makes a son love and cherish with an equal affection a selfish, negligent mother, or a tyrannical, harsh father. No failure in their duty can excuse you if you fail in yours; and, even if they are wicked, you are not to be their judge, but, while you detest and avoid their sin, you must still love the sinner. Nothing but the grossest and most revolting brutality could make a man reproach his parents with the feebleness of age or illness, or the incapacity to exert their talents for support.

An eminent writer, in speaking of a man's duties, says: "Do all in your power to render your parents comfortable and happy; if they are aged and infirm, be with them as often as you can, carry them tokens of your love, and show them that you feel a tender interest in their happiness. Be all to your parents, which you would wish your children to be to you." .

Next, in the home circle, come your brothers and sisters, and here you will find the little courtesies, which, as a gentleman, should be habitual to you, will ensure the love a man should most highly prize, the love of his brother and sister. Next to his filial love, this is the first tie of his life, and should be valued as it deserves.

If you are the eldest of the family, you may, by your example, influence your brothers to good or evil, and win or alienate the affections of your little sisters. There is scarcely a more enthusiastic affection in the world than that a sister feels for an elder brother. Even though he

may not repay the devotion as it deserves, she will generally cherish it, and invest him with the most heroic
qualities, while her tender little heart, though it may
quiver with the pain of a harsh word or rude action, will
still try to find an excuse for "brother's" want of affection. If you show an interest in the pursuits of the
little circle at whose head your age entitles you to stand,
you will soon find they all look up to you, seek your advice, crave your sympathy, and follow your example.
The eldest son holds a most responsible position. Should
death or infirmity deprive him of a father's counsel, he
should be prepared to stand forth as the head of the
family, and take his father's place towards his mother
and the younger children.

Every man should feel, that in the character and dignity of his sisters his own honor is involved. An insult
or affront offered to them, becomes one to him, and he
is the person they will look to for protection, and to
prevent its repetition. By his own manner to them he
can ensure to them the respect or contempt of other
men whom they meet when in his society. How can he
expect that his friends will treat his sisters with gentleness, respect, and courtesy, if they see him constantly
rude, disrespectful, and contemptuous towards them?
But, if his own manner is that of affectionate respect,
he need not fear for them rudeness from others, while
they are under his protection. An American writer
says: —

"Nothing in a family strikes the eye of a visitor with
more delight than to see brothers treat their sisters with
kindness, civility, attention, and love. On the contrary,

nothing is more offensive or speaks worse for the honor
of a family, than that coarse, rude, unkind manner which
brothers sometimes exhibit."

The same author says:—

"Beware how you speak of your sisters. Even gold
is tarnished by much handling. If you speak in their
praise—of their beauty, learning, manners, wit, or attentions—you will subject them to taunt and ridicule;
if you say anything against them, you will bring re-
proach upon yourself and them too. If you have occasion to speak of them, do it with modesty and few words.
Let others do all the praising and yourself enjoy it. If
you are separated from them, maintain with them a correspondence. This will do yourself good as well as them.
Do not neglect this duty, nor grow remiss in it. Give
your friendly advice and seek theirs in return. As they
mingle intimately with their sex, they can enlighten your
mind respecting many particulars relating to female
character, important for you to know; and, on the other
hand, you have the same opportunity to do them a
similar service. However long or widely separated from
them, keep up your fraternal affection and intercourse.
It is ominous of evil when a young man forgets his
sister.

"If you are living at home with them, you may do
them a thousand little services, which will cost you nothing but pleasure, and which will greatly add to theirs.
If they wish to go out in the evening—to a lecture, concert, a visit, or any other object,—always be happy, if
possible, to wait upon them. Consider their situation.

and think how you would wish them to treat you if the case were reversed."

A young man once said to an elderly lady, who expressed her regret at his having taken some trouble and denied himself a pleasure to gratify her :—

"Madam, I am far away from my mother and sisters now, but when I was at home, my greatest pleasure was to protect them and gratify all their wishes; let me now place you in their stead, and you will not have cause again to feel regret, for you can think 'he *must love* to deny himself for one who represents his mother.' "

The old lady afterwards spoke of him as a perfect gentleman, and was contradicted by a younger person who quoted some fault in etiquette committed by the young man in company. "Ah, that may be," said her friend; "but what I call a gentleman, is not the man who performs to the minutest point all the little ceremonies of society, but the one whose *heart* prompts him to be polite at home."

If you have left the first home circle, that comprising your parents, brothers, and sisters, to take up the duties of a husband and father, you must carry to your new home the same politeness I have advised you to exert in the home of your childhood.

Your wife claims your courtesy more now, even, than when you were courting her. She has given up, for your sake, all the freedom and pleasures of her maidenhood, and to you she looks for a love that will replace them all. Can you disappoint that trusting affection? Before your marriage you thought no stretch of courtesy too great, if the result was to afford her pleasure ; why, then, not strive to *keep* her love, by the same gentle courtesy you exerted to *win* it?

"A delicate attention to the minute wants and wishes of your wife, will tend, more than anything else, to the promotion of your domestic happiness. It requires no sacrifices, occupies but a small degree of attention, yet is the fertile source of bliss; since it convinces the object of your regard, that, with the duties of a husband, you have united the more punctilious behaviour of a lover. These trivial tokens of regard certainly make much way in the affections of a woman of sense and discernment, who looks not to the value of the gifts she receives, but perceives in their frequency a continued evidence of the existence and ardor of that love on which the superstructure of her happiness has been erected. The strongest attachment will decline, if you receive it with diminished warmth."

Mrs. Thrale gives the following advice, which is worth the consideration of every young man:

"After marriage," she says, "when your violence of passion subsides, and a more cool and tranquil affection takes its place, be not hasty to censure as indifferent, or to lament yourself as unhappy; you have lost that only which it is impossible to retain; and it were graceless amidst the pleasures of a prosperous summer, to regret the blossoms of a transient spring. Neither unwarily condemn your bride's insipidity, till you have recollected that no object, however sublime, no sound, however charming, can continue to transport us with delight, when they no longer strike us with novelty. The skill to renovate the powers of pleasing is said, indeed, to be possessed by some women in an eminent degree, but the artifices of maturity are seldom seen to adorn the inno cence of youth. You have made your choice and ought to approve it.

"To be happy, we must always have something in view. Turn, therefore, your attention to her mind, which will daily grow brighter by polishing. Study some easy science together, and acquire a similarity of tastes, while you enjoy a community of pleasures. You will, by this means, have many pursuits in common, and be freed from the necessity of separating to find amuse- ment; endeavor to cement the present union on every side: let your wife never be kept ignorant of your in- come, your expenses, your friendships, or your aver- sions; let her know your very faults, but make them amiable by your virtues; consider all concealment as a breach of fidelity; let her never have anything to find out in your character, and remember that from the mo- ment one of the partners turns spy upon the other, they have commenced a state of hostility.

"Seek not for happiness in singularity, and dread a refinement of wisdom as a deviation into folly. Listen not to those sages who advise you always to scorn the counsel of a woman, and if you comply with her requests pronounce you to be wife-ridden. Think not any priva- tion, except of positive evil, an excellence; and do not congratulate yourself that your wife is not a learned lady, or is wholly ignorant how to make a pudding. Cooking and learning are both good in their places, and may both be used with advantage. With regard to ex- pense, I can only observe, that the money laid out in the

purchase of luxuries is seldom or ever profitably em
ployed. We live in an age when splendid furniture and
glittering equipage are grown too common to catch the
notice of the meanest spectator; and for the greater
ones, they can only regard our wasteful folly with silent
contempt or open indignation.

"This may, perhaps, be a displeasing reflection; but
the following consideration ought to make amends. The
age we live in pays, I think, a peculiar attention to the
higher distinctions of wit, knowledge, and virtue, to
which we may more safely, more cheaply, and more
honorably aspire.

"The person of your lady will not grow more pleasing
to you; but, pray, let her not suspect that it grows less
so. There is no reproof, however pointed, no punishment, however severe, that a woman of spirit will not
prefer to neglect; and if she can endure it without complaint, it only proves that she means to make herself
amends by the attention of others for the slights of her
husband. For this, and for every other reason, it be-
hoves a married man not to let his politeness fail, though
his ardour may abate; but to retain, at least, that general
civility towards his own lady which he is willing to pay
to every other, and not show a wife of eighteen or twenty
years old, that every man in company can treat her with
more complaisance than he who so often vowed to her
eternal fondness.

"It is not my opinion that a young woman should be
indulged in every wild wish of her gay heart, or giddy
head; but contradiction may be softened by domestic
kindness, and quiet pleasures substituted in the place of

noisy ones.   Public amusements, indeed, are not so ex
pensive as is sometimes imagined ; but they tend to alienate
the minds of married people from each other.   A well-
chosen society of friends and acquaintances, more eminent for virtue and good sense than for gaiety and
splendor, where the conversation of the day may afford
comment for the evening, seems the most rational pleasure that can be afforded.   That your own superiority
should always be seen, but never felt, seems an excellent
general rule.

"If your wife is disposed towards jealousy of you,
let me beseech you be always explicit with her, never mysterious.   Be above delighting in her pain in all things."

After your duty to your wife comes that towards the
children whom God lends to you, to fit them to return
pure and virtuous to him.   This is your task, responsibility, and trust, to be undertaken prayerfully, earnestly
and humbly, as the highest and most sacred duty this
life ever can afford you.

The relationship between parent and child, is one that
appears to have been ordained by Providence, to bring
the better feelings of mankind and many domestic virtues
into active exercise.   The implicit confidence with which
children, when properly treated, look up to their elders
for guidance is not less beautiful than endearing; and no
parents can set about the work of guiding aright, in
real earnest, without deriving as much good as they impart.   The feeling with which this labor of love would
be carried forward is, as the poet writes of mercy twice
blessed :—

"It blesses him that gives and him that takes."

And yet, in daily life and experience, how seldom do we find these views realized! Children, in too many instances, are looked on as anything but a blessing; they are treated as incumbrances, or worse; and the neglect in which they are brought up, renders it almost impossible for them, when they grow older, to know anything properly of moral or social duties. This result we know, in numerous cases, is not willful, does not arise from ill intentions on the part of parents, but from want of fixed plans and principles. There are hundreds of families in this country whose daily life is nothing better than a daily scramble, where time and place, from getting up in the morning to going to bed at night, are regarded as matters of chance. In such homes as these, where the inmates are willing to do well, but don't know how, a word in season is often welcome. "Great principles," we are told, "are at the bottom of all things; but to apply them to daily life, many little rules, precautions, and insights are needed."

The work of training is, in some degree, lightened by the fact, that children are very imitative; what they see others do, they will try to do themselves, and if they see none but good examples, good conduct on their part may naturally be looked for. Children are keen observers, and are very ready at drawing conclusions when they see a want of correspondence between profession and practice, in those who have the care of them. At the age of seven, the child's brain has reached its full growth; it seldom becomes larger after that period, and it then contains the germ of all that the man ever accomplishes. Here is an additional reason for laying down the precept:—be yourselves what you wish the children to be. When correction is necessary, let it be administered in such a way as to make the child refrain from doing wrong from a desire to do right, not for the sole reason that wrong brings punishment. All experience teaches us that if a good thing is to be obtained, it must be by persevering diligence; and of all good things, the pleasure arising from a well-trained family is one of the greatest. Parents, or educators, have no right to use their children just as whim or prejudice may dictate. Children are smaller links in the great social chain, and bind together in lasting ties many portions which otherwise would be completely disjointed; their joyousness enlivens many a home, and their innocence is a powerful check and antidote to much that is evil. The implicit obedience which is required of them, will always be given when called forth by a spirit of forbearance, self-sacrifice, and love :—

> "Ere long comes the reward,
> And for the cares and toils we have endured,
> Repays us joys and pleasures manifold."

If you cherish and honor your own parents, then do you give your children the most forcible teaching for their duty, *example*. And your duty to your children requires your example to be good in all things. How can you expect counsel to virtue to have any effect, if you constantly contradict it by a bad example? Do not forget, that early impressions are deep and lasting, and from their infancy let them see you keep an upright, noble walk in life, then may you hope to see them follow in your footsteps.

Justice, as a sentiment, is inborn, and no one distin guishes its niceties more quickly than a child. There fore in your rewards and punishments examine carefully every part of their conduct, and judge calmly, not hastily, and be sure you are just. An unmerited reward will make a child question your judgment as much as an unmerited punishment.

Guard your temper. Never reprove a child in the heat of passion.

If your sons see that you regard the rules of polite- ness in your home, you will find that they treat their mother and sisters with respect and courtesy, and observe, even in play, the rules of etiquette your example teaches; but if you are a domestic tyrant, all your elder and stronger children will strive to act like "father," by ill- treating or neglecting the younger and weaker ones.

Make them, from the moment they begin to talk, use pure and grammatical language, avoid slang phrases, and, above all, profanity. You will find this rule, enforced during childhood, will have more effect than a library full of books or the most unwearied instruction can accom- plish, after bad habits in conversation have once been formed.

Make them, from early childhood, observe the rules of politeness towards each other. Let your sons treat your daughters as, when men, you would have them treat other females, and let your daughters, by gentleness and love, repay these attentions. You may feel sure that the brothers and sisters, who are polite one to another, will not err in etiquette when abroad.

In the home circle may very properly be included the
16

humble portion, whose onerous duties are too often repaid by harshness and rudeness; I mean the servancs.
A true gentleman, while he never allows familiarity from
his servants, will always remember that they are human
beings, who feel kindness or rudeness as keenly as the
more favored ones up stairs.   Chesterfield says :—

"There is a certain politeness *due* to your inferiors,
and whoever is without it, is without good nature.   We
do not need to compliment our servants, nor to talk of
their doing us the honor, &c., but we ought to treat them
with benevolence and mildness.   We are all of the same
species, and no distinction whatever is between us, except that which arises from fortune.   For example, your
footman and cook would be your equals were they as
rich as you.   Being poor they are obliged to serve you.
Therefore, you must not add to their misfortunes by insulting or ill-treating them.   If your situation is preferable to theirs, be thankful, without either despising them
or being vain of your better fortune.   You must, therefore, treat all your inferiors with affability and good
manners, and not speak to them in a surly tone, nor
with harsh expressions, as if they were of a different
species.   A good heart never reminds people of their
inferiority, but endeavors to alleviate their misfortunes,
and make them forget them."

"Example," says Mrs. Parkes, "is of the greatest importance to our servants, particularly those who are
young, whose habits are frequently formed by the first
service they enter.   With the mild and good, they become softened and improved, but with the dissipated and
violent, are too often disorderly and vicious.   It is

therefore, not among the least of the duties incumbent
on the head of the family, to place in their view such
examples as are worthy their imitation. But these examples, otherwise praiseworthy, should neither be rendered disagreeable, nor have their force diminished by
any accompaniment of ill humor. Rather by the happiness and comfort resulting from our conduct towards
our domestics, should they be made sensible of the
beauty of virtue. What we admire, we often strive to
imitate, and thus they may be led on to imitate good
principles, and to form regular and virtuous habits."

CHAPTER XIV.

TRUE COURTESY.

POLITENESS is the art of pleasing. It is to the deportment what the finer touches of the pencil are to the picture, or what harmony is to music. In the formation of character, it is indispensably requisite. "We are all," says Locke, "a kind of chameleons, that take a tincture from the objects which surround us." True courtesy, indeed, chiefly consists in accommodating ourselves to the feelings of others, without descending from our own dignity, or denuding ourselves of our own principles. By constant intercourse with society, we acquire what is called politeness almost intuitively, as the shells of the sea are rendered smooth by the unceasing friction of the waves; though there appears to be a natural grace about the well-bred, which many feel it difficult to attain.

Religion itself teaches us to honor all men, and to do unto others as we would others do unto us. This includes the whole principle of courtesy, which in this we may remark, assimilates to the principle of justice. It comprises, indeed, all the moral virtues in one, consisting not merely in external show, but having its principle in the heart. The politeness which superficial writers are fond of describing, has been defined as "the appearance of all the virtues, without possessing one of them;" but by this is meant the mere outward parade, or that kind of artificial adornment of demeanor, which owes its existence to an over-refinement of civility. Anything forced or formal is contrary to the very character of courtesy, which does not consist in a becoming deportment alone, but is prompted and guided by a superior mind, impelling the really polite person to bear with the failings of some, to overlook the weakness of others, and to endure patiently the caprices of all. Indeed, one of the essential characteristics of courtesy is good nature, and an inclination always to look at the bright side of things.

The principal rules of politeness are, to subdue the temper, to submit to the weakness of our fellow men, and to render to all their due, freely and courteously. These, with the judgment to recommend ourselves to those whom we meet in society, and the discrimination to know when and to whom to yield, as well as the discretion to treat all with the deference due to their reputation, station, or merit, comprise, in general, the character of a polite man, over which the admission of even one blot or shade will throw a blemish not easily removed.

Sincerity is another essential characteristic of courtesy; for, without it, the social system would have no permanent foundation or hope of continuance. It is the want of this which makes society, what it is said to be, artificial.

Good breeding, in a great measure, consists in being

easy, but not indifferent; good humored, but not familiar; passive, but not unconcerned. It includes, also, a sensibility nice, yet correct; a tact delicate, yet true. There is a beautiful uniformity in the demeanor of a polite man; and it is impossible not to be struck with his affable air. There is a golden mean in the art, which it should be every body's object to attain, without descending to obsequiousness on the one hand, or to familiarity on the other. In politeness, as in everything else, there is the medium betwixt too much and too little, betwixt constraint and freedom; for civilities carried to extreme are wearisome, and mere ceremony is not politeness, but the reverse.

The truly pious people are the truly courteous. "Religion," says Leighton, "is in this mistaken sometimes, in that we think it imprints a roughness and austerity upon the mind and carriage. It doth, indeed, bar all vanity and lightness, and all compliance;" but it softens the manners, tempers the address, and refines the heart.

Pride is one of the greatest obstacles to true courtesy that can be mentioned. He who assumes too much on his own merit, shows that he does not understand the simplest principles of politeness. The feeling of pride is, of itself, highly culpable. No man, whether he be a monarch on the throne, or the meanest beggar in his realm, possesses any right to comport himself with a haughty or discourteous air towards his fellow men. The poet truly says:

"What most ennobles human nature,
  Was ne'er the portion of the proud."

It is easy to bestow a kind word, or assume a gracious

smile; these will recommend us to every one; while a
haughty demeanor, or an austere look, may forfeit forever the favor of those whose good opinion we may be
anxious to secure. The really courteous man has a
thorough knowledge of human nature, and can make al
lowances for its weaknesses. He is always consistent
with himself. The polite alone know how to make others
polite, as the good alone know how to inspire others with
a relish for virtue.

Having mentioned pride as being opposed to true politeness, I may class affectation with it, in that respect.
Affectation is a deviation from, at the same time that it
is an imitation of, nature. It is the result of bad taste,
and of mistaken notions of one's own qualities. The
other vices are limited, and have each a particular object; but affectation pervades the whole conduct, and
detracts from the merit of whatever virtues and good
dispositions a man may possess. Beauty itself loses its
attraction, when disfigured by affectation. Even to copy
from the best patterns is improper, because the imitation
can never be so good as the original. Counterfeit coin
is not so valuable as the real, and when discovered, it
cannot pass current. Affectation is a sure sign that
there is something to conceal, rather than anything to
be proud of, in the character and disposition of the persons practicing it.

In religion, affectation, or, as it is fitly called, hypocrisy, is reprehensible in the highest degree. However
grave be their deportment, of all affected persons, those
who, without any real foundation, make too great pretensions to piety, are certainly the most culpable. The

mask serves to conceal innumerable faults, and, as has been well remarked, a false devotion too often usurps the place of the true. We can less secure ourselves against pretenders in matters of religion, than we can against any other species of impostors; because the mind being biased in favor of the subject, consults not reason as to the individual. The conduct of people, which cannot fail to be considered an evidence of their principles, ought at all times to be conformable to their pretensions. When God alone is all we are concerned for, we are not solicitous about mere human approbation.

Hazlitt says:—" Few subjects are more nearly allied than these two—vulgarity and affectation. It may be said of them truly that 'thin partitions do their bounds divide.' There cannot be a surer proof of a low origin or of an innate meanness of disposition, than to be always talking and thinking of being genteel. One must feel a strong tendency to that which one is always trying to avoid; whenever we pretend, on all occasions, a mighty contempt for anything, it is a pretty clear sign that we feel ourselves very nearly on a level with it. Of the two classes of people, I hardly know which is to be regarded with most distaste, the vulgar aping the genteel, or the genteel constantly sneering at and endeavoring to distinguish themselves from the vulgar. These two sets of persons are always thinking of one another; the lower of the higher with envy, the more fortunate of their less happy neighbors with contempt. They are habitually placed in opposition to each other; jostle in their pretensions at every turn; and the same objects and train of thought (only reversed by the rela-

tive situations of either party) occupy their whole time
and attention. The one are straining every nerve, and
outraging common sense, to be thought genteel; the
others have no other object or idea in their heads than
not to be thought vulgar. This is but poor spite; a
very pitiful style of ambition. To be merely not that
which one heartily despises, is a very humble claim to
superiority; to despise what one really is, is still worse.

"Gentility is only a more select and artificial kind of
vulgarity. It cannot exist but by a sort of borrowed
distinction. It plumes itself up and revels in the homely
pretensions of the mass of mankind. It judges of the
worth of everything by name, fashion, opinion; and
hence, from the conscious absence of real qualities or
sincere satisfaction in itself, it builds its supercilious and
fantastic conceit on the wretchedness and wants of
others. Violent antipathies are always suspicious, and
betray a secret affinity. The difference between the
'Great Vulgar and the Small' is mostly in outward circumstances. The coxcomb criticises the dress of the
clown, as the pedant cavils at the bad grammar of the
illiterate. Those who have the fewest resources in
themselves, naturally seek the food of their self-love
elsewhere. The most ignorant people find most to laugh
at in strangers; scandal and satire prevail most in coun-
try-places; and a propensity to ridicule every the slightest or most palpable deviation from what we happen to
approve, ceases with the progress of common sense.
True worth does not exult in the faults and deficiencies
of others; as true refinement turns away from grossness
and deformity instead of being tempted to indulge in an

unmanly triumph over it. Raphael would not faint
away at the daubing of a sign painter, nor Homer hold
his head the higher for being in the company of the
poorest scribbler that ever attempted poetry. Real
power, real excellence, does not seek for a foil in inferiority, nor fear contamination from coming in contact
with that which is coarse and homely. It reposes on itself, and is equally free from spleen and affectation.
But the spirit of both these small vices is in *gentility* as
the word stands in vulgar minds: of affected delight in
its own would-be qualifications, and of ineffable disdain
poured out upon the involuntary blunders or accidental
disadvantages of those whom it chooses to treat as inferiors.

"The essence of vulgarity, I imagine, consists in
taking manners, actions, words, opinions on trust from
others, without examining one's own feelings or weighing
the merits of the case. It is coarseness or shallowness
of taste arising from want of individual refinement, together with the confidence and presumption inspired by
example and numbers. It may be defined to be a pros-
titution of the mind or body to ape the more or less ob-
vious defects of others, because by so doing we shall secure the suffrages of those we associate with. To affect
a gesture, an opinion, a phrase, because it is the rage
with a large number of persons, or to hold it in abhor-
rence because another set of persons very little, if at all,
better informed, cry it down to distinguish themselves
from the former, is in either case equal vulgarity and
absurdity. A thing is not vulgar merely because it is
common. 'Tis common to breathe, to see, to feel, to

live. Nothing is vulgar that is natural, spontaneous, unavoidable. Grossness is not vulgarity, ignorance is not vulgarity, awkwardness is not vulgarity; but all these become vulgar when they are affected, and shown off on the authority of others, or to fall in with *the fashion* or the company we keep. Caliban is coarse enough, but surely he is not vulgar. We might as well spurn the clod under our feet, and call it vulgar.

"All slang phrases are vulgar; but there is nothing vulgar in the common English idiom. Simplicity is not vulgarity; but the looking to affectation of any sort for distinction is."

To sum up, it may be said, that if you wish to possess the good opinion of your fellow men, the way to secure it is, to be actually what you pretend to be, or rather to appear always precisely what you are. Never depart from the native dignity of your character, which you can only maintain irreproachable by being careful not to imitate the vices, or adopt the follies of others. The best way in all cases you will find to be, to adhere to truth, and to abide by the talents and appliances which have been bestowed upon you by Providence.

CHAPTER XV.

LETTER WRITING.

THERE is no branch of a man's education, no portion of his intercourse with other men, and no quality which will stand him in good stead more frequently than the capability of writing a good letter upon any and every subject. In business, in his intercourse with society, in, I may say, almost every circumstance of his life, he will find his pen called into requisition. Yet, although so important, so almost indispensable an accomplishment, it is one which is but little cultivated, and a letter, perfect in every part, is a great rarity.

In the composition of a good letter there are many points to be considered, and we take first the simplest and lowest, namely, the spelling.

Many spell badly from ignorance, but more from carelessness. The latter, writing rapidly, make, very often, mistakes that would disgrace a schoolboy. If you are in doubt about a word, do not from a feeling of false shame let the spelling stand in its doubtful position hoping that, if wrong, it will pass unnoticed, but get a dictionary, and see what is the correct orthography. Besides the actual misplacing of letters in a word there is another fault of careless, rapid writing, frequently

seen. This is to write two words in one, running them
together. I have more than once seen *with him* written
withim, and *for her* stand thus, *forer*. Strange, too, as
it may seem, it is more frequently the short, common
words that are misspelled than long ones. They flow
from the pen mechanically, while over an unaccustomed
word the writer unconsciously stops to consider the orthography. Chesterfield, in his advice to his son, says.

"I come now to another part of your letter, which is
the orthography, if I may call bad spelling *orthography*.
You spell induce, *enduce;* and grandeur, you spell
grandure; two faults of which few of my housemaids
would have been guilty. I must tell you that orthography, in the true sense of the word, is so absolutely necessary for a man of letters, or a gentleman, that one false
spelling may fix ridicule upon him for the rest of his
life; and I know a man of quality, who never recovered
the ridicule of having spelled *wholesome* without the *w*.

"Reading with care will secure everybody from false
spelling; for books are always well spelled, according to
the orthography of the times. Some words are indeed
doubtful, being spelled differently by different authors
of equal authority; but those are few; and in those
cases every man has his option, because he may plead
his authority either way; but where there is but one
right way, as in the two words above mentioned, it is unpardonable and ridiculous for a gentleman to miss it;
even a woman of tolerable education would despise and
laugh at a lover, who sent her an ill-spelled *billet-doux*.
I fear, and suspect, that you have taken it into your
head, in most cases, that the matter is all, and the man-

ner little or nothing. If you have, undeceive yourself, and be convinced that, in everything, the manner is full as important as the matter. If you speak the sense of an angel in bad words, and with a disagreeable utterance, nobody will hear you twice, who can help it. If you write epistles as well as Cicero, but in a very bad hand, and very ill-spelled, whoever receives, will laugh at them.''

After orthography, you should make it a point to write a good hand; clear, legible, and at the same time easy, graceful, and rapid. This is not so difficult as some persons imagine, but, like other accomplishments, it requires practice to make it perfect. You must write every word so clearly that it *cannot* be mistaken by the reader, and it is quite an important requisite to leave sufficient space between the words to render each one separate and distinct. If your writing is crowded, it will be difficult to read, even though each letter is perfectly well formed. An English author, in a letter of advice, says:—

"I have often told you that every man who has the use of his eyes and his hand can write whatever hand he pleases. I do not desire that you should write the stiff, labored characters of a writing master; a man of business must write quick and well, and that depends simply upon use. I would, therefore, advise you to get some very good writing master, and apply to it for a month only, which will be sufficient; for, upon my word, the writing of a genteel, plain hand of business is of much more importance than you think. You say, it may be, that when you write so very ill, it is because

you are in a hurry; to which, I answer, Why are you
ever in a hurry? A man of sense may be in haste, but
can never be in a hurry, because he knows, that what
ever he does in a hurry, he must necessarily do very ill.
He may be in haste to dispatch an affair, but he will take
care not to let that haste hinder his doing it well. Little
minds are in a hurry, when the object proves (as it commonly does) too big for them; they run, they puzzle, con-
found, and perplex themselves; they want to do everything at once, and never do it at all. But a man of
sense takes the time necessary for doing the thing he is
about, well; and his haste to dispatch a business, only
appears by the continuity of his application to it; he
pursues it with a cool steadiness, and finishes it before he
begins any other. * *

"The few seconds that are saved in the course of the
day by writing ill instead of well, do not amount to an
object of time by any means equivalent to the disgrace
or ridicule of a badly written scrawl."

By making a good, clear hand habitual to you, the
caution given above, with regard to hurry, will be entirely useless, for you will find that even the most rapid
pennmanship will not interfere with the beauty of your
hand-writing, and the most absorbing interest in the subject of your epistle can be indulged; whereas, if you
write well only when you are giving your entire attention to guiding your pen, then, haste in writing or interest in your subject will spoil the beauty of your sheet.

Be very careful that the wording of your letters is in
strict accordance with the rules of grammar. Nothing
stamps the difference between a well educated man and an

ignorant one more decidedly than the purely grammatical language of the one compared with the labored sentences, misplaced verbs, nouns, adjectives. and adverbs of the other. Chesterfield caricatures this fault in the following letter, written as a warning to his son, to guard him against its glaring faults:

"My Lord: I *had*, last night, the honor of your Lordship's letter of the 24th; and will *set about doing* the orders contained *therein;* and *if so be* that I can get that affair done by the next post, I will not fail *for to* give your Lordship an account of it, by *next post.* I have told the French Minister, *as how that if* that affair be not soon concluded, your Lordship would think it *all long of him;* and that he must have neglected *for to* have wrote to his court about it. I must beg leave to put your Lordship in mind, *as how*, that I am now full three quarters in arrear; and if *so be* that I do not very soon receive at least one half year, I shall *cut a very bad figure; for this here* place is very dear. I shall be *vastly beholden* to your Lordship for *that there* mark of your favor; and so I *rest* or *remain*, Your, &c."

This is, I admit, a broad burlesque of a letter written by a man holding any important government office, but in the more private correspondence of a man's life letters quite as absurd and ungrammatical are written every day.

Punctuation is another very important point in a letter. because it not only is a mark of elegance and education to properly punctuate a letter, but the omission of this point will inevitably confuse your correspondent, for if you write to your friend:

"I met last evening Mr James the artist his son a lawyer Mr Gay a friend of my mother's Mr Clarke and Mr Paul:"

he will not know whether Mr. Gay is a lawyer or your mother's friend, or whether it is Mr. James or his son who is an artist; whereas, by the proper placing of a few punctuation marks you make the sentence clear and intelligible, thus:

"I met, last evening, Mr. James, the artist; his son, a lawyer; Mr. Gay, a friend of my mother's; Mr. Clarke and Mr. Paul."

Without proper regard being paid to punctuation, the very essence of good composition is lost; it is of the utmost importance, as clearness, strength, and accuracy depend upon it, in as great a measure as the power of an army depends upon the skill displayed in marshalling and arranging the troops. The separation of one portion of a composition from another; the proper classification and division of the subjects; the precise meaning of every word and sentence; the relation each part bears to previous or following parts; the connection of one portion and separation of others—all depend upon punctuation. Many persons seem to consider it sufficient to put in a period at the end of a long sentence, leaving all the little niceties which a comma, semicolon, or colon would render clear, in a state of the most lamentable obscurity. Others use all the points, but misplace them in a most ludicrous manner. A sentence may be made by the omission or addition of a comma to express a meaning exactly opposite to the one it expressed before the little mark was written or erased. The best mode

17

of studying punctuation is to read over what you write, aloud, and put in the points as you would dwell a longer or shorter time on the words, were you speaking.

We now come to the use of capital letters, a subject next, in importance to punctuation, and one too often neglected, even by writers otherwise careful.

The first word of every piece of writing, whether it be a book, a poem, a story, a letter, a bill, a note, or only a line of directions, must begin with a capital letter.

Quotations, even though they are not immediately preceded by a period, must invariably begin with a capital letter.

Every new sentence, following a period, exclamation mark, or interrogation point, must begin with a capital letter.

Every proper name, whether it be of a person, a place, or an object, must begin with a capital letter. The pronoun I and exclamation O must be always written in capital letters.

Capitals must never, except in the case of proper names or the two letters mentioned in the last paragraph, be written in the middle of a sentence.

A capital letter must never be used in the middle of a word, among the small letters; nor must it be used at the end of a word.

Nothing adds more to the beauty of a letter, or any written composition, than handsomely written capital letters, used in their proper places.

Having specified the most important points in a correct letter, we next come to that which, more than anything else, shows the mind of the writer; that which proves his good or bad education; that which gives him rank as an elegant or inelegant writer—Style.

It is style which adorns or disfigures a subject; which makes the humblest matter appear choice and elegant, or which reduces the most exalted ideas to a level with common, or vulgar ones.

Lord Chesterfield says, "It is of the greatest importance to write letters well; as this is a talent which unavoidably occurs every day of one's life, as well in business as in pleasure; and inaccuracies in orthography or in style are never pardoned. Much depends upon the manner in which they are written; which ought to be easy and natural, not strained and florid. For instance, when you are about to send a *billet-doux*, or love letter to a fair friend, you must only think of what you would say to her if you were both together, and then write it; that renders the style easy and natural; though some people imagine the wording of a letter to be a great undertaking, and think they must write abundantly better than they talk, which is not at all necessary. Style is the dress of thoughts, and let them be ever so just, if your style is homely, coarse, and vulgar, they will appear to as much disadvantage and be as ill received as your person, though ever so well proportioned, would, if dressed in rags, dirt, and tatters. It is not every understanding that can judge of matter; but every one can and does judge, more or less, of style; and were I either to speak or write to the public, I should prefer moderate matter, adorned with all the beauties and elegancies of style, to the strongest matter in the world, ill worded and ill delivered."

Write legibly, correctly, and without erasures upon a whole sheet of paper, never upon half a sheet. Choose paper which is thick, white, and perfectly plain. The initials stamped at the top of a sheet are the only ornament allowed a gentleman.

It is an unpardonable fault to write upon a sheet which has anything written or drawn upon it, or is soiled; and quite as bad to answer a note upon half the sheet it is written upon, or write on the other side of a sheet which has been used before.

Write your own ideas in your own words, neither borrowing or copying from another. If you are detected in a plagiarism, you will never recover your reputation for originality, and you may find yourself in the position of the hero of the following anecdote:

Mr. O., a man of but little cultivation, fell in love with Miss N., whose fine intellect was duly improved by a thorough course of study and reading, while her wit, vivacity, and beauty made Mr. O. one only amongst many suitors. Fascinated by her beauty and gracious manner he determined to settle his fate, and ask her to go forward in the alphabet and choose the next letter to put to her surname. But how? Five times he tried to speak, and five times the gay beauty so led the discourse that he left at the end of each interview, no wiser than when he came. At length he resolved to write. It was the first time he had held the pen for any but a business letter. After commencing twice with "Dear sir," once with, "I write to inform you that I am well and hope this letter will find you the same," and once with, "Your last duly received," he threw the pen aside in disgust and despair. A love letter was beyond his feeble capacities. Suddenly a brilliant idea struck him. He had lately seen, in turning the leaves of a popular novel, a letter, perhaps a love letter. He procured the book, found the letter. It was full of fire and passion, words of love, protestations of never failing constancy, and contained an offer of marriage. With a hand that trembled with ecstasy, O. copied and signed the letter, sealed, directed, and sent it. The next day came the answer—simply :

"My Friend,
"Turn to the next page and you will find the reply.
"A. N."

He did so, and found a polite refusal of his suit.

The secret of letter writing consists in writing as you would speak. Thus, if you speak well, you will write well; if you speak ill, you will also write ill.

Endeavor always to write as correctly and properly as possible. If you have reason to doubt your own spelling, carefully read and correct every letter before you fold it. An ill-formed letter is, however, better let alone. You will not improve it by trying to reform it, and the effort will be plainly visible.

Let your style be simple, concise, and clear, entirely void of pretension, without any phrases written merely for effect, without useless flowery language, respectful towards superiors, women, and older persons, and it will be well.

Abbreviations are only permitted in business letters, and in friendly correspondence must never be used.

Figures are never to be used excepting when putting a date or a sum of money. In a business letter the money is generally specified both in figures and words, thus; $500 Five hundred dollars.

You may put the name, date, and address of a letter either at the top of the page or at the end. I give a specimen of each style to show my meaning.

PHILADELPHIA, *June 25th*, 1855.

MR. JAMES SMITH,
    Dear Sir,
            The goods ordered in your letter of the 19th inst. were sent this morning by Adam's Express. We shall be always happy to hear from you. and will promptly fill any further orders.
            Yours, truly,
                        JONES, BROWN & Co.

            or,

Dear Sir,
            Your favor of the 5th inst. received to day. Will execute your commissions with pleasure.
                        Yours, truly.
                                    J. Jones,

MR. JAMES SMITH.
    PHILA., *June 25th*, 1854.

If you send your own address put it under your own signature, thus:

J. JONES,
17 W—— st.,
NEW YORK.

The etiquette of letter-writing, should, as much as possible, be influenced by principles of truth. The superscription and the subscription should alike be in accordance with the tone of the communication, and the domestic or social relation of those between whom it passes. Communications upon professional or business matters, where no acquaintance exists to modify the circumstances, should be written thus:—"Mr. Gillot will feel obliged by Mr. Slack's sending by the bearer," &c. It is an absurdity for a man who writes a challenge, or an offensive letter, to another, to subscribe himself, "Your obedient Servant." I dislike this form of subscription, also, when employed by persons of equal rank. It is perfectly becoming when addressed by a servant to an employer. But in other cases, "Yours truly," "Yours very truly," "Your Friend," "Your sincere Friend," "Your Well-wisher," "Your grateful Friend," "Your affectionate Friend," &c., &c., appears to be much more truthful, and to be more in keeping with the legitimate expression of good feeling. It is impossible to lay down a set of rules that shall govern all cases. But as a principle, it may be urged, that no person should address another as, "Dear Sir," or, "Dear Madam," without feelings and relations that justify the use of the adjective. These compliments are mockeries

No one who entertains a desire to write another as "dear," need feel afraid of giving offence by familiarity; for all mankind prize the esteem even of their humblest fellows too much to be annoyed by it. And in proportion as the integrity of the forms of correspondence increase, so will these expressions of good feeling be more appreciated.

The next point to be considered is the *subject* of your letter, and without a good subject the epistle will be apt to be dull. I do not mean by this that it is necessary to have any extraordinary event to relate, or startling news to communicate; but in order to write a *good* letter, it is necessary to have a *good* subject, that you may not rival the Frenchman who wrote to his wife—"I write to you because I have nothing to do: I stop because I have nothing to say." Letters written without aim or object, simply for the sake of writing, are apt to be stupid, trivial, or foolish.

You may write to a friend to congratulate him upon some happy event to himself, or to condole with him in some misfortune, or to ask his congratulations or condolence for yourself. You may write to enquire for his health, or to extend an invitation, a letter of thanks, felicitations, upon business, or a thousand other subjects, which it is useless for me to enumerate.

LETTERS OF BUSINESS. The chief object in a letter of business is to communicate or enquire about some one fact, and the epistle should be confined entirely to that fact. All compliments, jests, high-flown language and sentiment, are entirely out of place in a business letter, and brevity should be one of the most important aims. Do not let your desire to be brief, however, make your meaning obscure; better to add a few words, or even lines, to the length of your letter, than to send it in confused, unintelligible language. Chesterfield's advice on business letters is excellent. He says:

"The first thing necessary in writing letters of business is, extreme clearness and perspicuity; every paragraph should be so clear and unambiguous that the dullest fellow in the world may not be able to mistake it, nor obliged to read it twice in order to understand it. This necessary clearness implies a correctness, without excluding an elegance of style. Tropes, figures, antithesis, epigrams, &c., would be as misplaced and as impertinent in letters of business as they are sometimes (if judiciously used) proper and pleasing in familiar letters, upon common and trite subjects. In business, an elegant simplicity, the result of care, not of labor, is required. Business must be well, not affectedly dressed; but by no means negligently. Let your first attention be to clearness, and read every paragraph after you have written it, in the critical view of discovering whether it is possible that any one man can mistake the true sense of it; and correct it accordingly.

Our pronouns and relatives often create obscurity and ambiguity; be, therefore, exceedingly attentive to them, and take care to mark out with precision their particular relations. For example, Mr. Johnson acquainted me, that he had seen Mr. Smith, who had promised him to speak to Mr. Clarke, to return him (Mr. Johnson) those papers, which he (Mr. Smith) had left some time ago with him (Mr. Clarke); it is better to repeat a name, though

unnecessarily, ten times, than to have the person mistaken once.

" *Who*, you know, is singly relative to persons, and
cannot be applied to things; *which* and *that* are chiefly
relative to things, but not absolutely exclusive of persons; for one may say the man, *that* robbed or killed
such-a-one; but it is better to say, the man *who* robbed
or killed.   One never says, the man or woman *which*.
Which and *that*, though chiefly relative to things, cannot
be always used indifferently as to things.   For instance,
the letter *which* I received from you, *which* you referred
to in your last, *which* came by Lord Albemarle's messenger, *which* I showed to such-a-one; I would change it
thus—The letter that I received from you, *which* you
referred to in your last, *that* came by Lord Albemarle's
messenger, and *which* I showed to such-a-one.

"Business does not exclude (as possibly you wish it
did) the usual terms of politeness and good breeding;
but, on the contrary, strictly requires them; such as, I
*have the honor to acquaint you ; Permit me to assure you ;
or, If I may be allowed to give my opinion, &c.*

"LETTERS OF BUSINESS will not only admit of, but be
the better for *certain graces*—but then, they must be scat-
tered with a skillful and sparing hand; they must fit
their place exactly.   They must adorn without encum-
bering, and modestly shine without glaring.   But as this
is the utmost degree of perfection in letters of business,
I would not advise you to attempt those embellishments,
till you have just laid your foundation well.

"Carefully avoid all Greek or Latin quotations; and
bring no precedents from the *virtuous Spartans, the po-*

like Athenians, and the brave Romans. Leave all that
to futile pedants. No flourishes, no declamations. But
(I repeat it again) there is an elegant simplicity and dignity of style absolutely necessary for *good letters of business;* attend to that carefully. Let your periods be
harmonious, without seeming to be labored; and let
them not be too long, for that always occasions a degree
of obscurity. I should not mention correct orthography,
but that to fail in that particular will bring ridicule upon
you; for no man is allowed to spell ill. The hand
writing, too, should be good; and I cannot conceive why
it is ever otherwise, since every man may, certainly, write
whatever hand he pleases. Neatness in folding up,
sealing, and directing your packets is, by no means, to
be neglected. There is something in the exterior, even
of a packet or letter, that may please or displease; and,
consequently, worth some attention."

If you are writing a letter, either upon your own business or upon that of the person you are addressing,
not in answer to him, but opening the subject between
you, follow the rule of clearness and of business brevity.
Come to the point at once, in order that the person addressed may easily comprehend you. Put nobody to
the labor of *guessing* what you desire, and be careful
that half-instructions do not lead your correspondent
astray. If you have so clear an idea of your operation
in your mind, or if it is so simple a one that it needs no
words, except specific directions, or a plain request, you
need not waste time, but, with the proper forms of
courtesy, instruct him of your wishes. In whatever you
write, remember that time is valuable; and that embar

rassing or indefinite letters are a great nuisance to a bu siness man. I need hardly remark, that punctuality in answering correspondents is one of the cardinal business virtues. Where it is possible, answer letters by return of post, as you will thus save your own time, and pay your correspondent a flattering compliment. And in opening a correspondence or writing upon your own business, let your communication be made at the earliest proper date in order that your correspondent, as well as yourself, may have the benefit of thought and deliberation.

LETTERS OF INQUIRY should be written in a happy medium, between tedious length and the brevity which would betoken indifference. As the subject is generally limited to questions upon one subject, they will not admit of much verbiage, and if your inquiry relates simply to a matter of business, it is better to confine your words strictly to that business; if, however, you are writing to make inquiry as to the health of a friend, or any other matter in which feeling or affection dictates the epistle, the cold, formal style of a business letter would become heartless, and, in many cases, positively insulting. You must here add some words of compliment, express your friendly interest in the subject, and your hope that a favorable answer may be returned, and if the occasion is a painful one, a few lines of regret or condolence may be added.

If you are requesting a favor of your correspondent, you should apologize for the trouble you are giving him, and mention the necessity which prompts you to write.

If you are making inquiries of a friend, your letter

will then admit of some words of compliment, and may be written in an easy, familiar style.

If writing to a stranger, your request for information becomes a personal favor, and you should write in a manner to show him that you feel this. Speak of the obligation he will confer, mention the necessity which compels you to trouble him, and follow his answer by a note of thanks.

Always, when sending a letter of inquiry, enclose a stamp for the answer. If you trouble your correspondent to take his time to write you information, valuable only to yourself, you have no right to tax him also for the price of postage.

ANSWERS TO LETTERS OF INQUIRY should be written as soon as possible after such letters are received. If the inquiry is of a personal nature, concerning your health, family affairs, or the denial or corroboration of some report concerning yourself, you should thank your correspondent for the interest he expresses, and such a a letter should be answered immediately. If the letter you receive contains questions which you cannot answer instantly, as, for instance, if you are obliged to see a third party, or yourself make inquiry upon the subject proposed, it is best to write a few lines acknowledging the receipt of your friend's letter, expressing your pleasure at being able to serve him, and stating why you cannot immediately give him the desired information, with the promise to write again as soon as such information is yours to send.

LETTERS REQUESTING FAVORS are trying to write, and must be dictated by the circumstances which make them necessary. Be careful not to be servile in such letters. Take a respectful, but, at the same time, manly tone; and, while you acknowledge the obligation a favorable answer will confer, do not adopt the cringing language of a beggar.

LETTERS CONFERRING FAVORS should never be written in a style to make the recipient feel a weight of obligation; on the contrary, the style should be such as will endeavor to convince your correspondent that in his acceptance of your favor *he* confers an obligation upon *you*.

LETTERS REFUSING FAVORS call for your most courteous language, for they must give some pain, and this may be very much softened by the manner in which you write. Express your regret at being unable to grant your friend's request, a hope that at some future time it may be in your power to answer another such letter more favorably, and give a good reason for your refusal.

LETTERS ACKNOWLEDGING FAVORS, or letters of thanks, should be written in a cordial, frank, and grateful style. While you earnestly thank your correspondent for his kindness, you must never hint at any payment of the obligation. If you have the means of obliging him near you at that instant, make your offer of the favor the subject of another letter, lest he attribute your haste to a desire to rid yourself of an obligation. To hint at a future payment is still more indelicate. When you can show your gratitude by a suitable return, then let your actions, not your words, speak for the accuracy of your memory in retaining the recollection of favors conferred.

ANONYMOUS LETTERS. The man who would write

an anonymous letter, either to insult the person addressed, or annoy a third person, is a scoundrel, "whom
'twere gross flattery to name a coward." None but a
man of the lowest principles, and meanest character,
would commit an act to gratify malice or hatred without
danger to himself. A gentleman will treat such a communication with the contemptuous silence which it deserves.

LETTERS OF INTÉLLIGENCE. The first thing to be regarded in a letter of intelligence is *truth*. They are
written on every variety of subjects, under circumstances
of the saddest and the most joyful nature. They are
written often under the pressure of the most crushing
grief, at other times when the hand trembles with ec-
stacy, and very frequently when a weight of other cares
and engagements makes the time of the writer invaluable.
Yet, whether the subject communicated concerns yourself or another, remember that every written word is a
record for your veracity or falsehood. If exaggeration,
or, still worse, malice, guide your pen, in imparting
painful subjects, or if the desire to avoid causing grief
makes you violate truth to soften trying news, you are
signing your name to a written falsehood, and the letter
may, at some future time, rise to confront you and prove
that your intelligence cannot be trusted. Whatever the
character of the news you communicate, let taste and
discretion guide you in the manner of imparting it. If
it is of so sorrowful a character that you know it must
cause pain, you may endeavor to open the subject
gradually, and a few lines of sympathy and comfort, if
unheeded at the time, may be appreciated when the

mourner re-reads your letter in calmer moments. Joyful news, though it does not need the same caution, also admits of expressions of sympathy.

Never write the gossip around you, unless you are *obliged* to communicate some event, and then write only what you know to be true, or, if you speak of doubtful matters, state them to be such. Avoid mere scandal and hearsay, and, above all, avoid letting your own malice or bitterness of feeling color all your statements in their blackest dye. Be, under such circumstances, truthful, just, and charitable.

LETTERS OF RECOMMENDATION should be written only when they are positively necessary, and great caution should be used in giving them. They make you, in a measure, responsible for the conduct of another, and if you give them frequently, on slight grounds, you will certainly have cause to repent your carelessness. They are letters of business, and should be carefully composed; truthful, while they are courteous, and just, while they are kind. If you sacrifice candor to a mistaken kindness, you not only make yourself a party to any mischief that may result, but you are committing a dishonest act towards the person to whom the letter will be delivered.

LETTERS OF INTRODUCTION should be short, as they are generally delivered in person, and ought not to occupy much time in reading, as no one likes to have to wait while a long letter of introduction is read. While you speak of the bearer in the warm language of friendship, do not write praises in such a letter; they are about as much in place as they would be if you spoke them at a personal introduction. Leave letters of in troduction unsealed, for it is a gross breach of politeness to prevent the bearer from reading what you have written, by fastening the envelope. The most common form is :—

Dear Sir,

It gives me much pleasure to introduce to you, the bearer of this letter, as my friend Mr. J——, who is to remain a few days in your city on his way to New Orleans. I trust that the acquaintance of two friends, for whom I have so long entertained so warm an esteem, will prove as pleasant as my intercourse with each has always been. Any attention which it may be in your power to pay to Mr. J——, whilst he is in your city, will be highly appreciated and gratefully acknowledged by

Your sincere friend
JAMES C. RAY.

MR. L. G. EDMONDS.
June 23d, 18—.

If your letter is to introduce any gentleman in his business or professional capacity, mention what that business is ; and if your own acquaintance with the bearer is slight, you may also use the name of the persons from whom he brought letters to yourself. Here, you may, with perfect propriety, say a few words in praise of the bearer's skill in his professional labors. If he is an artist, you need not hesitate to give a favorable opinion of whatever of his pictures you have seen, or, if a musician, express the delight his skill has afforded you.

A LETTER REQUESTING AN AUTOGRAPH should always enclose a postage stamp for the reply. In such a letter

18

some words of compliment, expressive of the value of
the name for which you ask, is in good taste.   You may
refer to the deeds or celebrity which have made the name
so desirable, and also express your sense of the greatness of the favor, and the obligation the granting of it
will confer.

AUTOGRAPH LETTERS should be short; containing
merely a few lines, thanking the person addressed for
the compliment paid in requesting the signature, and expressive of the pleasure it gives you to comply with the
request.   If you wish to refuse (though none but a churl
would do so), do not fall into the error of an eccentric
American whose high position in the army tempted a
collector of autographs to request his signature.   The
general wrote in reply:—

"Sir,
"I'll be hanged if I send my autograph to anybody.
"Yours,
"_____."

and signed his name in full in the strong, bold letters
which always characterized his hand writing.

INVITATIONS TO LADIES should be written in the third
person, unless you are very intimate with them, or can
claim relationship.   All letters addressed to a lady
should be written in a respectful style, and when they
are short and to a comparative stranger, the third person
is the most elegant one to use.   Remember, in directing
letters to young ladies, the eldest one in a family is addressed by the surname alone, while the others have also
the proper name ; thus, if you wrote to the daughters

of Mr. Smith, the eldest one is Miss Smith, the others, Miss Annie Smith and Miss Jane Smith.

Invitations should be sent by your own servant, or clerk. Nothing is more vulgar than sending invitations through the despatch, and you run the risk of their being delayed. The first time that you invite a lady to accompany you to ride, walk, or visit any place of public amusement, you should also invite her mother, sister, or any other lady in the same family, unless you have a mother or sister with whom the lady invited is acquainted, when you should say in your note that your mother or sister will accompany you.

LETTERS OF COMPLIMENT being confined to one subject should be short and simple. If they are of thanks for inquiry made, they should merely echo the letter they answer, with the acknowledgement of your correspondent's courtesy.

LETTERS OF CONGRATULATION. Letters of congratulation are the most agreeable of all letters to write; your subject is before you, and you have the pleasure of sympathizing in the happiness of a friend. They should be written in a frank, genial style, with warm expressions of pleasure at your friend's joy, and admit of any happy quotations or jest.

When congratulating your friend on an occasion of happiness to himself, be very careful that your letter has no word of envy at his good fortune, no fears for its short duration, no prophecy of a change for the worse; let all be bright, cheerful, and hopeful. There are few men whose life calls for letters of congratulation upon many occasions, let them have bright, unclouded ones when they can claim them. If you have other friends whose sorrow makes a contrast with the joy of the person to whom you are writing, nay, even if you yourself are in affliction, do not mention it in such a letter.

At the same time avoid the satire of exageration in your expressions of congratulation, and be very careful how you underline a word. If you write a hope that your friend may be *perfectly happy*, he will not think that the emphasis proves the strength of your wish, but that you are fearful that it will not be fulfilled.

If at the same time that you are writing a letter of congratulation, you have sorrowful news to communicate, do not put your tidings of grief into your congratulatory letter; let that contain only cheerful, pleasant words; even if your painful news must be sent the same day, send it in a separate epistle.

LETTERS OF CONDOLENCE are trying both to the writer and to the reader. If your sympathy is sincere, and you feel the grief of your friend as if it were your own, you will find it difficult to express in written words the sorrow that you are anxious to comfort.

Even the warmest, most sincere expressions, sound cold and commonplace to the mourner, and one grasp of the hand, one glance of the eye, will do more to express sympathy than whole sheets of written words. It is best not to try to say *all* that you feel. You will fail in the attempt and may weary your friend. Let your letter, then, be short, (not heartlessly so) but let its words, though few, be warm and sincere. Any light, cheerful jesting will be insulting in a letter of condolence. If you wish to comfort by bringing forward blessings or hopes for the future, do not do it w.th gay, or jesting expressions, but in a gentle, kind manner, drawing your words of comfort, not from trivial, passing events, but from the highest and purest sources.

If the subject for condolence be loss of fortune or any similar event, your letter will admit of the cheering words of every-day life, and kindly hopes that the wheel of fortune may take a more favorable turn; but, if death causes your friend's affliction, there is but little to be said in the first hours of grief. Your letter of sympathy and comfort may be read after the first crushing grief .is over, and appreciated then, but words of comfort are but little heeded when the first agony of a life-long separation is felt in all the force of its first hours.

LETTERS SENT WITH PRESENTS should be short, mere cards of compliment, and written in the third person.

LETTERS ACKNOWLEDGING PRESENTS should also be quite short, written in the third person, and merely containing a few lines of thanks, with a word or two of admiration for the beauty, value, or usefulness of the gift.

LETTERS OF ADVICE are generally very unpalatable for the reader, and had better not be written unless solicited, and not then unless your counsel will really benefit your correspondent. When written, let them be courteous, but, at the same time, perfectly frank. If you can avert an evil by writing a letter of advice, even when unsolicited, it is a friendly office to write, but it is usually a thankless one.

To write after an act has been performed, and state
what your advice would have been, had your opinion
been asked, is extremely foolish, and if you disapprove
of the course that has been taken, your best plan is,
certainly, to say nothing about it.

In writing your letter of advice, give your judgement
as an opinion, not a law, and say candidly that you will
not feel hurt if contrary advice offered by any other,
more competent to judge in the case, is taken. While
your candor may force you to give the most unpalatable
counsel, let your courtesy so express it, that it cannot
give offence.

LETTERS OF EXCUSE are sometimes necessary, and
they should be written promptly, as a late apology for
an offence is worse than no apology at all. They should
be written in a frank, manly style, containing an ex-
planation of the offence, and the facts which led to it,
the assurance of the absence of malice or desire to
offend, sorrow for the circumstances, and a hope that
your apology will be accepted. Never wait until circumstances force an apology from you before writing a
letter of excuse. A frank, prompt acknowledgement
of an offence, and a candidly expressed desire to atone
for it, or for indulgence towards it, cannot fail to con-
ciliate any reasonable person.

CARDS OF COMPLIMENT must always be written in the
third person.

ANSWERS. The first requisite in answering a letter
upon any subject, is promptness. If you can answer
by return of mail, do so; if not, write as soon as possi-

ble. If you receive a letter making inquiries about facts which you will require time to ascertain, then write a few lines acknowledging the receipt of the letter of inquiry and promising to send the information as soon as possible

CHAPTER XVI.

WEDDING ETIQUETTE.

From an English work, "The Habits of Good Society," I quote some directions for the guidance of the happy man who proposes to enter the state of matrimony. I have altered a few words to suit the difference of country, but when weddings are performed in church, the rules given here are excellent. They will apply equally well to the evening ceremony.

"At a time when our feelings are or ought to be most susceptible, when the happiness or misery of a condition in which there is no medium begins, we are surrounded with forms and etiquettes which rise before the unwary like spectres, and which even the most rigid ceremonialists regard with a sort of dread.

"Were it not, however, for these forms, and for this necessity of being *en règle*, there might, on the solemn ization of marriage, be confusion, forgetfulness, and, even—speak it not aloud—irritation among the parties most intimately concerned. Excitement might ruin all. Without a definite programme, the old maids of the family would be thrusting in advice. The aged chronicler of past events, or grandmother by the fireside, would have it all her way; the venerable bachelor in tights,

with his blue coat and metal buttons, might throw every
thing into confusion by his suggestions. It is well that
we are indepenent of all these interfering advisers; that
there is no necessity to appeal to them. Precedent has
arranged it all; we have only to put in or understand
what that stern authority has laid down; how it has been
varied by modern changes; and we must just shape our
course boldly. 'Boldly?' But there is much to be
done before we come to that. First, there is the offer to
be made. Well may a man who contemplates such a
step say to himself, with Dryden:

'These are the realms of everlasting fate;'

for, in truth, on marriage one's well-being not only here
but even hereafter mainly depends. But it is not on this
bearing of the subject that we wish to enter, contenting
ourselves with a quotation from the *Spectator:*

"'It requires more virtues to make a good husband or
wife, than what go to the finishing any the most shining
character whatsoever.'

"In France, an engagement is an affair of negotiation
and business; and the system, in this respect, greatly
resembles the practice in England, on similar occasions,
a hundred and fifty or two hundred years ago, or even
later. France is the most unchanging country in the
world in her habits and domestic institutions, and fore-
most among these is her '*Marriage de convenance,*' or
'*Marriage de raisou.*'

"It is thus brought about. So soon as a young girl
quits the school or convent where she has been educated,
her friends cast about for a suitable *parti.* Most parents

in France take care, so soon as a daughter is born, to put aside a sum of money for her '*dot*,' as they well know that, whatever may be her attractions, *that* is indispensable in order to be married. They are ever on the look out for a youth with, at least, an equal fortune, or more; or, if they are rich, for title, which is deemed tantamount to fortune; even the power of writing those two little letters *De* before your name has some value in the marriage contract. Having satisfied themselves, they thus address the young lady:—'It is now time for you to be married; I know of an eligible match; you can see the gentleman, either at such a ball, or [if he is serious] at church. I do not ask you to take him if his appearance is positively disagreeable to you; if so, we will look out for some one else.'

"As a matter of custom, the young lady answers that the will of her parents is hers; she consents to take a survey of him to whom her destiny is to be entrusted; and let us presume that he is accepted, though it does not follow, and sometimes it takes several months to look out, as it does for other matters, a house, or a place, or a pair of horses. However, she consents; a formal introduction takes place; the *promis* calls in full dress to see his future wife; they are only just to speak to each other, and those few unmeaning words are spoken in the presence of the bride-elect's mother; for the French think it most indiscreet to allow the affections of a girl to be interested before marriage, lest during the arrangements for the contract all should be broken off. If she has no dislike, it is enough; never for an instant are the engaged couple left alone, and in very few cases do they

go up to the altar with more than a few weeks' acquaintance, and usually with less. The whole matter is then
arranged by notaries, who squabble over the marriage-
contract, and get all they can for their clients.

"The contract is usually signed in France on the day
before the marriage, when all is considered safe; the re
ligious portion of their bond takes place in the church,
and then the two young creatures are left together to
understand each other if they can, and to love each other
if they will; if not they must content themselves with
what is termed, *un ménage de Paris*.

"In England, formerly, much the same system pre-
vailed. A boy of fourteen, before going on his travels,
was contracted to a girl of eleven, selected as his future
wife by parents or guardians; he came back after the
grande tour to fulfil the engagement. But by law it was
imperative that forty days should at least pass between
the contract and the marriage; during which dreary in-
terval the couple, leashed together like two young grey-
hounds, would have time to think of the future. In
France, the perilous period of reflection is not allowed.
'I really am so glad we are to take a journey,' said a
young French lady to her friends; 'I shall thus get to
know something about my husband; he is quite a stranger
to me.' Some striking instances of the *Marriage de
convenance* being infringed on, have lately occurred in
France. The late Monsieur de Tocqueville married for
love, after a five years' engagement. Guizot, probably
influenced by his acquaintance with England, gave his
daughters liberty to choose for themselves, and they

married for *love**—'a very indelicate proceeding,' re
marked a French comtesse of the old *régeme*, when
speaking of this arrangement.

"Nothing can be more opposed to all this than the
American system. They are so tenacious of the freedom
of choice, that even persuasion is thought criminal.

"In France negotiations are often commenced on the
lady's side; in America, never. Even too encouraging
a manner, even the ordinary attentions of civility, are,
occasionally, a matter of reproach. We are jealous of
the delicacy of that sacred bond, which we presume to
hope is to spring out of mutual affection. A gentleman
who, from whatever motives, has made up his mind to
marry, may set about it in two ways. He may propose
by letter or in words. The customs of society imply
the necessity of a sufficient knowledge of the lady to be
addressed. This, even in this country, is a difficult
point to be attained; and, after all, cannot be calculated
by time, since, in large cities, you may know people a
year, and yet be comparative strangers; and, meeting
them in the country, may become intimate in a week.

"Having made up his mind, the gentleman offers—
wisely, if he can, in speech. Letters are seldom expressive of what really passes in the mind of man; or, if
expressive, seem foolish, since deep feelings are liable to
exaggeration. Every written word may be the theme
of cavil. Study, care, which avail in every other species
of composition, are death to the lover's effusion. A few
sentences, spoken in earnest, and broken by emotion,
are more eloquent than pages of sentiment, both to

* Two brothers, named *De Witte*.

parent and daughter. Let him, however, speak and be accepted. He is, in that case, instantly taken into the intimacy of his adopted relatives. Such is the notion of American honor, that the engaged couple are henceforth allowed to be frequently alone together, in walking and at home. If there be no known obstacle to the engagement, the gentleman and lady are mutually introduced to the respective relatives of each. It is for the gentleman's family to call first; for him to make the first present; and this should be done as soon as possible after the offer has been accepted. It is a sort of seal put upon the affair. The absence of presents is thought to imply want of earnestness in the matter. This present generally consists of some personal ornament, say, a ring, and should be handsome, but not so handsome as that made for the wedding-day. During the period that elapses before the marriage, the betrothed man should conduct himself with peculiar deference to the lady's family and friends, even if beneath his own station. It is often said: 'I marry such a lady, but I do not mean to marry her whole family.' This disrespectful pleasantry has something in it so cold, so selfish, that even if the lady's family be disagreeable, there is a total absence of delicate feeling to her in thus speaking of those nearest to her. To her parents especially, the conduct of the betrothed man should be respectful; to her sisters kind without familiarity; to her brothers, every evidence of good-will should be testified. In making every provision for the future, in regard to settlements, allowance for dress, &c., the *extent* of liberality convenient should be the spirit of all arrangements. Perfect candor as to his own affairs, respectful consideration for those of the family he is about to enter, mark a true gentleman.

"In France, however gay and even blameable a man may have been before his betrothal, he conducts himself with the utmost propriety after that event. A sense of what is due to a lady should repress all habits unpleasant to her; smoking, if disagreeable; frequenting places of amusement without her; or paying attention to other women. In this respect, indeed, the sense of honor should lead a man to be as scrupulous when his future wife is absent as when she is present, if not more so.

"In equally bad taste is exclusiveness. The devotions of two engaged persons should be reserved for the *tête-à-tête*, and women are generally in fault when it is otherwise. They like to exhibit their conquest; they cannot dispense with attentions; they forget that the demonstration of any peculiar condition of things in society must make some one uncomfortable; the young lady is uncomfortable because she is not equally happy; the young man detests what he calls nonsense; the old think there is a time for all things. All sitting apart, therefore, and peculiar displays, are in bad taste; I am inclined to think that they often accompany insincerity, and that the truest affections are those which are reserved for the genuine and heartfelt intimacy of private interviews. At the same time, the airs of indifference and avoidance should be equally guarded against; since, however strong and mutual attachment may be, such a line of conduct is apt needlessly to mislead others, and so produce mischief. True feeling, and a lady-like consideration for others, a point in which the present gene ration essentially fails, are the best guides for steering between the extremes of demonstration on the one hand, and of frigidity on the other.

"During the arrangement of pecuniary matters, a young lady should endeavor to understand what is going on, receiving it in a right spirit. If she has fortune, she should, in all points left to her, be generous and confid-ing, at the same time prudent. Many a man, she should remember, may abound in excellent qualities, and yet be improvident. He may mean to do well, yet have a pas-sion for building; he may be the very soul of good na-ture, yet fond of the gaming-table; he may have no wrong propensities of that sort, and yet have a confused notion of accounts, and be one of those men who muddle away a great deal of money, no one knows how; or he may be a too strict economist, a man who takes too good care of the pence, till he tires your very life out about an extra dollar; or he may be facile or weakly good natured, and have a friend who preys on him, and for whom he is disposed to become security. Finally, the beloved Charles, Henry, or Reginald may have none of these propensities, but may chance to be an honest merchant, or a tradesman, with all his floating capital in business, and a consequent risk of being one day rich, the next a pauper.

"Upon every account, therefore, it is desirable for a young lady to have a settlement on her; and she should not, from a weak spirit of romance, oppose her friends who advise it, since it is for her husband's advantage as well as her own. By making a settlement there is always a fund which cannot be touched—a something, however small, as a provision for a wife and children ; and whether she have fortune or not, this ought to be made. An allowance for dress should also be arranged; and this should be administered in such a way that a wife should not have to ask for it at inconvenient hours, and thus irritate her husband.

"Every preliminary being settled, there remains nothing except to fix the marriage-day, a point always left to the lady to advance; and next to settle how the ceremonial is to be performed is the subject of consideration.

"It is to be lamented that, previous to so solemn a ceremony, the thoughts of the lady concerned must necessarily be engaged for some time upon her *trousseau*. The *trousseau* consists, in this country, of all the habiliments necessary for a lady's use for the first two or three years of her married life; like every other outfit there are always a number of articles introduced into it that are next to useless, and are only calculated for the vainglory of the ostentatious.

"The *trousseau* being completed, and the day fixed, it becomes necessary to select the bridesmaids and the bridegroom's man, and to invite the guests.

"The bridesmaids are from two to eight in number. It is ridiculous to have many, as the real intention of the bridesmaid is, that she should act as a witness of the marriage. It is, however, thought a compliment to include the bride's sisters and those of the bridegroom's relations and intimate friends, in case sisters do not exist.

"When a bride is young the bridesmaids should be young; but it is absurd to see a 'single woman of a certain age,' or a widow, surrounded by blooming girls, making her look plain and foolish. For them the discreet woman of thirty-five is more suitable as a bridesmaid. Custom decides that the bridesmaids should be spinsters, but there is no legal objection to a married woman being a bridesmaid, should it be necessary, as it might be abroad, or at sea, or where ladies are few in number. Great care should be taken not to give offence in the choice of bridesmaids by a preference, which is always in bad taste on momentous occasions.

"The guests at the wedding should be selected with similar attention to what is right and kind, with consideration to those who have a claim on us, not only to what we ourselves prefer.

"For a great wedding breakfast, it is customary to send out printed cards from the parents or guardians from whose house the young lady is to be married.

"Early in the day, before eleven, the bride should be dressed, taking breakfast in her own room. In America they load a bride with lace flounces on a rich silk, and even sometimes with ornaments. In France it is always remembered, with better taste, that when a young lady goes up to the altar, she is '*encore jeune fille ;*' her dress, therefore, is exquisitely simple; a dress of tulle over white silk, a long, wide veil of white tulle, going down to the very feet, a wreath of maiden-blush-roses interspersed with orange flowers. This is the usual costume of a French bride of rank, or in the middle classes equally.

"The gentleman's dress should differ little from his full morning costume. The days are gone by when
19

gentlemen were married—as a recently deceased friend of mine was—in white satin breeches and waistcoat. In these days men show less joy in their attire at the fond consumation of their hopes, and more in their faces. A dark-blue frock-coat—black being superstitiously considered ominous—a white waistcoat, and a pair of light trousers, suffice for the 'happy man.' The neck-tie also should be light and simple. Polished boots are not amiss, though plain ones are better. The gloves must be as white as the linen. Both are typical—for in these days types are as important as under the Hebrew lawgivers—of the purity of mind and heart which are supposed to exist in their wearer. Eheu! after all, he cannot be too well dressed, for the more gay he is the greater the compliment to his bride. Flowers in the button-hole and a smile on the face show the bridegroom to be really a 'happy man.'

"As soon as the carriages are at the door, those bridesmaids, who happen to be in the house, and the other members of the family set off first. The bride goes last, with her father and mother, or with her mother alone, and the brother or relative who is to represent her father in case of death or absence. The bridegroom, his friend, or bridegroom's man, and the bridesmaids ought to be waiting in the church. The father of the bride gives her his arm, and leads her to the altar. Here her bridesmaids stand near her, as arranged by the clerk, and the bridegroom takes his appointed place.

"It is a good thing for the bridegroom's man to distribute the different fees to the clergyman or clergymen the clerk, and pew-opener, before the arrival of the bride, as it prevents confusion afterwards.

" The bride stands to the left of the bridegroom, and takes the glove off her right hand, whilst he takes his glove off his right hand. The bride gives her glove to the bridesmaid to hold, and sometimes to keep, as a good omen.

" The service then begins. During the recital, it is certainly a matter of feeling how the parties concerned should behave; but if tears can be restrained, and a quiet modesty in the lady displayed, and her emotions subdued, it adds much to the gratification of others, and saves a few pangs to the parents from whom she is to part.

" It should be remembered that this is but the closing scene of a drama of some duration—first the offer, then the consent and engagement. In most cases the marriage has been preceded by acts which have stamped the whole with certainty, although we do not adopt the contract system of our forefathers, and although no event in this life can be certain.

" I have omitted the mention of the bouquet, because it seems to me always an awkward addition to the bride; and that it should be presented afterwards on her return to the breakfast. Gardenies, if in season, white azalia, or even camellias, with very little orange flowers, form the bridal bouquet. The bridesmaids are dressed, on this occasion, so as to complete the picture with effect. When there are six or eight, it is usual for three of them to dress in one color, and three in another. At some of the most fashionable weddings in London, the brides maids wear veils—these are usually of net or tulle; white tarlatan dresses, over muslin or beautifully-worked dresses, are much worn, with colors introduced—pink or blue, and scarves of those colors; and white bonnets, if bonnets are worn, trimmed with flowers to correspond. These should be simple, but the flowers as natural as possible, and of the finest quality. The bouquets of the bridesmaids should be of mixed flowers. These they may have at church, but the present custom is for the gentlemen of the house to present them on their return home, previous to the wedding breakfast.

"The register is then signed. The bride quits the church first with the bridegroom, and gets into his carriage, and the father and mother, bridesmaids, and bridegroom's man, follow in order in their own.

"The breakfast is arranged on one or more tables, and is generally provided by a confectioner when expense is not an object.

"Presents are usual, first from the bridegroom to the bridesmaids. These generally consist of jewelry, the device of which should be unique or quaint, the article more elegant than massive. The female servants of the family, more especially servants who have lived many years in their place, also expect presents, such as gowns or shawls; or to a very valued personal attendant or housekeeper, a watch. But on such points discretion must suggest, and liberality measure out the *largesse of* the gift."

When the ceremony is performed at the house of the bride, the bridegroom should be ready full half an hour before the time appointed, and enter the parlor at the head of his army of bridesmaids and groomsmen, with his fair bride on his arm. In America a groomsman is allowed for each bridesmaid, whilst in England one poor man is all that is allowed for six, sometimes eight brides maids. The brothers or very intimate friends of the bride and groom are usually selected for groomsmen.

CHAPTER XVII.

ETIQUETTE FOR PLACES OF AMUSEMENT.

WHEN you wish to invite a lady to accompany you to the theatre, opera, a concert, or any other public place of amusement, send the invitation the day previous to the one selected for taking her, and write it in the third person. If it is the first time you have invited her, in clude her mother, sister, or some other lady in the invita tion.

If she accepts your invitation, let it be your next care to secure good seats, for it is but a poor compliment to invite a lady to go to the opera, and put her in an uncomfortable seat, where she can neither hear, see, nor be seen.

Although, when alone, you will act a courteous part in giving your seat to a strange lady, who is standing, in a crowded concert room, you should not do so when you are with a lady. By giving up your place beside her, you may place a lady next her, whom she will find an unpleasant companion, and you are yourself separated from her, when the conversation between the acts makes one of the greatest pleasures of an evening spent in this way. In case of accident, too, he deprives her of his protection, and gives her the appearance of having come alone. Your first duty, when you are escorting a lady, is to that lady before all others.

When you are with a lady at a place of amusement, you must not leave your seat until you rise to escort her home.   If at the opera, you may invite her to promenade between the acts, but if she declines, do you too remain in your seat.

Let all your conversation be in a low tone, not whispered, nor wi'h any air of mystery, but in a tone that will not disturb those seated near you.

Any lover-like airs or attitudes, although you may have the right to assume them, are in excessively bad taste in public.

If the evening you have appointed be a stormy one, you must call for your companion with a carriage, and this is the more elegant way of taking her even if the weather does not make it absolutely necessary.

When you are entering a concert room, or the box of a theatre, walk before your companion up the aisle, until you reach the seats you have secured, then turn, offer your hand to her, and place her in the inner seat, taking the outside one yourself; in going out, if the aisle is too narrow to walk two abreast, you again precede your companion until you reach the lobby, where you turn and offer your arm to her.

Loud talking, laughter, or mistimed applause, are all in very bad taste, for if you do not wish to pay strict attention to the performance, those around you probably do, and you pay but a poor compliment to your companion in thus implying her want of interest in what she came to see.

Secure your programme, libretto, or concert bill, before taking your seat, as, if you leave it, in order to ob
tain them, you may find some one else occupying your
place when you return, and when the seats are not secured, he may refuse to rise, thus giving you the alternative of an altercation, or leaving your companion without
any protector. Or, you may find a lady in your seat,
in which case, you have no alternative, but must accept
the penalty of your carelessness, by standing all the
evening.

In a crowd, do not push forward, unheeding whom
you hurt or inconvenience, but try to protect your companion, as far as possible, and be content to take your
turn.

If your seats are secured, call for your companion in
time to be seated some three or four minutes before the
performance commences, but if you are visiting a
hall where you cannot engage seats, it is best to go
early.

If you are alone and see ladies present with whom
you are acquainted, you may, with perfect propriety, go
and chat with them between the acts, but when with a
lady, never leave her to speak to another lady.

At an exhibition of pictures or statuary, you may
converse, but let it be in a quiet, gentlemanly tone, and
without gesture or loud laughter. If you stand long
before one picture or statue, see that you are not interfering with others who may wish to see the same work
of art. If you are engaged in conversation, and wish
to rest, do not take a position that will prevent others

from seeing any of the paintings, but sit down, or stand near the centre of the room.

Never, unless urgently solicited, attach yourself to any party at a place of amusement, even if some of the members of it are your own relatives or intimate friends.

CHAPTER XVIII.

MISCELLANEOUS.

WHEN you are walking with a lady who has your arm, be careful to *keep step* with her, and do not force her to take long, unladylike steps, or trot beside you with two steps to one of yours, by keeping your usual manly stride.

Never allow a lady, with whom you are walking, to carry a bundle, shawl, or bag, unless both your hands are already occupied in her service.

When you attend a wedding or bridal reception, it is the bridegroom whom you are to *congratulate*, offering to the bride your wishes for her future happiness, but not *congratulation*. If you you are acquainted with the bridegroom, but not with the bride, speak to him first, and he will introduce you to his bride, but in any other case, you must speak first to the bride, then to the bridegroom, then the bridesmaids, if you have any previous acquaintance with them, then to the parents and family of the bride, and after all this you are at liberty to seek your other friends among the guests. If you are personally a stranger to the newly married couple, but have received a card from being a friend of one of the families

r from any other reason, it is the first groomsman's place to introduce you, and you should give him your card, or mention your name, before he leads you to the bride.

Always remove a chair or stool that stands in the way of a lady passing, even though she is an entire stranger to you.

You may hand a chair to a strange lady, in a hotel, or upon a boat; you may hand her water, if you see her rise to obtain it, and at a hotel table you may pass her the dishes near you, with perfect propriety.

In this country where every other man uses tobacco, it may not be amiss to say a few words on smoking.

Dr. Prout says, "Tobacco is confessedly one of the most virulent poisons in nature. Yet such is the fascinating influence of this noxious weed, that mankind resort to it in every form they can devise, to ensure its stupifying and pernicious agency. Tobacco disorders the assimilating functions in general, but particularly, as I believe, the assimilation of the saccharine principle. I have never, indeed, been able to trace the development of oxalic acid to the use of tobacco; but that some analogous, and equally poisonous principle (probably of an acid nature), is generated in certain individuals by its abuse, is evident from their cachetic looks, and from the dark, and often greenish yellow tint of the blood. The severe and peculiar dyspeptic symptoms sometimes produced by inveterate snuff-taking are well known; and I have more than once seen such cases terminate fatally with malignant disease of the stomach and liver. Great smokers, also, especially those who employ short pipes and cigars, are said to be liable to cancerous affections of the lips.''

Yet, in spite of such warnings met with every day, Young America, Middle-aged America, and Old America will continue to use the poison, and many even use it in excess. An English writer gives some very good rules for the times and places where smoking may be allowed, which I quote for the use of smokers on this side of the water.

He says:

"But what shall I say of the fragrant weed which Raleigh taught our gallants to puff in capacious bowls; which a royal pedant denounced in a famous 'Counterblast;' which his flattering laureate, Ben Jonson, ridiculed to please his master; which our wives and sisters protest gives rise to the dirtiest and most unsociable habit a man can indulge in; of which some fair favorers declare that they love the smell, and others that they will never marry an indulger (which, by the way, they generally end in doing); which has won a fame over more space and among better men than Noah's grape has ever done; which doctors still dispute about, and boys still get sick over; but which is the solace of the weary laborer; the support of the ill-fed; the refresher of over-wrought brains; the soother of angry fancies, the boast of the exquisite; the excuse of the idle; the companion of the philosopher; and the tenth muse of the poet. I will go neither into the medical nor the moral question about the dreamy, calming cloud. I will content myself so far with saying what may be said for everything that can bless and curse mankind, that, in moderation, it is at least harmless; but what is moderate and what is not, must be determined in each individual case, according to the habits and constitution of the subject. If it cures asthma, it may destroy digestion; if it soothes the nerves, it may, in excess, produce a chronic irritability.

"But I will regard it in a social point of view; and, first, as a narcotic, notice its effects on the individual character. I believe, then, that in moderation it diminishes the violence of the passions, and, particularly, that of the temper. Interested in the subject, I have taken care to seek instances of members of the same family having the same violent tempers by inheritance, of whom the one has been calmed down by smoking, and the other gone on in his passionate course. I believe that it induces a habit of calm reflectiveness, which causes us to take less prejudiced, perhaps less zealous views of life, and to be, therefore, less irritable in our converse with our fellow creatures. I am inclined to think that the clergy, the squirearchy, and the peasantry are the most prejudiced and most violent classes in this country; there may be other reasons for this, but it is noteworthy that these are the classes which smoke least. On the other hand, I confess that it induces a certain lassitude, and a lounging, easy mode of life, which are fatal both to the precision of manners and the vivacity of conversation. The mind of a smoker is contemplative rather than active; and if the weed cures our irritability, it kills our wit. I believe that it is a fallacy to suppose that it encourages drinking. There is more drinking and less smoking in England than in any other country of the civilized world. There was more drinking among the gentry of last century, who never smoked at all. Smoke and wine do not go well together. Coffee or beer are its best accompaniments, and the one cannot intoxicate, the other must be largely imbibed to do so. I have observed among young bachelors that very little wine is drunk in their chambers, and that beer is gra lually taking its place. The cigar, too, is an excuse for rising from the dinner-table where there are no ladies to go to.

"In another point of view, I am inclined to think that smoking has conduced to make the society of men, when alone, less riotous, less quarrelsome, and even less vicious than it was. Where young men now blow a common cloud, they were formerly driven to a fearful consumption of wine, and this in their heads, they were ready and roused to any iniquity. But the pipe is the bachelor's wife. With it he can endure solitude longer, and is not forced into low society in order to shun it. With it, too, the idle can pass many an hour, which otherwise he would have given, not to work, but to extravagant devilries. With it he is no longer restless and impatient for excitement of any kind. We never hear now of young blades issuing in bands from their wine to beat the watch or disturb the slumbering citizens, as we did thirty or forty years ago, when smoking was still a rarity; they are all puffing harmlessly in their chambers now. But, on the other hand, I foresee with dread a too tender allegiance to the pipe, to the destruction of good society, and the abandonment of the ladies. No wonder they hate it, dear creatures; the pipe is the worst rival a woman can have, and it is one whose eyes she cannot scratch out; who improves with age, while she herself declines; who has an art which no woman possesses, that of never wearying her devotee; who is silent, yet a companion; costs little, yet gives much pleasure; who, lastly, never upbraids, and always yields the same joy. Ah! this is a powerful rival to wife or maid, and no wonder that at last the woman succombs, consents, and, rather than lose her lord or master, even supplies the hated herb with her own fair hands.

"There are rules to limit this indulgence. One must never smoke, nor even ask to smoke, in the company of the fair. If they know that in a few minutes you will be running off to your cigar, the fair will do well—say it is in a garden, or so—to allow you to bring it out and smoke it there. One must never smoke, again, in the streets; that is, in daylight. The deadly crime may be committed, like burglary, after dark, but not before. One must never smoke in a room inhabited at times by the ladies; thus, a well-bred man who has a wife or sisters, will not offer to smoke in the dining-room after dinner. One must never smoke in a public place, where ladies are or might be, for instance, a flower-show or promenade. One may smoke in a railway-carriage in spite of by-laws, if one has first obtained the consent of every one present; but if there be a lady there, though she give her consent, smoke not. In nine cases out of ten, she will give it from good nature. One must never smoke in a close carriage; one may ask and obtain leave to smoke when returning from a pic-nic or expedition in an open carriage. One must never smoke in a theatre, on a race-course, nor in church. This last is not, perhaps, a needless caution. In the Belgian churches you see a placard announcing, 'Ici on ne mâche pas du tabac.' One must never smoke when anybody shows an objection to it. One must never smoke a pipe in the streets; one must never smoke at all in the coffee-room of a hotel. One must never smoke, without consent, in the presence of a clergyman, and one must never offer a cigar to any ecclesiastic.

"But if you smoke, or if you are in the company of smokers, and are to wear your clothes in the presence of ladies afterwards, you must change them to smoke in. A host who asks you to smoke, will generally offer you an old coat for the purpose. You must also, after smoking, rinse the mouth well out, and, if possible, brush the teeth. You should never smoke in another person's house without leave, and you should not ask leave to do so if there are ladies in the house. When you are going to smoke a cigar you should offer one at the same time to anybody present, if not a clergyman or a very old man. You should always smoke a cigar given to you, whether good or bad, and never make any remarks on its quality.

"Smoking reminds me of spitting, but as this is at all times a disgusting habit, I need say nothing more than —never indulge in it. Besides being coarse and atrocious, it is very bad for the health."

Chesterfield warns his son against faults in good breeding in the following words, and these warnings will be equally applicable to the student of etiquette in the present day. He says:—

"Of the lesser talents, good breeding is the principal and most necessary one, not only as it is very important

in itself, but as it adds great lustre to the more solid advantages both of the heart and the mind.   I have often
touched upon good breeding to you before; so that this
letter shall be upon the next necessary qualification to it,
which is a genteel and easy manner and carriage, wholly
free from those odd tricks, ill-habits, and awkwardnesses,
which even many very worthy and sensible people have
in their behaviour.   However trifling a genteel manner
may sound, it is of very great consequence towards
pleasing in private life, especially the women, which one
time or other, you will think worth pleasing; and I have
known many a man from his awkwardness, give people
such a dislike of him at first, that all his merit could not
get the better of it afterwards.   Whereas a genteel
manner prepossesses people in your favor, bends them
towards you, and makes them wish to be like you.
Awkwardness can proceed but from two causes; either
from not having kept good company, or from not having
attended to it.   In good company do you take care to
observe their ways and manners, and to form your own
upon them.   Attention is absolutely necessary for this,
as, indeed, it is for everything else; and a man without
attention is not fit to live in the world.   When an awkward fellow first comes into a room, it is highly probable
that he goes and places himself in the very place of the
whole room where he should not; there he soon lets his
hat fall down, and, in taking it up again, throws down
his cane; in recovering his cane, his hat falls a second
time, so that he is quarter of an hour before he is in
order again.   If he drinks tea or coffee, he certainly
scalds his mouth, and lets either the cup or saucer fall.
   20

and spills either the tea or coffee. At dinner his awkwardness distinguishes itself particularly, as he has more
to do; there he holds his knife, fork, and spoon differently from other people, eats with his knife, to the great
danger of his mouth, picks his teeth with his fork, and
puts his spoon, which has been in his throat twenty
times, into the dishes again. If he is to carve, he can
never hit the joint: but, in his vain efforts to cut through
the bone, scatters the sauce in everybody's face. He
generally daubs himself with soup and grease, though
his napkin is commonly stuck through a button-hole, and
tickles his chin. When he drinks, he infalliably coughs
in his glass, and besprinkles the company. Besides all
this, he has strange tricks and gestures; such as snuffing
up his nose, making faces, putting his finger in his nose,
or blowing it and looking afterwards in his handkerchief
so as to make the company sick. His hands are troublesome to him, when he has not something in them, and he
does not know where to put them; but they are in perpetual motion between his bosom and his breeches; he
does not wear his clothes, and, in short, he does nothing
like other people. All this, I own, is not in any degree
criminal; but it is highly disagreeable and ridiculous in
company, and ought most carefully to be avoided, by
whoever desires to please.

"From this account of what you should not do, you
may easily judge what you should do; and a due attention to the manners of people of fashion, and who have
seen the world, will make it habitual and familiar to
you.

"There is, likewise, an awkwardness of expression and

words, most carefully to be avoided; such as false English, bad pronunciation, old sayings, and common proverbs; which are so many proofs of having kept bad and low company. For example, if, instead of saying that tastes are different, and that every man has his own peculiar one, you should let off a proverb, and say, That what is one man's meat is another man's poison; or else, Every one as they like, as the good man said when he kissed his cow; everybody would be persuaded that you had never kept company with anybody above footmen and housemaids.

"Attention will do all this, and without attention nothing is to be done; want of attention, which is really want of thought, is either folly or madness. You should not only have attention to everything, but a quickness of attention, so as to observe, at once, all the people in the room, their motions, their looks, and their words, and yet without staring at them, and seeming to be an observer. This quick and unobserved observation is of infinite advantage in life, and is to be acquired with care; and, on the contrary, what is called absence, which is thoughtlessness, and want of attention about what is doing, makes a man so like either a fool or a madman, that, for my part, I see no real difference. A fool never has thought; a madman has lost it; and an absent man is, for the time, without it.

"I would warn you against those disagreeable tricks and awkwardnesses, which many people contract when they are young, by the negligence of their parents, and cannot get out of them when they are old; such as odd motions, strange postures, and ungenteel carrriage.

But there is likewise an awkwardness of the mind, th **·t** ought to be, and with care may be, avoided; as, for instance, to mistake names; to speak of Mr. What-d'ye-call-him, or Mrs. Thingum, or How-d'ye-call-her, is excessively awkward and ordinary. To call people by improper titles and appellations is so too. To begin a story or narration when you are not perfect in it, and cannot go through with it, but are forced, possibly, to say, in the middle of it, 'I have forgotten the rest,' is very unpleasant and bungling. One must be extremely exact, clear, and perspicuous, in everything one says, otherwise, instead of entertaining, or informing others, one only tires and puzzles them. The voice and manner of speaking, too, are not to be neglected; some people almost shut their mouths when they speak, and mutter so, that they are not to be understood; others speak so fast, and sputter, that they are not to be understood neither; some always speak as loud as if they were talking to deaf people; and others so low that one cannot hear them. All these habits are awkward and disagreeable, and are to be avoided by attention; they are the distinguishing marks of the ordinary people, who have had no care taken of their education. You cannot imagine how necessary it is to mind all these little things; for I have seen many people with great talents ill-received, for want of having these talents, too; and others well received, only from their little talents, and who have had no great ones."

Nothing is in worse taste in society than to repeat the witticisms or remarks of another person as if they were your own. If you are discovered in the larceny of another's ideas, you may originate a thousand brilliant ones afterwards, but you will not gain the credit of one. If you quote your friend's remarks, give them as quotations.

Be cautious in the use of your tongue. Wise men say, that a man may repent when he has spoken, but he will not repent if he keeps silence.

If you wish to retain a good position in society, be careful to return all the visits which are paid to you, promptly, and do not neglect your calls upon ladies, invalids, and men older than yourself.

Visiting cards should be small, perfectly plain, with your name, and, if you will, your address *engraved* upon it. A handsomely written card is the most elegant one for a gentleman, after that comes the engraved one; a printed one is very seldom used, and is not at all elegant. Have no fanciful devices, ornamented edges, or flourishes upon your visiting cards, and never put your profession or business upon any but business cards, unless it is as a prefix or title: as, Dr., Capt., Col., or Gen., in case you are in the army or navy, put U. S. N., or U. S. A. after your name, but if you are only in the militia, avoid the vulgarity of using your title, excepting when you are with your company or on a parade. Tinted cards may be used, but plain white ones are much more elegant. If you leave a card at a hotel or boarding house, write the name of the person for whom it is intended above your own, on the card.

In directing a letter, put first the name of the person for whom it is intended, then the name of the city, then that of the state in which he resides. If you send it to the care of another person, or to a boarding house, or hotel, you can put that name either after the name of your correspondent, or in the left hand corner of the letter—thus:—

Mr. J. S. Jones,
Care of Mr. T. C. Jones,
Boston,
Mass.

or,

Mr. J. S. Jones,
Boston,
Mass.

Revere House.

If your friend is in the army or navy, put his title before his station after his name, thus:—

Capt. L. Lewis, U. S. A.,

or,

Lieutenant T. Roberts, U. S. N.

If you send your letter by a private hand, put the name of the bearer in the lower left hand corner of the envelope, but put the name only. "Politeness of,"—or "Kindness of," are obsolete, and not used now at all. Write the direction thus:—

J. L. Holmes, Esq.,
Revere House,
Boston,
Mass.

C. L. Cutts, Esq.

This will let your friend, Mr. Holmes, know that Mr. Cutts is in Boston, which is the object to be gained by putting the name of the bearer on a letter, sent by a private hand.

GUARD AGAINST VULGAR LANGUAGE. There is as much connection between the words and the thoughts as there is between the thoughts and the words; the latter are not only the expression of the former, but they have a power to re-act upon the soul and leave the stains of their corruption there. A young man who allows himself to use one profane or vulgar word, has not only shown that there is a foul spot on his mind, but by the utterance of that word he extends that spot and inflames it, till, by indulgence, it will soon pollute and ruin the whole soul. Be careful of your words as well as your thoughts. If you can control the tongue, that no improper words are pronounced by it, you will soon be able to control the mind and save it from corruption. You extinguish the fire by smothering it, or by preventing bad thoughts bursting out in language. Never utter a word anywhere, which you would be ashamed to speak in the presence of the most religious man. Try this practice a little, and you will soon have command of yourself.

Do not be known as an egotist. No man is more dreaded in society, or accounted a greater "bore" than he whose every other word is "I," "me," or "my." Show an interest in all that others say of themselves, but speak but little of your own affairs.

It is quite as bad to be a mere relater of scandal or the affairs of your neighbors. A female gossip is detestable, but a male gossip is not only detestable but utterly despicable.

A celebrated English lawyer gives the following directions for young men entering into business. He says:—

"SELECT THE KIND OF BUSINESS THAT SUITS YOUR NATURAL INCLINATIONS AND TEMPERAMENT.—Some men are naturally mechanics; others have a strong aversion to anything like machinery, and so on; one man has a natural taste for one occupation in life, and another for another.

"I never could succeed as a merchant. I have tried it, unsuccessfully, several times. I never could be content with a fixed salary, for mine is a purely speculative disposition, while others are just the reverse; and therefore all should be careful to select those occupations that suit them best.

"LET YOUR PLEDGED WORD EVER BE SACRED.—Never promise to do a thing without performing it with the most rigid promptness. Nothing is more valuable to a man in business than the name of always doing as he agrees, and that to the moment. A strict adherence to this rule gives a man the command of half the spare funds within the range of his acquaintance, and encircles him with a host of friends, who may be depended upon in any emergency.

"WHATEVER YOU DO, DO WITH ALL YOUR MIGHT.—Work at it, if necessary, early and late, in season and out of season, not leaving a stone unturned, and never deferring for a single hour that which can just as well be done now. The old proverb is full of truth and meaning—"Whatever is worth doing at all, is worth doing well." Many a man acquires a fortune by doing his business *thoroughly*, while his neighbor remains poor for life, because he only *half* does his business. Ambition, energy, industry, and perseverance, are indispensable requisites for success in business.

"SOBRIETY. USE NO DESCRIPTION OF INTOXICATING DRINKS.—As no man can succeed in business unless he has a *brain* to enable him to lay his plans, and *reason* to guide him in their execution, so, no matter how bountifully a man may be blessed with intelligence, if his brain is muddled, and his judgment warped by intoxicating drinks, it is impossible for him to carry on business successfully. How many good opportunities have passed never to return, while a man was sipping a 'social glass' with a friend! How many a foolish bargain has been made under the influence of the wine-cup, which temporarily makes his victim so *rich!* How many important chances have been put off until to-morrow, and thence for ever, because indulgence has thrown the system into a state of lassitude, neutralizing the energies so essential to success in business. The use of intoxicating drinks as a beverage is as much an infatuation as is the smoking of opium by the Chinese, and the former is quite as destructive to the success of the business man as the latter.

"LET HOPE PREDOMINATE, BUT BE NOT TOO VISIONARY. —Many persons are always kept poor because they are too *visionary*. Every project looks to them like certain success, and, therefore, they keep changing from one business to another, always in hot water, and always 'under the harrow.' The plan of 'counting the chickens before they are hatched,' is an error of ancient date, but it does not seem to improve by age.

"Do not scatter your powers.—Engage in one kind of business only, and stick to it faithfully until you succeed, or until you conclude to abandon it. A constant hammering on one nail will generally drive it home at last, so that it can be clinched. When a man's undivided attention is centered on one object, his mind will continually be suggesting improvements of value, which would escape him if his brain were occupied by a dozen different subjects at once. Many a fortune has slipped through men's fingers by engaging in too many occupations at once.

"Engage proper employees.—Never employ a man of bad habits when one whose habits are good can be found to fill his situation. I have generally been extremely fortunate in having faithful and competent persons to fill the responsible situations in my business; and a man can scarcely be too grateful for such a blessing. When you find a man unfit to fill his station, either from incapacity or peculiarity of character or disposition, dispense with his services, and do not drag out a miserable existence in the vain attempt to change his nature. It is utterly impossible to do so, 'You cannot make a silk purse,' &c. He has been created for some other sphere; let him find and fill it."

If you wish to succeed in society, and be known as a man who converses well, you must cultivate your memory. Do not smile and tell me that this is a gift, not an acquirement. It is true that some people have naturally a

more retentive memory than others, but those naturally
most deficient may strengthen their powers by cultivation.

Cultivate, therfore, this glorious faculty, by stoiing
and exercising it with trains of imagery. Accustom
yourselves to look at any natural object, and then consider how many facts and thoughts may be associated
with it—how much of poetic imagery and refined combinations. Follow out this idea, and you will find that
imagination, which is too often in youth permitted to
build up castles in the air, tenantless as they are unpro-
fitable, will become, if duly exercised, a source of much
enjoyment. I was led into this train of thought while
walking in a beautiful country, and seeing before me a
glorious rainbow, over-arching the valley which lay in
front. And not more quickly than its appearance, came
to my remembrance an admirable passage in the "Art
of Poetic Painting," wherein the author suggests the
great mental advantage of exercising the mind on all
subjects, by considering—

" What use can be made of them ?
What remarks they will illustrate ?
What representations they will serve ?
What comparison they will furnish?"

And while thus thinking, I remembered that the in
genicus author has instanced the rainbow as affording a
variety of illustrations, and capable, in the imagery
which it suggests, of numerous combinations. Thus:

THE HUES OF THE RAINBOW

Tinted the green and flowery banks of the stream ;
Tinged the white blossoms of the apple orchards;

Shed a beauteous radiance on the grass;
Veiled the waning moon and the evening star;
Over-arched the mist of the waterfall;
Reminded the looker-on of peace opposed to turbulence,
And illustrated the moral that even the most beautiful things
   of earth must pass away.

Every book you read, every natural object which meets your view, may be the exercise of memory, be made to furnish food both for reflection and conversation, enjoyment for your own solitary hours, and the means of making you popular in society. Believe me, the man who—"saw it, to be sure, but really forgot what it looked like," who is met every day in society, will not be sought after as will the man, who, bringing memory and fancy happily blended to bear upon what he sees, can make every object worthy of remark familiar and interesting to those who have not seen it.

If you have leisure moments, and what man has not? do not consider them as spare atoms of time to be wasted, idled away in profitless lounging. Always have a book within your reach, which you may catch up at your odd minutes. Resolve to edge in a little reading every day, if it is but a single sentence. If you can give fifteen minutes a day, it will be felt at the end of the year. Thoughts take up no room. When they are right they afford a portable pleasure, which one may travel or labor with without any trouble or incumbrance.

In your intercourse with other men, let every word that falls from your lips, bear the stamp of perfect truth. No reputation can be more enviable than that of being known as a man who no consideration could force to soil his soul with a lie.

"Truth is naturally so acceptable to man, so charming in herself, that to make falsehood be received, we are compelled to dress it up in the snow-white robes of Truth; as in passing base coin, it must have the impress of the good ere it will pass current. Deception, hypocrisy, and dissimulation, are, when practised, direct compliments to the power of Truth; and the common custom of passing off Truth's counterfeit for herself, is strong testimony in behalf of her intrinsic beauty and excel lence."

Next to being a man of talent, a well-read man is the most agreeable in society, and no investment of money or time is so profitable as that spent in good, useful books, and reading. A good book is a lasting companion. Truths, which it has taken years to glean, are therein at once freely but carefully communicated. We enjoy communion with the mind, though not with the person of the writer. Thus the humblest man may surround himself by the wisest and best spirits of past and present ages. No one can be solitary who possesses a book; he owns a friend that will instruct him in moments of leisure or of necessity. It is only necessary to turn open the leaves, and the fountain at once gives forth its streams. You may seek costly furniture for your homes, fanciful ornaments for your mantel-pieces, and rich carpets for your floors; but, after the absolute necessaries for a home, give me books as at once the cheapest, and certainly the most useful and abiding embellishments

A true gentleman will not only refrain from ridiculing

the follies, ignorance, or infirmities of others, but he will not even allow himself to smile at them. He will treat the rudest clown with the same easy courtesy which he would extend to the most polished gentleman, and will never by word, look, or gesture show that he notices the faults, or vulgarity of another. *Personal deformity is a cross* sent by God, and none but a depraved, wicked, and brutal man could ridicule, or even greet with a passing smile the unfortunate thus stamped. Even a word or look of pity will wound the sensitive, but frank, gentle courtesy, the regard paid by a feeling man to the comfort of a cripple, or that easy grace which, while it shows no sign of seeing the deformity, shows more deference to the afflicted one than to the more fortunate, are all duly appreciated and acknowledged, and win for the man who extends them the respect and love of all with whom he comes in contact.

Remember that true wit never descends to personalities. When you hear a man trying to be "funny" at the expense of his friends, or even his enemies, you may feel sure that his *humor* is forced, and while it sinks to ill-nature, cannot rise to the level of true *wit*.

Never try to make yourself out to be a very important person. If you are so really, your friends will soon find it out; if not, they will not give you credit for being so, because you try to force your fancied importance upon them. A pompous fool, though often seen, is not much loved nor respected, and you may remember that the frog who tried to make himself as big as an ox, died in the attempt.

A severe wit once said, "If you do not wish to be the

mark for slanderous tongues, be the first to enter a room, and the last to leave it."

If you are ever tempted to speak against a woman, think first—"Suppose she were my sister!" You can never gain anything by bringing your voice against a woman, even though she may deserve contempt, and your forbearance may shame others into a similar silence. It is a cowardly tongue that will take a woman's name upon it to injure her; though many men do this, who would fear,—*absolutely be afraid*, to speak against a man, or that same woman, had she a manly arm to protect her.

I again quote from the celebrated Lord Chesterfield, who says:

"It is good-breeding alone that can prepossess people in your favour at first sight, more time being necessary to discover greater talents. This good-breeding, you know, does not consist in low bows and formal ceremony; but in an easy, civil, and respectful behaviour. You will take care, therefore, to answer with complaisance, when you are spoken to; to place yourself at the lower end of the table, unless bid to go higher; to drink first to the lady of the house, and next to the master; not to eat awkwardly or dirtily; not to sit when others stand; and to do all this with an air of complaisance, and not with a grave, sour look, as if you did it all unwillingly. I do not mean a silly, insipid smile, that fools have when they would be civil; but an air of sensible good-humor. I hardly know anything so difficult to attain, or so necessary to possess, as perfect good-breeding; which is equally inconsistent with a still formality, and imperti-

neat forwardness, and an awkward bashfulness. A little
ceremony is often necessary; a certain degree of firmness
is absolutely so; and an outward modesty is extremely
becoming; the knowledge of the world, and your own
observations, must, and alone can tell you the proper
quantities of each.

"I mentioned the general rules of common civility,
which, whoever does not observe, will pass for a bear, and
be as unwelcome as one, in company; there is hardly
any body brutal enough not to answer when they are
spoken to. But it is not enough not to be rude; you
should be extremely civil, and distinguished for your
good breeding. The first principle of this good breeding
is never to say anything that you think can be disagree
able to any body in company; but, on the contrary, you
should endeavor to say what will be agreeable to them;
and that in an easy and natural manner, without seeming
to study for compliments. .There is likewise such a
thing as a civil look, and a rude look; and you should
look civil, as well as be so; for if, while you are saying
a civil thing, you look gruff and surly, as English
bumpkins do, nobody will be obliged to you for a civility
that seemed to come so unwillingly. If you have occasion to contradict any body, or to set them right from a
mistake, it would be very brutal to say, '*That is not so, I
know better*, or *You are out;* but you should say with a
civil look, *I beg your pardon, I believe you mistake*, or,
*If I may take the liberty of contradicting you, I believe
it is so and so;* for, though you may know a thing better
than other people, yet it is very shocking to tell them so
directly, without something to soften it; but remember

particularly, that whatever you say or do, with ever so civil an intention, a great deal consists in the manner and the look, which must be genteel, easy, and natural, and is easier to be felt than described.

"Civility is particularly due to all women; and remember, that no provocation whatsoever can justify any man in not being civil to every woman; and the greatest man would justly be reckoned a brute, if he were not civil to the meanest woman. It is due to their sex, and is the only protection they have against the superior strength of ours; nay, even a little flattery is allowable with women; and a man may, without meanness, tell a woman that she is either handsomer or wiser than she is. Observe the French people, and mind how easily and naturally civil their address is, and how agreeably they insinuate little civilities in their conversation. They think it so essential, that they call an honest man and a civil man by the same name, of *honnête homme;* and the Romans called civility *humanitas*, as thinking it inseparable from humanity. You cannot begin too early to take that turn, in order to make it natural and habitual to you."

Again, speaking of the inconveniency of bashfulness, he says:—

"As for the *mauvaise honte*, I hope you are above it. Your figure is like other people's; I suppose you will care that your dress shall be so too, and to avoid any singularity. What then should you be ashamed of? and why not go into a mixed company, with as much ease and as little concern, as you would go into your own room? Vice and ignorance are the only things I know,

21

which one ought to be ashamed of; keep but clear of them, and you may go anywhere without fear or concern. I have known some people, who, from feeling the pain and inconveniences of this *mauvaise honte*, have rushed into the other extreme, and turned impudent, as cowards sometimes grow desperate from the excess of danger; but this too is carefully to be avoided, there being nothing more generally shocking than impudence. The medium between these two extremes marks out the well-bred man; he feels himself firm and easy in all companies; is modest without being bashful, and steady without being impudent; if he is a stranger, he observes, with care, the manners and ways of the people most es-teemed at that place, and conforms to them with com-plaisance."

Flattery is always in bad taste. If you say more in a person's praise than is deserved, you not only say what is *false*, but you make others doubt the wisdom of your judgment. Open, palpable flattery will be re-garded by those to whom it is addressed as an insult. In your intercourse with ladies, you will find that the delicate compliment of seeking their society, showing your pleasure in it, and choosing for subjects of conversa-tion, other themes than the weather, dress, or the opera, will be more appreciated by women of sense, than the more awkward compliment of open words or gestures of admiration.

Never imitate the eccentricities of other men, even though those men have the highest genius to excuse their oddities. Eccentricity is, at the best, in bad taste; but an imitation of it—second hand oddity—is detestable.

Never feign abstraction in society. If you have matters of importance which really occupy your mind, and prevent you from paying attention to the proper etiquette of society, stay at home till your mind is less preoccupied. Chesterfield says:—

"What is commonly called an absent man, is commonly either a very weak, or a very affected man; but be he which he will, he is, I am sure, a very disagreeable man in company. He fails in all the common offices of civility; he seems not to know those people to-day, whom yesterday he appeared to live in intimacy with. He takes no part in the general conversation; but, on the contrary, breaks into it from time to time, with some start of his own, as if he waked from a dream. This (as I said before) is a sure indication, either of a mind so weak that it is not able to bear above one object at a time; or so affected, that it would be supposed to be wholly engrossed by, and directed to, some very great and important objects. Sir Isaac Newton, Mr. Locke, and (it may be) five or six more, since the creation of the world, may have had a right to absence, from that intense thought which the things they were investigating required. But if a young man, and a man of the world, who has no such avocations to plead, will claim and exercise that right of absence in company, his pretended right should, in my mind, be turned into an involuntary absence, by his perpetual exclusion out of company. However frivolous a company may be, still, while you are among them, do not show them, by your inattention, that you think them so; but rather take their tone, and conform, in some degree, to their weakness, instead of manifesting your contempt for them. There is nothing that people bear more impatiently, or forgive less, than contempt; and an injury is much sooner forgotten than an insult. If, therefore, you would rather please than offend, rather be well than ill-spoken of, rather be loved than hated; remember to have that constant attention about you, which flatters every man's little vanity; and the want of which, by mortifying his pride, never fails to excite his resentment, or, at least, his ill will. For instance: most people (I might say all people) have their weaknesses; they have their aversions and their likings to such or such things; so that, if you were to laugh at a man for his aversion to a cat, or cheese, (which are common antipathies,) or, by inattention and negligence, to let them come in his way, where you could prevent it, he would, in the first case, think himself insulted, and, in the second, slighted, and would remember both. Whereas your care to procure for him what he likes, and to remove from him what he hates, shows him that he is, at least, an object of your attention; flatters his vanity, and makes him, possibly, more your friend than a more important service would have done. With regard to women, attentions still below these are necessary, and, by the custom of the world, in some measure due, according to the laws of good breeding."

In giving an entertainment to your friends, while you avoid extravagant expenditure, it is your duty to place before them the best your purse will permit you to purchase, and be sure you have plenty. Abundance without superfluity, and good quality without extravagance, are your best rules for an entertainment.

If, by the introduction of a friend, by a mistake, or in any other way, your enemy, or a man to whom you have the strongest personal dislike, is under your roof, or at your table, as a guest, hospitality and good breeding both require you to treat him with the same frank courtesy which you extend to your other guests; though you need make no violent protestations of friendship, and are not required to make any advances towards him after he ceases to be your guest.

In giving a dinner party, invite only as many guests as you can seat comfortably at your table. If you have two tables, have them precisely alike, or, rest assured, you will offend those friends whom you place at what they judge to be the inferior table. Above all, avoid having little tables placed in the corners of the room, when there is a large table. At some houses in Paris it is a fashion to set the dining room entirely with small tables, which will accommodate comfortably three or four people, and such parties are very merry, very sociable and pleasant, if four congenial people are around each table; but it is a very dull fashion, if you are not sure of the congeniality of each quartette of guests.

If you lose your fortune or position in society, it is wiser to retire from the world of fashion than to wait for that world to bow you out.

If you are poor, but welcome in society on account of your family or talents, avoid the error which the young are most apt to fall into, that of living beyond your means.

The advice of Polonius to Laertes is as excellent in the present day, as it was in Shakspeare's time:—

"Give thy thoughts no tongue,
Nor any unproportioned thought his act.
Be thou familiar, but by no means vulgar.
The friends thou hast, and their adoption tried,
Grapple them to thy soul with hooks of steel:
But do not dull thy palm with entertainments
Of each new hatch'd, unfledg'd comrade. Beware
Of entrance to a quarrel: but, being in,
Bear it that the opposer may beware of thee.
Give every man thine ear, but few thy voice;
Take each man's censure, but reserve thy judgment
Costly thy habit as thy purse can buy,
But not express'd in fancy; rich, not gaudy;
For the apparel oft proclaims the man.

    *   *   *   *   *

Neither a borrower nor a lender be:
For loan oft loses both itself and friend;
And borrowing dulls the edge of husbandry.
This above all,—To thine ownself be true;
And it must follow, as the night the day,
Thou canst not then be false to any man."

It is by no means desirable to be always engaged in the serious pursuits of life. Take time for pleasure, and you will find your work progresses faster for some recreation. Lord Chesterfield says:

"I do not regret the time that I passed in pleasures; they were seasonable; they were the pleasures of youth, and I enjoyed them while young. If I had not, I should probably have overvalued them now, as we are very apt to do what we do not know; but knowing them as I do, I know their real value, and how much they are generally overrated. Nor do I regret the time that I have passed

in business, for the same reason; those who see only the
outside of it, imagine it has hidden charms, which they
pant after; and nothing but acquaintance can undeceive
them. I, who have been behind the scenes, both of
pleasure and business, and have seen all the springs and
pullies of those decorations which astonish and dazzle
the audience, retire, not only without regret, but with
contentment and satisfaction. But what I do, and ever
shall regret, is the time which, while young, I lost in
mere idleness, and in doing nothing. This is the common effect of the inconsideracy of youth, against which
I beg you will be most carefully upon your guard. The
value of moments, when cast up, is immense, if well employed; if thrown away, their loss is irrecoverable.
Every moment may be put to some use, and that with
much more pleasure than if unemployed. Do not imagine that by the employment of time, I mean an unin-
terrupted application to serious studies. No; pleasures
are, at proper times, both as necessary and as useful;
they fashion and form you for the world; they teach you
characters, and show you the human heart in its un-
guarded minutes. But then remember to make that use
of them. I have known many people, from laziness of
mind, go through both pleasure and business with equal
inattention; neither enjoying the one nor doing the
other; thinking themselves men of pleasure, because
they were mingled with those who were, and men of business, because they had business to do, though they
did not do it. Whatever you do, do it to the purpose;
do it thoroughly, not superficially. *Approfondissez.*
go to the bottom of things. Anything half done or

half known, is, in my mind, neither done nor known at all. Nay worse, it often misleads. There is hardly any place or any company where you may not gain knowledge, if you please; almost every body knows some one thing, and is glad to talk upon that one thing. Seek and you will find, in this world as well as in the next. See everything; inquire into everything; and you may excuse your curiosity, and the questions you ask, which otherwise might be thought impertinent, by your manner of asking them; for most things depend a great deal upon the manner. As, for example, I *am afraid that I am very troublesome with my questions; but nobody can inform me so well as you;* or something of that kind."

The same author, speaking of the evils of pedantry, says:—

"Every excellency, and every virtue has its kindred vice or weakness; and, if carried beyond certain bounds, sinks into one or the other. Generosity often runs into profusion, economy into avarice, courage into rashness, caution into timidity, and so on:—insomuch that, I believe, there is more judgment required for the proper conduct of our virtues, than for avoiding their opposite vices. Vice, in its true light, is so deformed, that it shocks us at first sight, and would hardly ever seduce us, if it did not at first wear the mask of some virtue. But virtue is, in itself, so beautiful, that it charms us at first sight; engages us more and more upon further acquaintance; and, as with other beauties, we think excess impossible, it is here that judgment is necessary, to moderate and direct the effects of an excellent cause. I shall apply this reasoning, at present, not to any particular virtue, but to an excellency, which, for want of judgment, is often the cause of ridiculous and blameable effects; I mean great learning; which, if not accompanied with sound judgment, frequently carries us into error, pride, and pedantry. As, I hope, you will possess that excellency in its utmost extent, and yet without its too common failings, the hints, which my experience can suggest, may probably not be useless to you.

"Some learned men, proud of their knowledge, only speak to decide, and give judgment without appeal; the consequence of which is, that mankind, provoked by the insult, and injured by the oppression, revolt; and, in order to shake off the tyranny, even call the lawful authority in question. The more you know, the modester you should be; and (by the bye) that modesty is the surest way of gratifying your vanity. Even where you are sure, seem rather doubtful; represent, but do not pronounce; and, if you would convince others, seem open to conviction yourself.

"Others, to show their learning, or often from the prejudices of a school education, where they hear of nothing else, are always talking of the ancients, as something more than men, and of the moderns, as something less. They are never without a classic or two in their pockets; they stick to the old good sense; they read none of the modern trash; and will show you plainly that no improvement has been made in any one art of science these last seventeen hundred years. I would, by no means, have you disown your acquaintance with the ancients; but still less would I have you brag of an exclusive intimacy with them. Speak of the moderns without contempt, and of the ancients without idolatry, judge them all by their merits, but not by their ages; and if you happen to have an Elzevir classic in your pocket, neither show it nor mention it.

" Some great scholars, most absurdly, draw all their maxims, both for public and private life, from what they call parallel cases in the ancient authors; without con-sidering that, in the first place, there never were, since the creation of the world, two cases exactly parallel; and, in the next place, that there never was a case stated, or even known, by any historian, with every one of its circumstances; which, however, ought to be known in order to be reasoned from. Reason upon the case itself, and the several circumstances that attend it, and act accordingly; but not from the authority of ancient poets or historians. Take into your consideration, if you please, cases seemingly analogous; but take them as helps only, not as guides.

" There is another species of learned men who, though less dogmatical and supercilious, are not less impertinent. These are the communicative and shining pedants, who adorn their conversation, even with women, by happy quotations of Greek and Latin; and who have contracted such a familiarity with the Greek and Roman authors, that they call them by certain names or epithets denoting intimacy. As, *old* Homer; that *sly rogue* Horace, *Maro*, instead of Virgil; and *Naso*, instead of Ovid. These are often imitated by coxcombs who have no learning at all, but who have got some names and some scraps of ancient authors by heart, which they impro-

perly and impertinently retail in all companies, in hopes
of passing for scholars. If, therefore, you would avoid
the accusation of pedantry on one hand, or the suspicion
of ignorance on the other, abstain from learned ostenta
tion. Speak the language of the company that you are
in ; speak it purely, and unlarded with any other.
Never seem wiser nor more learned than the people you
are with. Wear your learning, like your watch, in a
private pocket; and do not pull it out and strike it,
merely to show that you have one. If you are asked
what o'clock it is, tell it, but do not proclaim it hourly
and unasked, like the watchman.

"Upon the whole, remember that learning (I mean
Greek and Roman learning) is a most useful and necessary ornament, which it is shameful not to be master of;
but, at the same time, most carefully avoid those errors
and abuses which I have mentioned, and which too often
attend it. Remember, too, that great modern knowledge
is still more necessary than ancient ; and that you had
better know perfectly the present, than the old state of
the world; though I would have you well acquainted with
both."

If you are poor, you must deprive yourself often of
the pleasure of escorting ladies to ride, the opera, or
other entertainments, because it is understood in society
that, in these cases, a gentleman pays all the expenses
for both, and in any emergency you may find your bill
for carriage hire, suppers, bouquets, or other unforeseen
demands, greater than you anticipated.

Shun the card table. Even the friendly games common in society, for small stakes, are best avoided. They

feed the love of gambling, and you will find that this love, if once acquired, is the hardest curse to get rid off.

It is in bad taste, though often done, to turn over the cards on a table, when you are calling. If your host or hostess finds you so doing, it may lead them to suppose you value them more for their acquaintances than them. selves.